Hebrews:
Christ Above All

Other books in the Hebron Series include:

FIRST JOHN: Confident Christianity (2022)

JAMES: Authentic Faith (2023)

FIRST TIMOTHY: Church Charter (2024)

Coming soon:

SECOND TIMOTHY: Sound Doctrine

HEBRON COMMENTARY SERIES

Hebrews: Christ Above All

SERIES EDITOR

Kenneth J. Spink

GENERAL EDITOR

Daryl A. Neipp

Hebron Association of Regular Baptist Churches

North-Central Region

KDP 2024

The Hebron Association of Regular Baptist Churches is a Northcentral Ohio regional fellowship of twenty-six independent Baptist churches. Most of these are in the greater Cleveland area.

Cover Design: Jon Casbohm, Executive Director, Skyview Ranch in Millersburg OH.

The authors have used Scripture citations from the *King James Version of the Holy Bible* KJV, in the public domain, unless otherwise noted. Others include *The New King James Version of the Bible* NKJV© 1982 Thomas Nelson, the *Holy Bible, New International Version* NIV© 1973, 1978, 1984 by International Bible Society, or *The Holy Bible, English Standard Version* ESV© 2001 by Crossway, a division of Good News Publishing, all within their kindly permitted parameters.

Copyright © 2024 Kenneth J. Spink

All rights reserved.

ISBN: 9798345001783

CONTENTS

CH	TITLE	AUTHOR	HEBREWS	
	Meet the Authors			vii
	Forward			ix
	Preface			xi
	Prelude: The Five Warnings			xiii
1	Introduction	Smallman		1
2	Unparalleled Greatness	Gardiner	1:1-2:4	10
3	Highlighting His Humanity	Beight	2:5-18	27
4	Listening to His Voice (Part 1)	Peck	3:1-11	39
5	Listening to His Voice (Part 2)	Anderson	3:12-4:13	57
6	Perfect Priest	Jenks	4:14-5:10	71
7	Choosing What is Better	Alber	5:11-6:12	84
8	Soul Anchor	Prosowski	6:13-20	102
9	King and High Priest	VanCuran	7:1-28	112
10	High Priest of a New Covenant	Strong	8:1-13	132
11	Our Mediator	Hixson	9:1-28	142
12	Once for All	Pausley	10:1-18	155
13	Faithful Living	Alexander	10:19-39	165
14	Marks of True Faith	Nocella	11:1-40	180
15	Disciplined Endurance	Odle	12:1-17	194
16	Unshakable Kingdom	Kopas	12:18-29	208
17	Life in Christ	Fowler	13:1-25	224
	Bibliography			243
	Meet the Editors			247

To the pastors and ministry leaders who selflessly invested their time in this project:

FOR GOD IS NOT UNJUST SO AS TO OVERLOOK YOUR WORK AND THE LOVE THAT YOU HAVE SHOWN FOR HIS NAME IN SERVING THE SAINTS, AS YOU STILL DO. ~ HEBREWS 6:10 (ESV)

MEET THE AUTHORS
HEBREWS Commentary Authors 2024

Alber, Kurt, First Baptist Church, Medina, OH; Senior Pastor since 2021; Staff Pastor Oak Pointe Church, Novi, MI 2010-2021; Associate Pastor Farmington Hills Baptist Church, Farmington Hills, MI 2003-2008; Staff Pastor The Chapel of Miami Valley, Franklin, OH 1999-2003; Music Pastor, Fredericktowne Baptist Church, Walkersville, MD 1998-1999; Music Pastor Calvary Baptist Church, Muskegon, MI 1997; Associate Pastor First Baptist Church, Albion, MI 1992-1996

Anderson, Gary, First Baptist Church, Elyria, OH; President Emeritus Baptist Mid-Missions since 2016; Interim Preaching Pastor, First Baptist Elyria 2020; President, BMM 1989-2017; Executive VP of BMM 1987-1989; Senior Pastor, Springville Baptist Church, Springville, PA 1975-1987

Alexander, Tom, First Baptist Church, Wellington, OH; Senior Pastor since 1996; Assistant Pastor, Lima Baptist Temple 1984-1996; Youth Staff Highland Baptist Church, Chattanooga, TN 1980-1983

Beight, James, Abram Creek Baptist Church, Brook Park, OH, Senior Pastor since 2009; Senior Pastor Madison Avenue Baptist Church, Cleveland, OH 1994-2009; Assistant Pastor, Calvary Baptist Church Ashland, OH 1989-1994

Fowler, Robb, Calvary Baptist Church, Chillicothe, OH; Pastor since 2020; Associate Pastor, Calvary Baptist Church, Sandusky, OH 2000-2019

Gardiner, Brian, New Community Baptist Church, Avon, OH; Lead Pastor since 2000; Missionary with Baptist Mid-Missions 1996-2002

Hixson, David, Calvary Baptist Church, Sandusky, OH; Senior Pastor since 1992; Youth and Music Pastor Pennsville Baptist Church, Mt. Pleasant, PA 1984-1992; Youth and Music Pastor Southgate Baptist Church, Scottsboro, AL 1981-1984

Jenks, Jon, Camden Baptist Church, Wellington, OH; President, Baptist Church Planters since 2020; Senior Pastor, Calvary Baptist Church, Wisconsin Rapids, WI, 2000-2020; Assistant Pastor, Calvary Baptist Church, Wisconsin Rapids, WI, 1996-2000

Kopas, Bill, Camden Baptist Church, Wellington, OH, Associate Pastor since 2001; Associate Pastor, fellowship Baptist, Lorain, OH 1998-2001

Neipp, Daryl A., New Community Baptist Church, Avon, OH, Associate Pastor since 2001; Professor & Instructional Mentor, Liberty University since 2010; Adjunct Instructor, California Baptist University, since 2017

Nocella, Larry, Camden Baptist Church, Wellington, OH; Senior Pastor since 2000; Youth Pastor 1994-2000; Youth Pastor, Memorial Baptist Church, Columbus, OH 1989-1994

Odle, Patrick, First Baptist Church, Elyria, OH, President, Baptist Mid-Missions since 2020; Senior Pastor First Baptist, Elyria 2011-2020; Vice President, Faith Baptist Bible College, 2008-2011; Pastor, Holmes Baptist Church, Clarion, IA, 1999-2008; Assistant Pastor, Ankeny Baptist Church, Ankeny, IA, 1991-1999

Pausley, Chuck, Ohio Association of Regular Baptist Churches State Representative since 2017; Pastor, Bethany Baptist Church, Avon Park, FL 2008-2017; Senior Pastor, Willow Creek (now Soteria) Baptist Church, West Des Moines, IA 1994-2007; Senior Pastor, Grace Baptist, Troy, OH 1986-1994, Assistant Pastor, 1978-1986

Peck, Michael – Interim Pastor/Pulpit supply to the following Ohio churches: First Baptist Church of Elyria; Abbe Road Baptist Church, Elyria; Norton Baptist Church, Norton; First Baptist Church, Strongsville; Rochester Baptist Church, Rochester; Vice President Baptist Church Planters 2001-2017; Pastor in New York State 31 years

Prosowski, Cory, Faith Baptist Church, Amherst, OH; Associate Pastor since 2012

Smallman, William H., First Baptist Church, Medina, OH since 1992; Professor, Berea Baptist Bible School since 2000; Vice President Baptist Mid-Missions, 1980-2009; BMM missionary to Brazil, 1968-1979; Founding Pastor, Galilee Baptist Church, Chicago Heights, IL 1968

Spink, Kenneth J., Berea Baptist Church, Berea, OH; Senior Pastor since 1984; Youth Pastor 1982-1984; Director, Berea Baptist Bible School since 2015

Strong, Steven T., Grace Baptist Church, Westlake, OH; Lead Pastor since 2012; Youth Pastor 1999-2012

VanCuran, Alex, Faith Baptist Church, Amherst, OH; Senior Pastor since 2018

FOREWORD

A new vehicle comes with an instruction manual, which is created to help the consumer know how to operate that vehicle properly and safely. Unfortunately, many people view the Bible in the same way—as nothing more than instructions and practical tips for helping a person successfully navigate life. And while following Scriptural principles will produce a better life, the book of Hebrews makes it clear that the theme of Scripture is not so much about instructions as it is about relationship—about man's relationship with God, how that was broken, and how it has been restored. Hebrews contrasts the temporary conditions that were set up in the Old Testament with the privileges offered in the New Testament and the result is something quite astounding. While the Israelite's access to God could be described as exceedingly limited, New Testament believers have open access and are encouraged to approach the throne of God with boldness. In God's grace and because of Christ's work on the cross, we can commune and walk with God in ways the Israelites could never fathom. The book of Hebrews opens our eyes to what a relationship with God can look like when the barrier of sin has been fully removed.

The Hebron Commentary series is designed so an ordinary follower of Christ, regardless of his/her biblical knowledge, can grow in his/her faith and understanding of the Bible. Technically speaking, an expositional method is utilized, which is just a fancy way of saying it has a teacher/student approach in mind. This means no technical Bible knowledge is necessary to begin this study. In short, our intent as pastors and ministry leaders is to 1) describe what the text says, 2) explain what it means, and 3) provide some ideas for how your reading can be applied in real life. In this specific commentary on Hebrews, study guide questions have been added to the end of each chapter to assist in the process of exploration and to encourage both reflection and discussion. While some may use this commentary for personal Bible study, we encourage you to find a friend or small group with whom you can work through each chapter together.

Daryl Neipp, General Editor

Christ Above All

PREFACE

THE HEBRON FELLOWSHIP

The Hebron Association of Regular Baptist Churches, also known as the Hebron Fellowship, is an association of independent Baptist churches in north-central Ohio. These churches identify with one another because of their common doctrinal beliefs. They also enjoy various aspects of fellowship together such as monthly pastors' meetings, bi-annual meetings of a women's missionary union, youth events, church planting initiatives, work projects, and an annual gathering.

Why does this fellowship of churches exist? The answer causes us to take a step back in history. In the late nineteenth century, theological liberalism, also known as modernism, was gaining a strong foothold in America. The rising popularity of the theory of evolution made belief in God unnecessary. The scientific method was seen as having equal or even greater authority than the Bible. The Bible itself was being attacked by higher criticism, a "scientific" method of studying the text of Scripture that cast doubt on the authorship of many of the books of the Bible. There was also an increasing mood of anti-supernaturalism. If something could not be scientifically demonstrated, it should not be believed. This resulted in a questioning or denial of all the miracles in the Bible, including the virgin birth and bodily resurrection of Jesus Christ.

These historic elements had a significant impact on many denominations in the United States, including Baptists. Core doctrines of the faith were being denied, including the inspiration and infallibility of Scripture, the virgin birth and deity of Christ, the substitutionary atonement of Christ, the literal resurrection of Christ from the dead, and the literal, physical return of Christ at the Second Coming.

Bible-believing pastors and theologians responded with a movement that became known as fundamentalism. They believed there were fundamental doctrines that, if denied, would result in the denial of true Christianity. There were core doctrines that a person must believe in order to truly be a Christian. These pastors and theologians tried, in vain, to turn the tide of modernism within their denominations.

In 1907, the Northern Baptist Convention was formally organized. From the beginning, its hierarchy, schools, publications, and missions programs were marked by modernism. Core doctrines of the faith were being denied by the Convention, even though many local Baptist churches and pastors continued to believe and preach what the Bible teaches. After trying and failing to bring the Convention back to its biblical roots, a number of churches in Ohio determined that they must separate and form a new organization.

So, in October of 1928, a significant group of Baptist churches in Ohio withdrew from the national, state, and local arms of the Northern Baptist Convention and formed the Union of Regular Baptist Churches of Ohio (now known as the Ohio Association of Regular Baptist Churches). Churches in north-central Ohio also formed the Hebron Fellowship. The churches that became the Hebron fellowship held strongly to these doctrines, and they still do today.

Why did these churches choose the name Hebron for their local fellowship? Rev. Robert T. Ketcham was serving as the pastor of the First Baptist Church of Elyria at that time. At the organizational meeting of the fellowship, he preached a message with thirteen points on the use of the term "Hebron" in the Bible. His message emphasized the need to stand for the truths of God's Word and separate from those who deny them. Standing for the truths of Scripture and the proclamation of those truths remains the doctrinal priority of the churches of the Hebron Fellowship still today.

Tom Alexander

Prelude

THE FIVE WARNINGS IN HEBREWS

Daryl Neipp, General Editor

The book of Hebrews contains five warning passages (2:14; 3:7-4:13; 5:11-6:12; 10:19-39; 12:14-29), which have been the source of debate among scholars, pastors, and theologians for countless years. In short, the differences in interpretation can be summed up with the question: For whom are the warning passages written? First, it must be established whether Hebrews was written to believers or unbelievers. A conclusion in this regard can be drawn from wording such as Holy (3:1), Brethren (3:1, 12), Companions (or partakers) of the heavenly calling (3:1), God's house (3:6), Companions (or partakers) of the Messiah (3:14), People who should have been mature enough to be teachers (5:12), Enlightened (6:4), Having tasted the heavenly gift (6:4), Companions (or partakers) of the Holy Spirit (6:4), Having tasted the good Word of God (6:5), Having tasted the powers of the age to come (6:5), Having loved the Lord's name (6:10), Sanctified (10:10, 29), and Perfected (10:14). Each of these words or phrases lends itself as evidence that the book was indeed written with believers in view.

Having established the intended audience, two other main positions should be explored. The first is to interpret the warned person as a believer who falls away from the faith and thus forfeits his/her salvation. However, this position must be rejected because Scripture makes it clear that true believers cannot lose their salvation (Jn. 1:12; Jn. 6:37-40; Jn. 10:28-29; Jn. 14:16; Rom. 4:21; Rom. 5:10; Rom. 8:1; Rom. 8:29-30; Rom. 8:34-35; Rom. 8:38-39; Rom. 11:29; 1 Cor. 1:8; 1 Cor. 5:5; 2 Cor. 1:21-22; 2 Cor. 5:17; Gal 3:3; Eph. 1:5; Eph. 1:13-14; Eph. 2:4-6; Eph. 2:8-9; Eph. 4:30; Phil. 1:6; Heb. 5:9; Heb. 6:19; Heb. 7:25; Heb. 9:12; Heb. 10:14; Heb. 13:20; 1 Pet. 1:3; 1 Pet. 1:4-5; 1 Pet. 3:18).

The second position upholds the doctrine of eternal security for the believer and thus assumes and interprets the warning passages through that filter. Stephen Ger (p. 57) provides the following rationale:

1. It recognizes that the recipients are indeed true believers.

2. It incorporates the New Testament's (including Hebrews) doctrine of the believers' assurance of salvation.

3. In perhaps the seemingly severest of Hebrews' warning passages (6:7-8), it is not the field that is destroyed by burning but the worthless vegetation. Thus, the believer's apostasy would be punished but the consequence would fall far short of loss of salvation.

4. There is a significant correlation between the historical punishment cited as an illustration, that is, the judgment on Israel's wilderness generation and their subsequent loss of reward, and the present threat of which the author warns the recipients.

5. Paul's expressed concern regarding the avoidance of disqualification (1 Cor. 9:27) as well as his teaching on each believer receiving commensurate reward or loss, depending on whether the quality of his work endures the assessment of divine fire (1 Cor. 3:11-15, note that it is the subpar work that is burned up, not the believer).

While it is impossible to address every potential nuanced position, for those who are committed to the Scriptural doctrine of eternal security, the most plausible interpretation seems to indicate that warning passages are referring to true believers who have fallen away from their faith and thus will experience a loss of blessing. An example of this reality can be seen in the life of King David. Having been called *a man after God's own heart*, very few probably question whether David will be in heaven. However, he is also known for committing horrendous sins including adultery and murder, and in so doing forfeiting fellowship *with* God and blessing *from* God for a season of his life. And of course, there were severe consequences for his actions that not only affected him but also his immediate family and even the larger kingdom. That said, David repented of his sin and found restoration—and that is the point of the warning passages in Hebrews. The author is warning believers who have fallen away as well as those who are considering falling away that consequences are sure to follow such a decision. And while salvation will not be lost, there are blessings, over and above salvation, that can surely be forfeited.

The contributors to this study will delve into the warning passages, but the editor deliberately ensured that the commentary would not become overly consumed by the debate, which is why this excursus was added at the beginning. Doing so helps set the tone without allowing these particular issues to dominate and deviate from the central focus of the study. That said, there is room for differences of opinion, and we encourage honest and respectful conversations on these matters. As differences within commentary chapters appear, editors will reference those various points of view and encourage further exploration through personal study.

1

INTRODUCTION TO HEBREWS

William H. Smallman

God speaks! He addressed specific people and expected them to respond positively to his message of love and judgment. We get to read over their shoulders.

Who Were Those First Readers?
This epistle was addressed to believers who were Jewish. They had recognized Jesus as the Messiah (Christ) and trusted him for salvation, but they were under such pressure to recant that they were considering denying the faith.

It seems most likely that there was a group of such Jewish believers at some location away from Jerusalem, very possibly in Rome. The final greeting, *They of Italy greet you* (13:24) is not definitive as to location but is a noteworthy clue. The anonymous writer hoped to visit them soon (13:22) and did not reside among them.

It could well be that these Jewish believers had set up a meeting of their own in a Messianic assembly away from the majority of the believers there who were Gentiles. This was more than a special-interest Bible study group. It was almost like a church split since there was some animosity between the factions. They were not to forsake meeting with the rest of the believers even while maintaining their own cultural identity. They can all learn to enjoy one another's cultural quirks while celebrating their oneness in Christ.

These were Hellenistic Jews, that is, adopting a Greek or gentile lifestyle and language rather than living entirely like those in Judea.

They still followed their traditional Jewish lifestyle as adapted to a gentile environment remote from direct access to the temple. The Judean Jewish community apparently demanded that they return "home" to them in "the right way" to be Christians.

The readers used the Greek Bible, the Septuagint, rather than the *Tanach* in Hebrew and Aramaic (which they did not speak, not being Judeans). This epistle is replete with citations from and informal references to the Old Testament with 86 specific quotations or allusions. All such references are from the LXX (Septuagint), the Greek translation of the Old Testament, indicating the Bible normally used by the original readers of Hebrews, non-Judean Jews. It is a commentary on the Tabernacle ceremonies from a New Testament perspective.

Is This Work Really an Epistle?

We are accustomed to the normal epistolary format as used by Paul and Peter. Hebrews is more like an essay or a teaching manual without the common introductory greetings, though it concludes with personal notes. Its opening paragraph is a grand literary portrait of the glorious Son and heir of God, soon regaled with praises from all over the Old Testament. This work of early Christology frames the person and work of Jesus in the familiar patterns of the Tabernacle (without even mentioning the temple in Jerusalem, still active at the time).

The Greek of this work is eloquent, expressive, even elegant, as a formal presentation of Jesus the Messiah in his resplendent self. While called an epistle, it is a fine literary work of art and a theological masterpiece. Our own teaching need not be dull. This might be considered a homily or sermon but is too long for a single session. It may well be the collection of a series of studies, wrapped up in a single document for circulation. It is the Spirit-inspired work of an inspiring teacher in a Messianic assembly far from Jerusalem.

Why Was This Work Written to Them and Us?

The Jewish brothers away from Judea were grappling with issues that simply were not as important to their gentile brothers and sisters. They needed to discern how much of Judaism to keep, what to toss out, and how this new Messianic faith was related to their beloved Judaism. That cultural sifting still follows the intrusion of the gospel into any environment that needs to change under its influence.

Being remote from the temple, they had developed some variations of the rituals, now superseded by Christian celebrations. They faced intense pressure from friends and neighbors, not to mention family members, as well as from non-Messianic Jews. The writer of Hebrews is showing them the continuity of faith in God the Creator and Lawgiver, the God of the Old Testament, who has now revealed himself fully and finally in God the Son! What a novel concept. The Old Testament was still the Word of God, revealing the nature of God, the origins of all things, principles for fallen people to return to God, and guidelines for living with spiritual integrity for a righteous life. The new focus came to be life in the Son, under the Father, empowered by the Spirit. That is a lot to incorporate into the deep tradition of the utter singularity of God in the face of multiple deities of paganism. That resonated well with Jewish people back in the pagan Roman "wilderness."

These Jewish believers are wondering whether it is worth all the suffering they face, mostly from fellow Jews. Some are seriously considering defecting from the faith, and the writer is encouraging them to grow spiritually, despite their suffering, and to remind them that outside of Jesus Christ, there is no salvation. Peter's question in John 6:68 reverberates in this letter. If Yeshua is not the promised redeemer, what hope do we have?

Who Wrote This Wonderful Letter?

From earliest Christian times people have wondered who wrote this epistle. Paul? Luke? Barnabas? Clement? (an early pastor and writer in Rome around 200 who quoted it a lot). An early church scholar wrote around AD 250, "I would say that... the thoughts are from the Apostle [Paul] but the style and composition are of one who called to mind the Apostle's teaching.... As to who wrote the epistle, God alone knows the truth of the matter" (Origen).

Early church consensus pointed to Paul as the author since he was such a prolific writer. However, Hebrews 2:3 would not likely have come from Paul's pen, about the word of salvation. The writer asserts that the message **was confirmed to us by those who heard Him** (NKJV), but Paul had carefully identified himself as receiving truth directly from Jesus.

My personal favorite candidate is Barnabas. He was favored in North African churches associated with the Montanists, an early Pentecostal-type movement. He was a Levite, trained in details of the Law, though not in the priestly line. The Levitical details of temple ceremonies seen in Hebrews would have been quite familiar to him. He was wealthy and so presumably well-educated. He was capable of writing elegant Greek as found in the Greek Old Testament. He was a man of apostolic stature, even called an *apostle* (Acts 14:14), and in the broader sense served as a missionary. He was a mentor to the radical convert Saul, something of a "Saul winner," recruiting him for church service and their first missionary journey. Barnabas was a healer and reconciler, well-equipped for mending fences between factions of fellow Jewish believers. His inherent modesty allowed him to play *second fiddle* as Paul emerged as a dynamic leader playing *first trumpet*, and also to leave his important epistle anonymous. There is a *First Epistle of Barnabas* from early times with some thematic affinity with Hebrews, regarded by some scholars as authentic. Still, only God knows. In reality, the Holy Spirit was the ultimate author, so we are not bothered to know which holy man held the pen in his hand. Someday we'll meet him in Heaven.

When Was This Letter Written?

Hebrews speaks of sacrifices as a current and familiar matter, so it clearly was written before AD 70 when the temple was destroyed with all of Jerusalem. The letter mentions **not suffering unto blood,** so we surmise that the first violent persecution in Rome by Nero had not yet begun. He was enthroned in 54 and ruled wisely for a decade. But in 64 he apparently went insane, burned Rome, blamed the Christians, and tried to kill them all – until he was invited to commit suicide in 68 (or they would help him do it). Hebrews was first quoted by Clement of Rome (around AD 95).

The writer refers to the Holy Spirit sparingly (2:4, 3:7, 6:4, 9:8, 14, 10:15), but of status equal to Christ and God, so this letter was late enough in Church times to normalize, at least casually, the mystery of the Holy Trinity. The principles of justification, explained so explicitly by Rabbi Paul, are here framed in the intended functions of the Law of the Offerings and the exchange of sinfulness for righteousness on the basis of the shed blood of an innocent substitute.

The expositions of salvation by grace through faith are fully compatible when we compare this letter with the Pauline Corpus along with the writings of John and Peter.

The casual mention of Timothy (13:23) as a familiar co-worker places the letter late enough for his involvement with Paul. So, we place the letter definitely before 95, before 70, and possibly before

64. That said, it is timeless and remains timely for churches today.

How Does the Old Testament Fit in Hebrews?

The unnamed author is clearly saturated with Old Testament themes, particularly from the Pentateuch and Psalms. All of the quotes and allusions are from the Septuagint (*siglum LXX*), translated into Greek around 250 BC at the request of the Alexandrian Library. Instead of citing the human authors, this writer says, **God says...** or explicitly, **the Holy Spirit also witnesses** to introduce a quotation. The Old Testament, even as translated from Hebrew, was regarded as the Word of God, not merely some historical document of Jewish traditions.

B.F. Westcott counted 29 direct quotations (mostly from Moses' and David's writings) and 53 allusions to Scripture in Hebrews (Morris, p. 7). There were no citations of Apocryphal writings, even though those books from the Intertestamental Period were known.
The focus of the Old Testament Scriptures was clearly on Jesus the person, and not merely on the concept of a Messiah. It is a clear affirmation like "Our most precious Book and foundation reaches its climax in Jesus the Messiah! The familiar rituals and rhythms of classical Judaism can now find joy and redemption in Jesus Christ."

What is the Epistle to the Hebrews All About?

In a word, this Christological syllabus is all about the Messiah: Who he was and what he accomplished. That work is *not* to be cast aside as a religious option too risky to embrace. It shows us that Christ is the superior way to God, not as a competing religion, but as the fulfillment of all that Judaism taught. Christ is superior in all of the aspects and dimensions of the relationship with God that the Law of Moses pointed to. Jesus the Messiah is not *a little better*, or merely *preferable*. He is the ONLY way to God! Christ is ALL that the Law provided and more.

- The practice of the Law was the rehearsal while Jesus Christ is the reality it anticipated.

- The Law and its offerings to God were object lessons about finding God; Christ is the true Lamb of God, just as John had expressed at Jesus' sudden appearance.

- The Law was temporary; Christ is permanent and final.

- Christ is superior to angels and superior to Moses. He is the better sacrifice, better Tabernacle, better offering, etc.

The whole letter flows to the conclusion that Jesus Christ is worthy of our trust, even if we must suffer for Him. There are several severe warnings, not about losing salvation but missing out on rewards. In other words, do not falter!

We tend to think of crossing a line of faith to embrace salvation. Under a microscope, we can see that transition as crossing a bridge. Just stepping onto the bridge is the major first step of faith in coming to Christ. Growth in Christ confirms the rightness of that step of trust.

Those readers who had committed themselves to trusting Christ and are most of the way across that bridge to firm and settled discipleship are urged to go all the way with him. Those who first received this letter are addressed as true believers, but they are seriously considering bailing out because of opposition from the larger Jewish community where they are deeply rooted. There is a Heroes Hall of Faith memorial in Chapter Eleven that demonstrates the great men and women in their Jewish ancestry who have gone on in triumph, people **of whom the world was not worthy**.

That cloud of witnesses encourages us today. They made it and so can we. God's special miracles supported the infant nation in their march to The Land. God continues to be faithful. You provide your own manna now. Keep running; trim the excess weight of threats and arguments that do not matter; keep running the race.

A glance at our Table of Contents gives an overview of this wonderful and meaty book. The book of Hebrews nourishes our spirits, focuses our worship, and encourages our shaky knees. It shows how the Old Testament is the foundation of our New Testament faith which is now the order of the day. It breathes confidence into our failing strength so we will keep running as our heroes of faith did.

Key Words and Phrases in Hebrews

- Better, or superior

- Rest in God's work

- Redemption
- High Priest
- New Covenant
- New assurance based on trust, not Law-keeping
- New community of faith
- No hope outside of Christ

Key Titles for Jesus Christ in Hebrews

- A **King**
- A **Priest** like Melchizedek
- A **Prophet** better than Moses, bearing our judgment rather than just declaring judgment from God.

Major Themes in Hebrews

- God spoke, and still speaks; we listen.
- Progression is from temporary to permanent. We grow.
- God is one and has a Son fully equal. We ponder.
- Judaism was correct; now obsolete. We refocus.
- The old Law embodied the Covenant, and led us into a New Covenant, always of grace but now more clearly of grace rather than human accomplishment. We marvel.
- The glory of God was seen in a rainbow, a bush, a cloud, a temple, and now in a human person. We worship.
- The Lord Jehovah of the Old Testament is now known as Jesus Christ in the New Testament. We serve.

- The Lord Jehovah became the Lamb who was offered up so God's holy wrath was satisfied. We trust.

- The gentle Shepherd rules His flock. We obey.

- The Redeemer suffered for us. We can suffer for Him.

- Redemption was always by grace; it still is. We persevere in trusting the blood of the Lamb to protect us.

- The true High Priest is seated in honor. We await.

- The loving Lord invites rather than compels. We continue.

- The Temple is replaced by the synagogues, and now by the churches. We gather.

Outline and Structure of Hebrews

The Superiority of the Messiah: Heb 1:1–3:6

The Superior Rest in God's Provision: Heb 3:7–4:13

The Superior High Priest Overcoming Unbelief: Heb 4:14–6:20

The Superior Priesthood: Heb 7

    Of Melchizedek: Heb 7:1-14

    Of Jesus Christ: Heb 7:15-28

The Superior Covenant: Heb 8, 9, 10

The Superior Ministry: Heb 8:1-23

    Better Temple: Heb 9:1-22

    Better Sacrifice: Heb 10:1-39

The Superior Relationship—Faith: Heb 11

The Superior Lifestyle—Jesus Living Through Us: Heb 12 & 13

    Better Response to Suffering: Heb 12:1-29

    Better Response to Serving: Heb 13:1-25

Welcome to the Epistle to the Hebrews!

2

UNPARALLELED GREATNESS

Hebrews 1:1-2:4

Brian Gardiner

Introduction

Floating somewhere in the North Atlantic is a ship. If you find it, you can turn it in for about 800,000 dollars. The only caveat is that you have to get it to a scrap yard. And oh, by the way, it is likely infested with cannibalistic rats. According to a 2014 CNN story, and like something from a bad movie plot, the broken-down Russian ship *Lyubov Orlova* was impounded in Canada after it was abandoned by its crew. The Canadians tried to move it from Newfoundland to the Dominican Republic where it was to be scrapped for cash, but a storm caused the ship to break loose from its towlines. Eventually, the Canadians gave up and abandoned it at sea. In the years since, some think it sank; others, however, believe it is slowly floating in the currents of the North Atlantic toward Great Britain. No doubt the British are overjoyed at the thought of a cannibalistic rat-infested ship inching its way toward their shores.

A ship with no power, no anchor, and no moorings is a ship in trouble. I have lived almost all my life near large bodies of water, Lake Erie, and the Atlantic and Pacific Oceans. Along the coast, when a hurricane is approaching, ships head to sea. It is safer for them to ride out the weather in deep water rather than be tossed about like corks in the storm surge near shore. As we recently witnessed after Hurricane Ian struck southwest Florida, boats can break free from their moorings and may crash into other boats, docks, or land itself. The story usually doesn't end well for boats that drift.

Similar to a ship, the heart of faith that is not anchored deeply to Christ is in trouble too. It is primed for problems and destined to drift toward spiritual disaster. So, to what or to whom are you anchored? Is it your job? The affirmation of others? A relationship? Some hidden or illicit pleasure? A material possession? A secure retirement? The trappings of success? Is it your sense of self-reliance? Is it something temporary or is it something eternal? Have you become more enamored with the tangible blessings of God rather than with God himself? We are all anchored to something. The question is to whom or to what? Is it worthy of your affection? Will it hold fast when the storms of life bear down on you?

In a chaotic world that seems upside down more than right side up, good anchorage is critical. The book of Hebrews has a message we need to hear—Jesus Christ is superior and is worthy to be the one to whom we anchor our souls.

The Unparalleled Greatness of Our Revealed Christ
Hebrews 1:1-3

Hebrews begins abruptly. There is no introduction, no author is identified, no destination is specified, and it contains no greeting. It gets down to business right away. Its rich grounding in Old Testament texts makes it evident that it was originally written to a Jewish audience who had a deep understanding of Old Testament worship. It is also clear the writer of the book was intimately aware of the Old Testament. Hebrews is second only to Romans in quoting the Old Testament. Seven of these quotes are found in Chapter One alone. The author of the book, whoever he might have been, points to the Christ of the New Testament as the fulfillment of the promises of the Old and demonstrates for us that Christ is unrivaled.

GOD, who at sundry times and in divers manners spake in time past unto the fathers by the prophets, (1:1). The book of Hebrews refers to God by his divine title (*Theos*) with more frequency than almost any other New Testament book. It does so an average of once every seventy-three words (Gaebelein, p. 12). From its beginning, Hebrews presents God as active. He has and continues to engage with mankind. His choice to constantly take the initiative is proof of his amazing love for us!

At the heart of this activity was his choice to reveal himself. In the Old Testament era, he primarily communicated through the prophets. But consider the various methods by which he got his message across. He spoke to Moses from out of a burning bush. The Children of Israel heard a thunderous voice at Sinai. God spoke with a still small voice to Elijah. Isaiah saw a vision of heaven's throne room. God's message was made clear to Jonah via the casting of lots and a giant fish. Amos saw a basket of fruit. His message through Hosea involved a very unique domestic situation. Even creation itself is part of God's general revelation to man.

Hath in these last days spoken... (1:2a). Something changed with the advent of Jesus Christ. Until he came, God's communication had been fragmentary. His revelation about himself was incomplete; it provided a limited picture. But then God chose to make himself known. The one who had been distant became touchable. He could be seen. He spoke with a human voice. God chose to take on flesh and live among men. In comparison, previous revelation was like a bad cell connection in which you hear every third word and are left to piece together the rest of the conversation. But then Jesus arrived. He was the climax. This message is not limited to Jesus' words. His actions and work are further revelation. Verses 1-4 are one sentence. In it, the author presents seven descriptive statements about the revealed Christ.

> **The one who had been distant became touchable. He could be seen. He spoke with a human voice. God chose to take on flesh and live among men.**

Seven Descriptive Statements About the Revealed Christ

1. He is the Heir of All Things

Whom he hath appointed heir of all things (1:2b). Christ has been appointed heir of all things by the Father. This speaks to the exalted place and status of the Son. Part of the unique privilege of being a son is the opportunity to inherit. Many scholars see a connection to Psalm 2:8 which says: *Ask of me, and I will make the nations your heritage, and the ends of the earth your possession* (Psalm 2:8 ESV). Christ is the heir of all that is and will ever be (MacArthur, p. 11). And this is in part due to the next descriptive statement.

2. He is the Creator

In these first two descriptive statements, God the Father is the subject who chose to act. He was the initiator. He appointed Jesus the heir and then in v2 he created through the Son. The text says **by whom also he made the worlds (1:2c).** The Father exerting his will does not in any way diminish the work of the Son. It has the opposite effect. These statements speak to Jesus' uniqueness and pre-eminence. The writer's word choice for *world* is interesting. He chose *aion*. It can be translated "world" as we see here or "age." In other words, Christ created all that is and has ever been. He is the creator of space and time! And, what an amazing creator he is! Kent Hughes (p. 25) writes:

> An average-sized galaxy like ours that looks like a spiral pastry is estimated to be 100,000 light-years across or about six hundred trillion miles. And ours is just one of some hundred thousand million that can be seen using modern telescopes. Each galaxy contains some hundred thousand million stars. It is commonly thought that the distance between these hundred thousand million galaxies (each six hundred million miles across and containing one hundred thousand million stars) is three million light years. Some estimates say that the most distant galaxy is eight billion light years away and racing away at two hundred million miles an hour.

And here is the point. Christ created all of it—every speck of dust. Every quark, every neutron, every electron in this vast universe, he created all of it—with his Word. Oh, what wonder that we have a God like that! Let us anchor ourselves to him!

3. He is the Radiance of Glory

Throughout the remaining descriptive statements, Jesus moves into the role of subject. In verse 3 he (Jesus) is referred to as the **brightness of his glory (1:3a).** Jesus radiates the glory of God. This phrase can be understood in two different ways: "to reflect" or "to radiate." Complicating the choice for the interpreter is the fact that the word used is found only here in the New Testament. While the ancient church fathers favored the idea of radiating, reflecting can also accurately be asserted about Jesus (Ellingworth, p. 98). Since he is fully God and completely equal to the Father, Christ radiates his own glory (John 17:5), but in his capacity as the Son he also reflects the Father's glory (John 17:1). Perhaps the duality is the point of this ambiguous statement. Jesus both radiates and reflects glory.

4. He is the Full Expression of God

And the express image of his person, (1:3b). The word translated "express image" is taken from the world of engraving. It described something stamped or impressed with a die. Though distinct from the Father, Jesus is the exact imprint of all that the Father is. As we noted above, he is fully God and not in any way diluted. Thus, we can confidently assert that to know the Son is to know God. If one wants to know what the Father is like, he need only look to the Son who is the express image of all that the Father is (Ellingworth, p. 99).

5. He Upholds the Universe by His Spoken Word

Not only is Christ the creator, but he is also the sustainer, **upholding all things by the word of his power (1:3c).** These words echo Colossians 1 where Paul writes that *He is before all things, and in him all things hold together* (Colossians 1:17 NIV). Interestingly, the words Christ speaks are in themselves the expression of his power, and with them, he holds the universe together. The idea of the phrase is to carry something toward a destination. Christ is sustaining directionally. He will do so until all things are consummated, a new heaven and new earth are created, and eternity begins. From our perspective, things frequently seem out of control, but with only a word, Jesus can calm the raging universe and bring it back into order.

6. He Made Purification for Sin

When he had by himself purged our sins (1:3d). With this phrase we move toward an even greater miracle—the redemption of mankind. In this simple statement, the writer of Hebrews introduces the high priestly ministry of Christ, one of several glorious themes of the book. Purification rites were ritual washings made by the priests. For example, on the Day of Atonement, the priest would ritually wash himself before he stood before the Lord in the Holy of Holies. Here it refers to a much greater washing, the permanent removal of sin from the believer. Christ through his death has purified the believer from sin. He has removed it. The word for sin, *hamartia*, occurs twenty-five times in Hebrews. Only the book of Romans uses it more. This phrase highlights the work of Christ. The next highlights the position of Christ.

7. He is Seated at the Right Hand of the Father

Jesus' work, as it relates to our salvation, was completed and so he **sat down on the right hand of the Majesty on high (1:3e).** Note two things about this little phrase: First, Jesus is in the position of honor and power at the right side of the Father, who is himself described beautifully as the *Majesty on High*. Second, with the completion of his work, Jesus sat down. In the Tabernacle and temple sanctuaries, there were no seats; the priest's work was never done. Day after day they had to make sacrifices for sin. However, Jesus' one sacrifice was enough. His work has been gloriously completed (MacArthur, p. 19-20).

The Unparalleled Greatness of Our Superior Savior
Hebrews 1:4-14

The story of Elgin Staples is fascinating, to say the least. According to the *Proceedings of the Naval Institute* (Berryman, p. 48):

> The USS Astoria (CA-34) was the first U.S. cruiser to engage the Japanese during the Battle of Savo Island, a night action fought 8-9 August 1942. Although she scored two hits on the Imperial flagship Chokai, the Astoria was badly damaged and sank shortly after noon, 9 August.
>
> About 0200 hours a young Midwesterner, Signalman 3rd Class Elgin Staples, was swept overboard by the blast when the Astoria's number one eight-inch gun turret exploded. Wounded in both legs by shrapnel and in semi-shock, he was kept afloat by a narrow lifebelt that he managed to activate with a simple trigger mechanism.
>
> At around 0600 hours, Staples was rescued by a passing destroyer and returned to the Astoria, whose captain was

attempting to save the cruiser by beaching her. The effort failed, and Staples, still wearing the same lifebelt, found himself back in the water. It was lunchtime. Picked up again, this time by the USS President Jackson (AP-37), he was one of 500 survivors of the battle who were evacuated to Noumea. On board the transport Staples, for the first time, closely examined the lifebelt that had served him so well. It had been manufactured by Firestone Tire and Rubber Company of Akron, Ohio, and bore a registration number.

Given home leave, Staples told his story and asked his mother, who worked for Firestone, about the purpose of the number on the belt. She replied that the company insisted on personal responsibility for the war effort, and that the number was unique and assigned to only one inspector. Staples remembered everything about the lifebelt and quoted the number. It was his mother's personal code and affixed to every item she was responsible for approving.

When it comes to choosing a life preserver you want the best.

You can't afford to settle for a life preserver that is second-rate and only temporarily or occasionally dependable. How much more important is it for the rescuer of your soul to be superior in every way?

In the space of one sentence that stretches over the first four verses, the author of Hebrews packed an abundance of truth. Verse 4 itself functions as a hinge. It concludes the first paragraph while pivoting our attention from the greatness of the revealed Christ to the superiority of Christ.

Being made so much better than the angels (1:4a). In verse four we find another key word in Hebrews. In the KJV it is translated "better." In modern translations, such as the ESV or NIV, it is often translated "superior." Of the nineteen times it is used in the New Testament, thirteen occur in Hebrews. This tight grouping helps to underscore the message of the book: Christ is above all. He is better. He

> **This tight grouping helps to underscore the message of the book: Christ is above all. He is better. He is superior.**

is superior.

How could Christ *be made* (KJV) or *become* (ESV) so much better than the angels? Is he not God? Is he not intrinsically superior? Of course, he is! He could not in that sense become *more superior* than he already was. But it was his incarnation, death, and resurrection that fully demonstrated why he is better and worthy of highest honor.

Jesus' greatness is attested throughout Hebrews. For example, he is the author of a better hope (7:19). He guarantees a better covenant (7:22) and he mediates that covenant with better promises (8:6). He has offered a better sacrifice—himself! (9:23).

Hebrews 1 establishes the superiority of Jesus via several quotes from the Old Testament. As we have already seen, Christ is the creator. Apparently, there were some, however, who were elevating the importance of angels to an unhealthy degree. Have things changed two thousand years later? People happily put angel figurines on their shelves or tattoo them on their shoulders. Sports teams are named after them. They make good subject matter for movies and television shows. They adorn Christmas trees. Apparently, angels are benign, safe, and noncontroversial. Yet how does culture respond to Jesus? Mention Christ in a public setting and be prepared for a much different reaction. Sadly, Jesus is considered too controversial, and too demanding. We elevate creation while rejecting the creator.

Six Reasons Why Christ is Superior to Angels

1. He is Called "Son" by the Father

First, Jesus possesses a more excellent name. A lot of ink has been spent writing about various theories about which name is meant in verse four when it says, **As he hath by inheritance obtained a more excellent name than they (1:4b).** Some suggest it was the name given to him at birth. Others suggest that it might be "Lord" based on Philippians 2:5-11. And still others think that it is the unknown name written on Christ in Revelation 19 (Allen, p. 130). But the simplest answer may be that Jesus is called "Son" by the Father.

Verse five quotes Psalm 2:7 when it states: **For unto which of the angels said he at any time, Thou art my Son, this day have I begotten thee? (1:5a).** Since before Christ was born, rabbis had been debating the identity of the "son" in Psalm 2. The writer of Hebrews clearly understood it was Christ! Then to make the argument stronger he quoted 2 Samuel 7:17 in the second part of verse 5. **And again, I will be to him a Father, and he shall be to me a Son? (1:5b).** In their original context God was expressing to David how he would treat David's son Solomon. But now we can see that these were also prophetic references to Jesus.

It is fitting that the author of Hebrews chose anonymity. By remaining nameless, he directed the spotlight more brightly upon Christ, the one who among his many titles, is called, "son." In the Old Testament, angels (Job 1:6; 2:1) and men (Exodus 4:22; Hosea 11:1) have been called sons of God. But no angel, no matter how impressive he may be, has ever been singled out as "The Son of God." This is a title that has been reserved for Christ alone.

2. He is Worthy of Worship

And again, when he bringeth in the firstbegotten into the world, he saith, And let all the angels of God worship him (1:6). Jesus is identified as the first begotten or firstborn. Firstborn here does not refer to time or birth order. It refers to position. This is similar to Colossians where Paul wrote that Jesus is the *firstborn of every creature* (Colossians 1:15). He wasn't the first one who was born; Paul was expressing that Jesus is preeminent over all creation. He is worthy of worship. And note, in verse 6 the angels are not the objects of worship, they are the worshippers! Angels are not deserving of worship. Lucifer sought it, but it was his downfall. Only God is worthy of worship. The final phrase in verse six is a quote from Deuteronomy 32:43 from a Greek translation of the Old Testament called the Septuagint. By connecting Jesus with this text, the writer is thus making the following argument: Jesus is worthy of worship. God alone is to be worshipped. Therefore, Jesus is God.

When does the worship of verse 6 take place? What is the meaning of "again"? It helps to know that the word "world" describes the place where people live. Reading the words of a different translation might help as well. For example, the NIV states: *And again, when God brings his firstborn into the world, he says, "Let all God's angels worship him."* Verse 6 is a future look at the Second Coming when Jesus returns to earth. But this time he does so in power and majesty with angelic hosts worshipping him (MacArthur, p. 30).

3. He Reigns, Angels Serve

Jesus reigns as king while the angels serve. Recently the world watched the passing of Queen Elizabeth and the enthronement of a new monarch, King Charles III. Whenever we think of royal figures, British or otherwise, we know there is a difference between the royalty and those who attend to them. Hebrews makes the same observation in verses 7-8 when it quotes Psalm 104 and then Psalm 45 saying: **And of the angels he saith, Who maketh his angels spirits, and his ministers a flame of fire. But unto the Son he saith, Thy throne, O God, is for ever and ever: a sceptre of righteousness is the sceptre of thy kingdom (1:7–8).** A clear distinction has been drawn between angels who serve (minister) and King Jesus who reigns on the throne. The character of Christ is highlighted. He reigns in uprightness. Goodness and moral uprightness did not originate with the angels. They originate with God and are synonymous with who he is. No angel or human leader, king, queen, or otherwise, can compare to the superior Christ who sits enthroned in the heavens.

4. He Was Set Apart for a Greater Purpose

Thou hast loved righteousness, and hated iniquity; therefore God, even thy God, hath anointed thee with the oil of gladness above thy fellows (1:9). Continuing to quote Psalm 45, Hebrews further demonstrates why Christ is better. It is because he alone was chosen to redeem humanity. Note the word "anointed." It means to set apart for a sacred function. What was that sacred function? It was his death on the cross. No angel could rescue us from sin. Only God coming in human flesh could fit that role. Nothing highlights the distinctive qualities of Christ more than this. The greatest demonstration of Christ's character is the cross. His love and his justice were expressed there. In complete obedience to the Father's will, Jesus lived a sinless life and obediently died the death he did not deserve. The greatest demonstration of his power is the resurrection. The greatest demonstration of his glory is *in* the gospel. Are you anchored to such a superior savior as this?

5. He is Eternal

And, Thou, Lord, in the beginning hast laid the foundation of the earth; and the heavens are the works of thine hands (1:10). In verses 10-12 the writer of Hebrews quotes Psalm 102:25-27. Using this Psalm, he directs us to the eternality of Jesus. Though we do not know exactly when the angels were created, because Scripture does not tell us, they are part of God's creation. Christ however is eternal, and as we noted in verse 2, he is the creator. Verse 10 returns to this idea reminding us that Christ laid the foundations of the earth and created the heavens.

They shall perish; but thou remainest; and they all shall wax old as doth a garment; And as a vesture shalt thou fold them up, and they shall be changed: but thou art the same, and thy years shall not fail (1:11-12). In these verses, Christ's eternality is in contrast to creation which passes away. Though all of creation will perish, Christ will not. One day God will create a new heaven and a new earth. Worlds come and go. They change, but our superior savior will remain the same. He will be unchanged. He will not fail. As Hebrews will later remind us. He is *the same yesterday, and today, and forever* (13:8). We also see the immensity of Christ's power. He can roll up the heavens like a garment. No angel can do that!

6. He is Seated in the Place of Honor

Psalm 110 has the distinction of being the most commonly quoted psalm in the New Testament. For the final time in Chapter One Hebrews turns to the Old Testament and specifically Psalm 110 when he states, **But to which of the angels said he at any time, Sit on my right hand, until I make thine enemies thy footstool?** Based upon Jesus' interaction with the Pharisees in Mark 12:35-37 it appears that Psalm 110 was considered Messianic even by his enemies and probably by Jewish scholars long before his birth (Gaebelein, p. 19). Again, as noted in verse 3, Jesus is seated in the place of honor on the right hand of the Father in contrast to the angels. They do not sit, they serve. **Are they not all ministering spirits, sent forth to minister for them who shall be heirs of salvation?** And take note, the angels

> **Angels are not independent contractors. They are created beings with a divine purpose. They follow the commands of the divine king.**

serve for our sake! However, contrary to the opinions of some who even sit in our pews, they do not freelance. Angels are not independent contractors. They are created beings with a divine purpose. They follow the commands of the divine king. Throughout the pages of Scripture, they point to one who is greater—Christ, who is the place of honor. Having been obedient to the Father's redemptive plan Christ now sits in the place he rightfully deserves. What a glorious and superior savior! Are you anchored tightly to him? If not, you are in danger.

Warning: The Danger of Drift
Hebrews 2:1-4

Throughout the book of Hebrews, the author presents a series of five warnings and admonitions. There was a very real danger that the Jewish audience to whom Hebrews was written would lose sight of their superior savior and drift back toward their roots in Judaism. These roots were full of religious practice but devoid of real faith and any understanding of the gospel of grace. The first warning begins in Hebrews 2:1 where we read: **Therefore we ought to give the more earnest heed to the things which we have heard, lest at any time we should let them slip (2:1).** We must remain anchored so that we do not drift. Similar to the way a boat without an anchor is prone to drift, so too is the child of God who is not anchored to the revealed Christ, the superior savior. The way we avoid spiritual drift is by paying close attention to what we have heard and know to be true from the Word of God. The meaning of "paying earnest heed" is to take careful note of something and then act upon what is seen. In simplest terms, it means to pay attention and if necessary, make corrections. When we sense that we are deviating from scriptural truth, we need to make sure that we bring ourselves back into line, so we stay anchored.

But here is the problem. **Drift is subtle.** It is easy to drift without realizing the current is carrying us away. The word that was translated *slip,* or in other translations *drift*, was used to describe things like a ring that slid off a finger or snow slipping off soldier's bodies (Wuest, p. 51). On my wedding day, the ring my wife presented to me was too big—way too big. A few days into our honeymoon I jumped into the deep end of a swimming pool and my ring slid off my finger. I watched helplessly as it pirouetted its way toward the bottom of the pool and landed on the very edge of an intake grate. It happened so subtly that I barely realized it. Drift is like that. Movement happens so subtly that at first, it seems harmless until one is far from where one should be.

> *In 2017, the BBC reported the story of a Ukrainian man who had been rescued from an inflatable toy that drifted out into the Black Sea. The Russian Coast Guard found the distressed man on a floating trampoline upon which he had been trapped without food for three days. The man had fallen asleep and was swept out to sea shortly afterward. He had drifted 35 nautical miles. The drifter said when he could no longer see the shore he started crying, he went into shock and tried to protect himself from the sun as best he could. When his attempts to flag down passing ships failed, he assumed he would be lost at sea.*

Drift may be subtle, but its dangers are real. Spiritual drift seems harmless. Time away from God's Word and worship at first have little noticeable effect. Inattentiveness to negative influences or small hiccups in personal holiness can feel harmless until we find ourselves floundering in a tumultuous sea of confusion, fear, and sinful entanglements. C. S. Lewis (p. 140-141) once remarked, "As a matter of fact, if you examined a hundred people who had lost their faith in Christianity, I wonder how many of them would turn out to have been reasoned out of it by honest argument? Do not most people simply drift away?" A slow seemingly gentle current is enough, over time, to push the believer to an entirely different "spiritual continent" where beliefs and behaviors they would never have considered become mainstreamed into the thinking process. Sadly, what follows is often a spiritual shipwreck.

Inattention Will Make Drift Inevitable

The current is real. We may find ourselves in currents of immorality, life pressures, busyness, affirmation, discouragement, or the pursuit of happiness, just to name a few. The Christian is called to point upstream and to strain against currents that constantly push against our souls. We know this. We feel it. And sometimes, if we are honest, we grow tired and feel the temptation to let the current have its way. We want to ride it out for a while or take a break. But we can't. The danger of shipwreck is too great. Like seasoned navigators, we must be able to read the currents. So, for this reason, the writer of Hebrews exhorts us to pay attention and give more earnest heed to the things we have heard so that we do not slip. The current is pushing. So, fellow Christian, to what or to whom are you anchored?

The Solution to Drift: Be Anchored to Our Great Salvation

This is the only sure way to avoid drift. We must be anchored to our great salvation. In verse two we read these cautionary words: **For if the word spoken by angels was stedfast (2:2a).** The Greek term translated "word" in verse two is *logos*. This is a familiar and important word for the New Testament reader. Jesus, of course, is the final *logos,* the ultimate revelation (John 1:1). But in this case, it does not refer to Christ, but to the law which both Acts 7:53 and Galatians 3:19 indicate was given with the aid of angels. For more specifics about that process, we will have to wait until we have had a conversation with Moses in heaven!

The text continues **and every transgression and disobedience received a just recompence of reward (2:2b).** The law spelled out the punishment for sin and disobedience. To transgress means to willfully disregard what God has said. The word for disobedience indicates a wrong that is the result of an incomplete hearing. However, it doesn't mean a failure to hear because one is deaf or in some way hearing impaired. It means to be unaware because one refused to listen (MacArthur, p. 47). By connecting these two words the writer encapsulates the rebellious nature of our sin.

At this point, the text drops the hammer. **How shall we escape, if we neglect so great salvation (2:3a).** If the message delivered by inferior angels proved to be reliable and men were held accountable to it, how much more reliable and how much more will we be held accountable to the message that has been revealed in Jesus Christ? The writer has been building his argument toward this crescendo. We must be anchored to the superior Christ and to the salvation that he made possible through his death on our behalf.

The potential for disaster is upon us if we ignore or neglect "so great a salvation." The word for neglect was used to describe politicians who made bold public statements and failed to follow through on them. I know, hard to imagine, right? It describes a willful neglect. Interestingly, Hebrews draws a line of connecting dots between a refusal to listen (disobedience) in verse 2 and willful neglect in verse 3. Romans uses the same word for disobedience in 5:19 where it says that by one man's disobedience, the many were made sinners. By one man's (Adam's) disregard for what had been revealed to him by God, many (all of humanity) were made sinners.

We have all been tainted by his unwillingness to listen. And from his experience as well as our own we know there are tragic implications for those who disregard God's commands.

To be clear, this text is not warning us of a potential loss of salvation. Note that the author includes himself in the warning. He says how shall we escape? It is not a rejection of the gospel that is in view, but a neglect of that message (Allen, p. 194). To reject the gospel by refusing Christ's offer of salvation brings eternal punishment. This, however, appears to be a warning to believers that neglect of our faith brings with it serious consequences, though the passage does not indicate what exactly those may be. He is setting the stage for other warnings yet to come in the book. There was a very real danger that those first-century Jewish believers could lose sight of their salvation and the ultimate victory over sin accomplished by Jesus (Walvoord & Zuck, p. 783).

Despite our natural rebellion, God didn't stop. Out of his abundant grace, he provided the message of salvation. The text lays out three important truths. First, the gospel was spoken by Jesus. Verse 3 states, **which at the first began to be spoken by the Lord (2:3b).** Jesus was the first to preach salvation. He promised that eternal life was available for all who would believe in him. Second, the author continues, **and was confirmed unto us by them that heard him (2:3c).** The Apostles were witnesses of Christ's message and his death and resurrection. They confirmed what he said was true. Finally, in verse 4 we read **God also bearing them witness, both with signs and wonders and with divers miracles and gifts of the Holy Ghost, according to his own will? (2:4).** God the Father continued to confirm the gospel message himself through the signs and miracles that we find recorded in the book of Acts. The special giftedness of the apostles was also God's confirmation that their message was true.

Once again, just as we noted in Chapter One, God took the initiative. Out of love for humanity, he sent the means and the message of our great salvation in Jesus Christ. He is the superior Savior. Don't drift. Anchor yourself and your eternal destiny to him!

ADDITIONAL COMMENTS

The writer of Hebrews makes the point that Christ is superior to the angels, and with good reason. People often elevate angels to God-like status and perceive them as something more than they are. The idea that an angel is looking out for us is a compelling idea, but the reality is they cannot take the place of God. David Jeremiah puts it this way: "Angels are always one-way messengers. They are God's messengers to us, and never our messengers to God. No one in Scripture ever prays to an angel, and neither should we. They are not go-betweens or mediators between us and heaven" (p. 61). Hebrews makes the point that neither priests nor angels can serve in the role of mediator between God and man—that alone is reserved for Christ Jesus (Heb 8:6, 9:15, 12:24; 1 Tim 2:5). (Neipp)

Jesus Christ is:
- The Spokesman (v2) "spoken unto us by his son"
- The Son (v2) "his son...heir of all things"
- The Sovereign Creator (v2) "He made the worlds"
- The Shekinah Glory (v3) "the brightness of his glory"
- The Substance of God (v3) "the express image of his person"
- The Sustaineer (v3) "upholding all things"
- The Savior (v3) "when he had purged our sins"
- The Supreme Lord (v3) "sat down on the right hand of the Majesty on high" (Spink)

STUDY GUIDE QUESTIONS

What is the main emphasis of the book of Hebrews and why is its central theme considered significant?

What makes us regard earthly entities or people as noteworthy, and how does Hebrews 1 shift your view of Jesus?

What qualities of Jesus highlighted in Chapter One stand out to you, and how do these characteristics have a direct impact on your life?

The opening verse reveals that God previously spoke to humanity via prophets, yet there has been a transition in his method of communication. Why is this change meaningful? What are the theological implications of this shift? And how does this exceed the function of the prophets?

Rivers naturally have a flow, suggesting that objects within them will inevitably be carried downstream. In a spiritual sense, remaining static doesn't mean we stay where we are; rather, we are likely to slowly move away from the truth. How does this metaphor reinforce the need for active engagement with our faith? What active steps can we take to counteract this drift?

3

HIGHLIGHTING HIS HUMANITY

Hebrews 2:5-18

James Beight

Introduction

The superiority of Jesus is once again the overall theme in Hebrews 2. God the Son was and is superior to everything else these Jewish readers had ever considered sacred. The Son is introduced as a superior spokesman for God over the prophets (1:1) and the angels (1:4). As God's messengers, prophets spoke for God and often prefaced their published messages with "thus saith the Lord." These Hebrews likewise esteemed angels as messengers of God. Towards the beginning of Chapter Two, the application is given that since the messages delivered by angels were binding, certainly the message of Jesus was as well. If disobedience to angelic directives brought swift and just punishment, ignoring Christ's offer of salvation was even more so without remedy or survival. Thus comes a natural question to the Jewish audience: Was the long-awaited Messiah going to come as an angel or spirit being? The unnamed author of Hebrews makes it clear the promised Messiah must be human. Hebrews 2:5-18 presents the case for the Messiah to be both the Son of God and the Son of Man!

> **Hebrews 2:5-18 presents the case for the Messiah to be both the Son of God and the Son of Man!**

Our writer is not done comparing and contrasting the ministry of Jesus, as the ultimate messenger of God, with the ministry of angels, who likewise delivered messages from God. However, for Jesus to accomplish his redemptive purpose, *he was made for a little while even lower than the angels.* You see, Jesus did not become an angel to save the fallen angels. No grace nor plan of salvation was established or extended to those evil spirits who followed Satan into rebellion. Their fall into sin was permanent and catastrophic. Jesus did, however, become a man to save lost humans. Our assigned text thus highlights *Jesus in his humanity.* We will focus the outline of our commentary on this fascinating truth.

The Humanity of Jesus was Predictable (v5-8)
Our author uses a selected portion of Psalm 8 to revisit and enhance the distinction that was made after Chapter One: The Son is clearly superior to angels.

> What is man, that thou art mindful of him? and the son of man, that thou visitest him? For thou hast made him a little lower than the angels, and hast crowned him with glory and honour. Thou madest him to have dominion over the works of thy hands; thou hast put all things under his feet (Ps. 8:4-6).

> But one in a certain place testified, saying, What is man, that thou art mindful of him? or the son of man that thou visitest him? Thou madest him a little lower than the angels; thou crownedst him with glory and honour, and didst set him over the works of thy hands: Thou hast put all things in subjection under his feet. For in that he put all in subjection under him, he left nothing that is not put under him. But now we see not yet all things put under him. But we see Jesus, who was made a little lower than the angels for the suffering of death, crowned with glory and honour; that he by the grace of God should taste death for every man (Heb. 2:6-9).

The notion that the Savior of mankind would be human, not angelic, is therefore a biblically viable truth. Psalm 8 primarily refers to the delegated dominion of humans over God's creation. This dominion was granted by God to Adam and his descendants at the end of the creation week.

> So God created man in his own image, in the image of God created he him; male and female created he them. And God blessed them, and God said unto them, Be fruitful, and

> multiply, and replenish the earth, and subdue it: and have dominion over the fish of the sea, and over the fowl of the air, and over every living thing that moveth upon the earth (Gen. 1:27-28).

Our writer's purpose in quoting Psalm 8:5-6 is made clear by his additional comments about angels in verse 5 of our text. Unlike the Son who was promised to rule over the heathen and all the kingdoms of the earth in Psalm 2 (cited by our author in 1:5), angels have not been promised any such honor or reign. Therefore, the promises of Psalm 8 cannot possibly be fulfilled by any normal angel. The Messiah had to be a human. Our writer uses this logic to reinforce his later conclusions about the Son. This meant that the genuine humanity of the promised Messiah and Savior could have been predicted by those who were students of the Scriptures.

The Humanity of Jesus was Proficient (v9)
But we see Jesus, who was made a little lower than the angels for the suffering of death, crowned with glory and honour; that he by the grace of God should taste death for every man.

In the Incarnation (Jn 1:14), the Son of God was made in the likeness of human flesh, and is, therefore, the perfect fulfillment of Psalm 8. You see, Jesus was fully human, just as he was fully divine. He, as the Son of Man, was obedient unto death and was thus crowned or exalted with glory and honor. Paul repeats these truths in his epistle to the church at Philippi:

> Let this mind be in you, which was also in Christ Jesus: Who, being in the form of God, thought it not robbery to be equal with God: But made himself of no reputation, and took upon him the form of a servant, and was made in the likeness of men: And being found in fashion as a man, he humbled himself, and became obedient unto death, even the death of the cross. Wherefore God also hath highly exalted him, and given him a name which is above every name: That at the name of Jesus every knee should bow, of things in heaven, and things in earth, and things under the earth; And that every tongue should confess that Jesus Christ is Lord, to the glory of God the Father (Phil. 2:5-11).

At the end of verse 9 in our text, our writer clarifies something that has confused and divided generations of Christians. This question is, "For whom did Christ die?" or "Was the atonement sufficient for the elect only?" The answer from our text isn't ambiguous. Please note: **that he** (Jesus Christ) **by the grace of God should taste death for every man.** There is something gracious about the death of Jesus Christ, that in some unexplained fashion benefited **every man**. This includes the lost. *Christ tasted death for every man.* This concept is reinforced by Paul in 2 Corinthians 5:14: *For the love of Christ constraineth us; because we thus judge, that if one died for all, then were all dead.*

Don't be confused. This verse does not teach that Jesus only died for the physically dead. It seems pretty clear that Paul has concluded that Jesus Christ died out of his love for all who were spiritually dead. Ephesians 2:1 clarifies those are spiritually dead because of trespasses and sins. For whom did Jesus die? Jesus died for sinners—all sinners!

Please note, however, that while these verses speak to the extent of the atonement, they do not speak at all to its application. Let me be very clear, they do not teach universalism (that everyone without exception is saved by Christ's sacrifice on the cross). These passages do teach, however, that every man could be rendered as savable because Christ died for all. I like to say that Christ died for everyone without distinction.

In my understanding, our text teaches the following truth, which could settle the question concerning limited atonement: The atonement from our Savior's death is graciously sufficient for all but is practically efficient only for elect believers! Paul is emphatic—the Gospel is the power of God unto salvation for all who believe (Rom. 1:16).

This biblical truth about an unlimited atonement is not isolated to these texts alone. Paul speaks of an unlimited ransom made for all by Christ Jesus to his young protégé, Timothy. I Timothy 2:5 states: *For there is one God, and one mediator between God and men, the man Christ Jesus; Who gave himself a ransom for all, to be testified in due time.*

I heard Dr. Paul Tassell give the following definition of the word *all*, which he claims originated from a fourth grader. When asked by his teacher the student replied, "All means all, and that's all that all means." Christ Jesus tasted death for every man. He was the ransom for *all*. This was God's gift of common grace even to those unbelievers who would never accept Jesus as their Savior. Thus, we can conclude that Jesus' humanity was supremely virtuous. It could never matter how many sinful people are born, nor how much sin these myriads of lost people commit. The death of Christ satisfied God's wrath upon sin because Jesus had more than enough righteousness to atone for all sin. Therefore, he was able and willing by the grace of God to taste death for every man!

> **Christ Jesus tasted death for every man. He was the ransom for *all*.**

The Humanity of Jesus was Perfected (v10)
For it became him, for whom are all things, and by whom are all things, in bringing many sons unto glory, to make the captain of their salvation perfect through sufferings.

God determined that for his own purposes, his only begotten son should suffer. This was the divine prerogative of the Almighty Creator, for whom and by whom all things exist. God the Father wanted Jesus the Son to suffer, learn obedience to his will, and thus become the only qualified human *captain of salvation*! Many believers might be unsettled by the notion from our author that physical suffering perfected our Savior in any way. They might protest, "Scriptures declares in 2 Corinthians 5:21, 'He knew no sin!'" This is correct. Jesus was and is and always will be perfectly sinless.

Since Jesus was already sinless, how could human suffering make him any more perfect? This does appear to be a paradox on its surface. This use of the English word *perfect* is not to be confused with enhancing his moral perfection in any way. Rather, it indicates that the real genuine humanity of Jesus was perfectly confirmed through these sufferings. Jesus was not a phantom; he was not a spirit, nor was he an angel. Spirit beings don't suffer physically. Jesus was a real human being, and his intense physical and emotional sufferings perfectly qualified him in his humanity to be the ideal **captain of our salvation**.

To reiterate, Jesus was already morally perfect, but suffering as he did, and as we do, made him the perfect, merciful, and sympathetic Savior for those who are not perfect. His suffering thus displayed Jesus to be victorious.

Please note, this verse also confirms that despite "tasting death for every man," not every man is ultimately saved. His death is sufficient for all but efficient only for those who believe. Praise God, the power of the gospel brings **many sons unto glory**. However, it does not save those who reject Jesus. Salvation is offered to us; it is not, however, forced upon us. Remember, our writer warns earlier in our chapter, "How shall we escape, if we neglect so great a salvation" (Heb. 2:3). In doing so, he warns, do not let your opportunity to trust in Jesus slip by and/or drift away.

The Humanity of Jesus was Productive (v10-13)

Hebrews 2:10 already declared that the "captain of our salvation" was able to bring many sons unto glory. This redemptive truth is supported as our text quotes Old Testament passages that confirm this joyous truth.

> **For both he that sanctifieth and they who are sanctified are all of one: for which cause he is not ashamed to call them brethren, Saying, I will declare thy name unto my brethren, in the midst of the church will I sing praise unto thee. And again, I will put my trust in him. And again, Behold I and the children which God hath given me** (Heb. 2:11-13).

These verses expand our understanding of the humanity of Jesus. The writer insists this is also how we are made children of God. Jesus is the sole qualified human *captain of salvation*. As such, he alone can sanctify (set apart from sin unto righteousness) those who were previously lost in sin. Jesus, who sanctifies sinners, is human. The ones he sanctifies are also human. They both are one—of the same flesh, blood, and bone. Thus, after salvation, they belong to the same spiritual family. He is willing to claim these transformed sinners as his family. This refers to some of the blessed results of

> **When a sinner is born again, God becomes their Heavenly Father because Jesus Christ becomes their Lord and Savior.**

regeneration. When a sinner is born again, (Jn. 3:3) God becomes their Heavenly Father because Jesus Christ becomes their Lord and Savior. In Christ, believers are a new creation (2 Cor. 5:17). They have new life and belong to a new family! Believers are now considered sons, (children) of God. John 1:12 reaffirms this truth: *But as many as received him, to them gave he power to become the sons of God, even to them that believe on his name: Which were born, not of blood, nor of the will of the flesh, nor of the will of man, but of God.*

Jesus is God's Son, who is now crowned with glory and honor. Jesus is the Son of Man, our Savior with a name that is above every other name. However, on a mere human level, Jesus is our Messiah. He is also our Jewish brother. He is not ashamed to claim us as his family! These somewhat random Old Testament proof texts (Ps. 22:22; & Isa. 8:17-18) cited by the author are simply supporting the idea of kinship. Notice the terms of family relationships, such as **brethren** and **children**. The church is the family of God, with God as our Father and Jesus as our Savior! The value in God's Son, the promised Messiah, becoming human, was that through him, many humans would become God's sons too!

The Humanity of Jesus was Pertinent (v14)

Forasmuch then as the children are partakers of flesh and blood, he also himself likewise took part of the same; that through death he might destroy him that had the power of death, that is, the devil;

As our writer highlights the humanity of Jesus, he gets to a critical consideration. God's Son took on real human flesh and blood so that he could be just as human as those he came to save. He needed to be human so that he could die a valid atoning death for sinners. Biblically, *the wages of sin is death* (Rom. 6:23). Thus, in order to absorb God's wrath upon sin and pay the penalty for sinners, Jesus had to actually die for sin. His real humanity gave him the ability to make a valid payment for sin! Jesus shed his blood as the prescribed atonement or covering for sin.

Our writer began our consideration of the Son by referencing this provision and purification. Remember, *he by himself, purged our sins* (Heb. 1:3). Make no mistake! Jesus died to purge us from our sins. He did not need to suffer or die for his own sin—for he had none! It was all for us.

> For I delivered unto you first of all that which I also received, how that Christ died for our sins according to the scriptures; (1 Cor. 15:3).
>
> But for us also, to whom it shall be imputed, if we believe on him that raised up Jesus our Lord from the dead; Who was delivered for our offences, and was raised again for our justification (Rom. 4:24).

So, the sinless humanity of Jesus allowed him to die as the perfect payment for our sin. However, our writer adds another tremendous result: His death also destroyed the devil's power over death. This was one of the first redemptive promises recorded in the Bible. It was stated during God's curse upon the serpent: *And the LORD God said unto the serpent, Because thou hast done this, thou art cursed above all cattle, and above every beast of the field; upon thy belly shalt thou go, and dust shalt thou eat all the days of thy life: And I will put enmity between thee and the woman, and between thy seed and her seed; it shall bruise thy head, and thou shalt bruise his heel* (Gen. 3:15).

Paul indicates that this promised undoing of the devil's power of death was accomplished at the cross: *Blotting out the handwriting of ordinances that was against us, which was contrary to us, and took it out of the way, nailing it to his cross; And having spoiled principalities and powers, he made a show of them openly, triumphing over them in it* (Col. 2:14). Jesus' real humanity allowed him to die in the place of sinners and to absorb the wrath of God upon sin. His death also disarmed the ability of the devil to ever accuse us again. You see, our death sentence for sin has been blotted out by the shed blood of Jesus Christ. Sin's penalty has been paid in full at the cross. Satan's slanderous accusations against me have been spoiled and defeated. Jesus triumphs and Satan is disgraced!

The Humanity of Jesus Provides a Prototype (v15-16)

And deliver them who through fear of death were all their lifetime subject to bondage. For verily he took not on him the nature of angels; but he took on him the seed of Abraham.

Jesus died as a human and he was raised back to life as a human. Jesus was the human prototype of victory over death and the devil! Our writer refers to our natural human fear of death as a type of bondage or slavery. You see, until Jesus was raised, death reigned supreme from Adam to all of his offspring. Death brought decay. Death brought separation. Death brought grief. Death always seemed to win. Death enslaved mankind. However, the real humanity of Jesus not only gave him the chance to die for sins but to be resurrected from death on the third day as the firstborn from the dead! Christ is now the first fruits or the prototype of all else who will eventually be resurrected. Death doesn't always win! The grave is not our hopeless end. The man Christ Jesus conquered sin, Satan, death, hell, and the grave! Our deliverer is living proof that death doesn't win.

> But now is Christ risen from the dead, and become the firstfruits of them that slept. For since by man came death, by man came also the resurrection of the dead. For as in Adam all die, even so in Christ shall all be made alive (1 Cor. 15:20).

> That as sin hath reigned unto death, even so might grace reign through righteousness unto eternal life by Jesus Christ our Lord (Rom. 5:21).

The mention of angels once again in verse 16 is proof that our writer has never left his aim of proving that the Son of God and of Man, our Savior Jesus Christ, needed to be human not simply angelic. To reiterate, Jesus did not leave heaven and become an angel to save fallen angels. However, he did become human, a Hebrew from the line of Abraham, to save all those of Adam's race who share Abraham's faith: *Nor because they are his descendants are they all Abraham's children. On the contrary, "It is through Isaac that your offspring will be reckoned." In other words, it is not the children by physical descent who are God's children, but it is the children of the promise who are regarded as Abraham's offspring* (Rom. 9:7-8 NIV).

In summary, Jesus became human in order to die for sin. His humanity was completely vindicated by his subsequent resurrection from the dead: *Regarding his Son, who as to his earthly life was a descendant of David, and who through the Spirit of holiness was appointed the Son of God in power by his resurrection from the dead: Jesus Christ our Lord* (Rom. 1:3-4 NIV). Jesus was declared to be God's Son with spiritual power by his resurrection from the dead. This should encourage every believer who has been adopted into God's family, that we too shall live even after we die.

Jesus said unto her, I am the resurrection, and the life: he that believeth in me, though he were dead, yet shall he live (Jn. 11:25).

We no longer fear death nor grieve departed believers *like the rest of mankind who have no hope* (1 Thess. 4:13 NIV).

The Humanity of Jesus was also Priest-like (v17-18)
Wherefore in all things it behoved him to be made like unto his brethren, that he might be a merciful and faithful high priest in things pertaining to God, to make reconciliation for the sins of the people. For in that he himself hath suffered being tempted, he is able to succour them that are tempted.

Chapter Two ends with a fitting summary of these truths about our Savior's humanity. In fact, the text states it emphatically: **in all things it behoved him to be made like his brethren**. Thus, he made **reconciliation** for sins. Additionally, he was **tempted** in order to assist other humans who were tempted. This simply means that Jesus is able help those who are in severe distress.

Our writer includes a conceptual exclamation point for these Hebrew readers. Remember, the author's thesis is that the Son is superior to all that they had ever held as sacred. One of these sacred elements, especially dear to Orthodox Jews, was and is their priesthood. In all of these ways in which the humanity of Jesus was highlighted, a new doctrine is emphasized in verse 17. The author indicates that because of Jesus' humanity, he was acting on our behalf, before God as **a merciful and faithful high priest**. This truth was only briefly alluded to earlier in 1:3 where the Son by himself purged sin and then *sat down on the right hand of the Majesty on High*. This assertion of an avenue for the Son of God and the Son of Man to be a legitimate **high priest** opens up new questions needing clarification. Our author explains and expands this truth throughout the middle portion of the book.

Conclusion
Angels are wonderful and mysterious ministering spirits. They are messengers of God and for God. However, angels are not the fulfillment of God's promises of a redeemer. In fact, some angels had fallen into sin. Yet, no plan of salvation was offered to demons. No

grace was extended to evil spirits. Mankind also fell into sin which demanded death! By the grace of God, a plan of salvation was devised in eternity past, to redeem lost humanity. That plan involved the Son of God becoming the Son of Man and *being made even lower than the angels for a little while*. At the point of redundancy—Jesus needed to be human in order to become the only qualified Savior for humans. We have attempted in this portion of our commentary to explain each of the reasons offered. God's plan of salvation required a human savior. The promised Messiah would have to suffer and taste death for every man. The process would end with a qualified **captain of salvation**. Jesus entered into human history with this as his mission. He took upon himself our flesh, blood, and bones so that he might die for us and reconcile us back to God. In so doing, he has destroyed the power of the devil to accuse us. He has become the **captain of our salvation**. He is now crowned with glory and honor! Jesus our Savior is amazing!

"All praise to him who reigns above in majesty supreme, who gave his Son for man to die, that he might man redeem! Blessed be the name of the Lord!" (William H. Clark)

ADDITIONAL COMMENTS

Limited atonement refers to the theological idea that restricts or limits the effect of Christ's death to the elect (Acts 13:48). This concept fits within a theological ideology popularized by John Calvin in which total depravity, unconditional election, irresistible grace, and perseverance of the saints are also emphasized. In contrast, James Arminius is the central figure equated with what has come to be known as Arminianism. Five points were drawn up in correlation to and as a response and form of protest to Calvinism. Those correlating points are free will, conditional election, unlimited atonement, effectual resistance, and falling from grace. In alignment with other tenets, Calvin argued the atonement was only applicable to the elect. However, Arminius viewed Christ's redeeming work in a way that made it possible for anyone to believe (Jn. 1:29; 1 Jn. 2:2). Well-known scholars and theologians have fallen on both sides of the debate for the simple reason that Scripture appears to teach that Christ died for all men (Jn. 3:16; 2 Cor. 5:19; 2 Pt. 2:1; 1 Jn. 2:2) **and** that he also secured the salvation of the elect (Jn. 10:15; Eph. 5:25).

There is room here for differences of theological opinion and my encouragement is that each person carefully study Scripture in the process of forming their convictions. (Neipp)

STUDY GUIDE QUESTIONS

In the preceding chapter, Christ's supremacy over angels was emphasized, but in this chapter, we find a passage stating that Jesus was "made a little lower than the angels." What is the central theme of this text, and why is Jesus depicted as somewhat lesser than the angels? How exactly was he "lower than the angels"?

What responsibilities does the role of a captain encompass, and why is Jesus referred to as a captain in verse 10?

Carefully analyze verses 2:10-18 and count the occurrences of terms related to familial connections. What significance does the prevalence of family-related references hold in this passage?

According to 2:8, Christ is granted authority over everything. How does this depiction resonate with your everyday experiences? In which areas of your life do you typically seek control, and where do you find it challenging to let go?

In times of great adversity, we may easily overlook the comfort and advice offered by others because they may not have firsthand experience with our circumstances. However, despite never yielding to temptation, Jesus genuinely encountered the allure of sin. Considering Christ's humanity, what comfort arises from knowing that he understands the depths of our experiences?

4

LISTENING TO HIS VOICE (PART 1)

Hebrews 3:1-11

Michael Peck

Introduction

Think of the word *better*. It is an adjective that means *of a superior quality or excellence*. While these words are adequate descriptors for many things in life, they fall woefully short as descriptors of our awesome Lord and Savior, Jesus Christ. The writer of Hebrews expresses with joyous confidence that the Lord Jesus Christ is better in every way. The word better *kreitton* (KRITE-tohn) means the best, more advantageous, or more excellent. Yes, the Lord Jesus is better than the prophets (1:1-3), than the angels (1:4-14), and even better than Moses (3:1-11). This wonderful Lord Jesus is actively involved in the lives of his people. Considering that the Lord Jesus Christ is better, more excellent, and superior to everyone and everything, it will be wise indeed to **Hear his voice** (v7) through his Word.

Why should I listen to him? He is building his church upon himself. He said: *Upon this rock I will build my church; and the gates of hell shall not prevail against it* (Matthew 16:18). Through his Word, he is speaking to his people: *And when he putteth forth his own sheep, he goeth before them, and the sheep follow him: for they know his voice. And a stranger will they not follow, but will flee from him: for they know not the voice of strangers* (John 10:4-5). Paul reminded us of this privilege as he wrote: *Let the word of Christ dwell in you richly in all wisdom; teaching and admonishing one another, in psalms, and hymns and spiritual songs, singing with grace in your hearts to the*

Lord (Colossians 3:16).

What a wonderful blessing and privilege it is to belong to the Lord Jesus. We are his people and so blessed to be part of his family, purpose, and work. It is imperative to have not only the right view of his superiority but in a very practical application to listen to his voice through his Word and encourage others to do the same. How significant it is to be intentional in our walk with the Lord.

Far greater than a long list of rules and regulations, believers have the joy of learning about the Lord (Matthew 11:29), being fruitful as we abide in him (John 15: 4-5), and seeking those things above where Christ is sitting on the right hand of God (Colossians 3:1). All of this is built upon the intentional decision to listen to his voice (v7).

Verse 1
Listen to His Voice! Think of the Connection (v1a)

It is an amazing display of the awesomeness of our Savior. This connection is presented in the word **Wherefore.** Whenever the writer of Scripture employs the word *therefore* or *wherefore*, a strategic pause ought to take place. **Wherefore,** *othen* (HOTH-en), is a connection that links the previously written section with what follows. It literally means *on account of.* It suggests that the writer is saying, "Think of what I've written before. Now think of what I am going to write." They are connected with the "wherefore!"

This word connects the incredible view of Christ in the previous chapter to the incredible blessing of Christ in this section. How superior is the one to whom we must listen! Glance very briefly back to the previous section that is connected to listening to his voice.

He bore powerful witness by miracles (2:4) and yet he is mindful of us (2:6). Wherefore!

He is crowned with glory and honor (2:7-8). Wherefore!

He was made lower than the angels for the suffering of death (2:9). Wherefore!

He is victorious over the devil (2:14). Wherefore!

He is the merciful and faithful High Priest (2:17a). Wherefore!

He is the incredible propitiation for our sins (2:17b). Wherefore!

He is fully capable of helping those who are tempted because he himself was tempted (2:18).

WHEREFORE! Because of all these wonderful blessings, what follows is logical.

Listen to His Voice! Think of the Calling (v1b)

It is a wonderful privilege to be part of the Lord's family. Wherefore, **holy** *hagios* (HAG-ee-os) means *that which is separated or dedicated to the Lord*. It is a breathtaking reminder that we who know the Lord Jesus Christ are referred to by him as *holy*. This is the amazing privilege of being set apart unto the Lord and cherished by him, resulting in a lifestyle that reflects his holiness. Holiness can be viewed from both a positional and practical perspective.

The position of being *holy* or sanctified is firm. Those who place their trust in Christ are declared positionally to be a fully sanctified or holy people in Christ. Think of what Paul wrote to the Corinthian believers: *Unto the church of God which is at Corinth, to them that are sanctified in Christ Jesus, called to be saints* (1 Corinthians 1:2). The word *sanctified* is *hagiazo* (hag-ee-AD-zo) which means *to make holy*. The word *saints* is actually *hagios*. The writer of Hebrews speaks of this wonderful calling that comes to the holy people of God.

The practical aspect of being holy or sanctified is demonstrated by the state of our lives and the way that we live. Think of what Peter wrote as he said: *As obedient children, not fashioning yourselves according to the former lusts in your ignorance; but as he which hath called you is holy, so be ye holy in all manner of conversation because it is written, be ye holy; for I am holy* (1 Peter 1:14-16). Peter uses the word *hagios* holy as the way believers are to live and conduct themselves.

As you pick up the Scriptures and carefully read the words, you will hear his voice. Often he speaks of holiness to his children as he reminds us of the tremendous privilege of being called saints: *To all that be in Rome, beloved of God, called to be saints; Grace to you and peace from God our Father, and the Lord Jesus Christ* (Romans 1:7). *And you, that were sometime alienated and enemies in your mind by wicked works, yet now hath He reconciled in the body of his flesh through death, to present you holy and unblameable and unreproveable in his sight: If ye continue in the faith grounded and settled, and be not moved away from the hope of the gospel, which ye have heard, and which was preached to every creature which is under heaven; whereof I Paul am made a minister (Colossians 1:21-23).*

Brethren *adelphos (ad-el-FOS)* denotes the sheer joy of familyhood. Profoundly stated, we are a close family, a community of like ones who have been born into God's household through faith in Christ's redemption. There is one way into the incredible family of the Lord and that is through the new birth. We who share the womb are highly privileged to be related to the Lord and each other. It is not just that we as the people of God are called to be holy; we are called to remember the oneness of our fellowship with the Lord Jesus and with one another.

The writer of the book of Hebrews expressed with great tenderness and with joy the incredible blessings of being brethren. He wrote: *For both he that sanctifieth, and they who are sanctified are all of one: for which cause he is not ashamed to call them brethren, Saying, I will declare thy name unto my brethren, in the midst of the church will I sing praise unto thee* (2:11-12).

We are humbled, blessed, amazed, and filled with wonder and awe as we are reminded: *Wherefore in all things it behooved him to be made like unto his brethren, that he might be a merciful and faithful high priest in all things pertaining to God, to make reconciliation for the sins of the people* (2:17).

The Lord Jesus calls us brethren, related family members! What a declaration the writer of Hebrews makes: *Having therefore, brethren, boldness to enter into the holiest by the blood of Jesus, By a new and living way, which he hath consecrated for us, through the veil, that is to say, his flesh* (10:19-20). The new and living way is a beautiful demonstration of the change he has made in our lives.

> **The new and living way is a beautiful demonstration of the change he has made in our lives.**

A note of caution must be sounded in the midst of these promises and privileges. As the family of the Lord, the writer of Hebrews cautions the brethren about a very real possibility. He wrote: *Take heed, brethren, lest there be in any of you an evil heart of unbelief, in departing from the living God* (3:12). Much will be written about this awful possibility of hardening one's heart in the next section. Suffice it to say that a hardened heart is not the fertile ground of the spiritual heart that is eager to hear from the Lord and to embrace what he tells us in the Word of God.

Reflection

Though we are created beings with the capability of a wide range of emotions, it is important to consider very carefully and make a deliberate decision to listen to his voice. How very important it is to stop and remember that we believers do not live by our feelings. We live by what the Word of God declares us to be.

How wonderfully blessed to listen to his voice as He tells us: *Be not thou therefore ashamed of the testimony of our Lord, nor of me his prisoner: but be thou partaker of the afflictions of the gospel according to the power of God; Who hath saved us, and called us with an holy calling, not according to our works, but according to his own purpose and grace, which was given us in Christ Jesus before the world began* (2 Timothy 1:8-9).

Think of this, **holy brethren**.

1. It is possible despite this wonderful calling to allow negative feelings to come along. We need to be on guard concerning our thoughts and the condition of our spiritual heart (Psalm 19:14).

2. Our testimony is that by which the Lord and we are known and observed by others. We have the amazing opportunity to live quietly, confidently, and in full trust of the Lord despite our circumstances (1 Timothy 2:1-3).

3. Sometimes we as **holy brethren** have hard things happen to us. Such was Paul's imprisonment (Philippians 1:12-13).

4. The Christian life is not always easy as demonstrated by the word *afflictions*. **Holy brethren** have hard things that happen to them (2 Timothy 4:5).

5. What wonderful transforming power is found in the gospel! **Holy brethren** have been taken from spiritual darkness and transformed into the Kingdom of his dear Son (Colossians 1:13).

6. True joy comes from the truth of being saved and called with a holy calling (2 Timothy 1:9).

7. Thankfully this holy calling is not according to our own self-effort (Titus 3:5).

8. God has a plan and purpose which for us is found in Christ and is of an eternal nature (Romans 12:1-2).

Go to his Word and listen to his voice!

Remember Christ being better, superior to all, he is the very one who calls you **holy brethren** or quite literally *My uniquely separated unto Myself holy family*! The writer of Hebrews continues with **partakers** *metochos* (MET-okh-os) which is one who completely shares with and is a partner in office and joyous position. No believer is left out. All participate as partakers.

The heavenly *epouranios* (ep-oo-RAN-ee-os) denotes the place where Christ sits and is in authority. Think of what the Lord reveals to us about this as we read: *The eyes of your understanding being enlightened; that ye may know what is the hope of his calling, and what the riches of the glory of his inheritance in the saints, And what is the exceeding greatness of his power to us-ward who believe, according to the working of his mighty power, Which he wrought in Christ, when he raised him from the dead, and set him at his own right hand in the heavenly places, Far above all principality and power, and might, and dominion, and every name that is named, not only in this world, but also in that which is to come: And hath put all things under his feet, and gave him to be the head over all things to the church, Which is his body, the fulness of him that filleth all in all* (Ephesians 1:18-23).

Line upon line we discover the power, glory, and dominion which is heavenly. The writer continues with the specific term **calling** *klesis* (KLAY-sis) which speaks of the heavenly summons or invitation to respond, to accept the blessings and benefits of salvation. It is not a light matter to understand that God has called his people. The Lord Jesus declared to his disciples: *Upon this rock I will build my church* (Matthew 16:18). Literally, the Lord Jesus declares that he is at work building a called-out people who are built upon him. The church, *ekklesia*, is composed of *ek* (out of) *klesis* (a calling). What a joy and privilege to be a follower of Christ, one of his own people and part of the great called-out ones of his church. This calling is to be considered carefully and with great joy.

Listen to his voice as a "called" one

1. God's calling is not on the basis of our merits.
   For ye see your calling, brethren, how that not many wise men after the flesh, not many mighty, not many noble, are called: But God hath chosen the foolish things of the world to confound the wise; and God hath chosen the weak things of the world to confound the things which are mighty; And base things of the world, and things which are despised, hath God chosen, yea, and things which are not, to bring to nought things that are: That no flesh should glory in his presence (1 Corinthians 1:26-29).

2. God's calling provides direction for daily living.
   Brethren, I count not myself to have apprehended: but this one thing I do, forgetting those things which are behind, and reaching forth unto those things which are before, I press toward the mark for the prize of the high calling of God in Christ Jesus (Philippians 3:13-14).

3. God's calling demands our alertness and a heart that is quick to obey.
   Wherefore also we pray always for you, that our God would count you worthy of this calling, and fulfil all the good pleasure of his goodness, and the work of faith with power: That the name of our Lord Jesus Christ may be glorified in you, and ye in him, according to the grace of our God and the Lord Jesus Christ (2 Thessalonians 1:11-12).

Listen to His Voice! Think of the Consideration (v1c)

It is an incredible blessing to consider who he is and what he is doing! The word **Consider** *katanoeo* (kat-an-o-EH-o) is much stronger than casually entertaining a thought or two about a given subject. This denotes the intentional action of one's mind in apprehending the revealed facts about the subject. It is the intentional frequent thinking, embracing, and apprehending of what the Word of God has revealed to the people of God.

> **In every way the Lord Jesus is better.**

Consider indeed that in every way the Lord Jesus is better. He is superior. He is incomparable. Among his many titles, He is called the Lord (Luke 2:11; Revelation 19:6); Son of God (John 20:31); The Word (John 1:1-3); great God and Savior (Titus 2:13); Advocate (1 John 2:1); Lord Jesus Christ (1 Thessalonians 1:1). Now the writer will open several more incredible blessings for us to consider about the Lord Jesus, the awesome One.

Blessedly the writer of Hebrews gives several titles describing the function of the Lord Jesus. Consider the titles and the many practical applications of these. **The Apostle** *Apostolos* (ap-OS-tol-os) is the one sent forth with orders and authority. The Father sent the Son for a purpose and plan to fulfill. The Lord Jesus himself proclaimed: *For I came down from heaven, not to do mine own will, but the will of him that sent me* (John 6:38). He explained to his disciples ahead of time what the plan would include. *From that time forth began Jesus to show unto his disciples, how that he must go unto Jerusalem, and suffer many things of the elders and chief priests and scribes, and be killed, and be raised again the third day.* Think of it. Moments before this, Peter answered the question as to who the Lord Jesus is. Peter proclaimed: *Thou art the Christ, the Son of the living God* (Matthew 16:16). Great answer, Peter, and so correct.

Very soon thereafter the Lord Jesus reveals the plan of redemption and Peter unwisely proclaims he would never permit Christ to do this. Listen to the discussion between the Lord Jesus and Peter and grasp how profoundly the Lord Jesus is committed to the Father's plan: *Then Peter took him, and began to rebuke him, saying, Be it far from thee, Lord: this shall not be unto thee. But he turned, and said unto Peter, Get thee behind me, Satan: thou art an offense unto me: for thou savourest not the things that be of God, but those that be of men* (Matthew 16:22-23). The Lord Jesus is the ultimate sent one with the ultimate orders.

In Gethsemane the night before the Lord Jesus would go to the cross, he reported to his Father: *For I have given unto them the word which thou gavest me; and they have received them, and have known surely that I came out from thee, and they have believed that thou didst send me* (John 17:8). He prayed on and said: *As thou hast sent me into the world, even so have I also sent them into the world. And for their sakes I sanctify myself, that they also might be sanctified through the truth* (John 17:18-19). Consider and intentionally focus on the Lord Jesus being our great Apostle. This will indeed cause you to hear with joy his voice in Scripture.

High Priest *archiereus* (ar-khee-er-YUCE). The Jewish readers immediately understood the role of the high priest and his relationship to the Lord as well as to the people. The High Priests of Israel were busy as they functioned as mediators between God and the people, teaching God's laws (Deuteronomy 33:8-10), offering sacrifices (Leviticus 16:3-16), and praying for the people (Exodus 28:29-30). Stop and consider that the Lord Jesus Christ is our merciful and faithful high priest (Hebrews 2:17). He is the high priest who has passed into the heavens (Hebrews 4:14). He is the high priest who can identify with us and yet he is without sin (Hebrews 4:15). What absolute amazing sinless, perfect, holiness alone describes our awesome high priest.

Of our profession *homologia* (hom-ol-og-EE-ah) also known and described as our confession, is that which we confess or profess to possess. This profession accepts by faith what the Scriptures declare about oneself. It is to say the same thing as does God's Word, to acknowledge and express the Word of Truth as it relates to one's individual life. It is to declare by faith what the Scripture declares. By faith "this is the place of my line being drawn in the sand." With conviction and purpose of heart, I cannot recant; I will not retreat. **Christ** *Christos* (Khris-TOS) is Anointed One; Messiah, the Son of God. **Jesus** *Iesous* (ee-ay-SOOCE) "Jehovah is Salvation" speaks of his work as Savior: *Being justified freely by his grace through the redemption that is in Christ Jesus* (Romans 3:24). *There is therefore now no condemnation to them which are in Christ Jesus, who walk not after the flesh, but after the Spirit* (Romans 8:1). *For we preach not ourselves, but Christ Jesus the Lord...* (2 Corinthians 4:5). *That in the ages to come he might show the exceeding riches of his grace in his kindness toward us through Christ Jesus* (Ephesians 2:7). *I press toward the mark for the prize of the high calling of God in Christ Jesus* (Philippians 3:14). *As ye have therefore received Christ Jesus the Lord, so walk ye in him* (Colossians 2:6).

Verses 2-6
Listen to His Voice! Think of the Construction (v2-6)

It is a joy to be part of his family! In this section, the word **house** is used seven times in five verses. It is important to understand that another reason we listen to his voice is because of his faithfulness in building his house. With his functioning in the role of the apostle and high priest of our profession, Christ Jesus himself is the absolute reason to listen to his voice. However, the writer of Hebrews is not finished with presenting the truth that not only encourages us to listen to his voice but also demands it. The Lord Jesus, in addition to all of this, is such a faithful builder.

Verse 2a

Discover the joy of seeing the superior Lord Jesus as the writer speaks of **Who was faithful** *pistos* (pis-TOS) fully trustworthy, reliable, without fail, being totally dependable. **To him that appointed** *poieo* (poy-EH-o) speaks of being placed, to make or ordain by one's authority. **Him that appointed** refers to the Father's role of appointing the Lord Jesus with a mission and purpose. On the day of his baptism which was the formal commencement of his public ministry, the Father declared: *This is my beloved Son, in whom I am well pleased* (Matthew 3:17). On the mountain where the transfiguration of Christ took place, the Father once again declared from the bright cloud: *This is my beloved Son, in whom I am well pleased; hear ye him* (Matthew 17:5). Rising from the dead on the third day is further confirmation of the Father's absolute pleasure in his son and all he accomplished: *Concerning his Son Jesus Christ our Lord, which was made of the seed of David according to the flesh; And declared to be the Son of God with power, according to the spirit of holiness, by the resurrection from the dead* (Romans 1:3-4).

Listen to his voice is exactly what the Father commanded. How precious indeed it is that the Lord Jesus reported to his Father on the night before he died for our sins and said: *I have glorified thee on the earth: I have finished the work which thou gavest me to do. And now, O Father, glorify thou me with thine own self with the glory which I had with thee before the world was* (John 17:4-5). From the cross, he said: *It is finished* (John 19:30). He was totally faithful in his appointment.

Verse 2b, 3

The author uses the illustration of the master builder to demonstrate the superiority of the Lord Jesus over Moses as a sufficient reason to listen to his voice. Not only is the Lord Jesus faithful to the Father, he exceeds the faithfulness of Moses, the national hero. **As also Moses was faithful in all his house** *oikos* (OY-kos) which can speak of a literal inhabited house, the tabernacle, the human body, or the persons forming one family or a household. Specifically, this is a reference to Moses being faithful in all his house as God's leader for the children of Israel.

Moses demonstrated faithfulness in his life choices. He could have had the very best of Egypt, but he chose to obey the Lord and to be identified with God's people (Acts 7:22; Hebrews 11:24-27).

He demonstrated faithfulness in trusting God concerning God's message and his mouth! At his call from the Lord at the burning bush (Exodus 3), Moses tried to explain to the Lord that he most certainly could not be the Lord's spokesman (Exodus 4:10). Patiently the Lord answered Moses (Exodus 4:11-12). Moses, the man who said, "I can't speak," is found in places where he would boldly speak as the Lord's representative to Pharaoh as well as to the people of Israel. He demonstrated obedience in responding to the warning of the Lord (Hebrews 11:24-28). He demonstrated faithfulness in his earnest intercession for the people of the Lord. Find him crying out to the Lord as Pharaoh and his army pursued them at the Red Sea (Exodus 14); at the sin of the Golden Calf and the lewdness of its worship (Exodus 32); in the incident of rebellion with Aaron and Miriam (Numbers 12) and in the rebellion of the people after hearing the report of the spies (Numbers 14). He demonstrated faithfulness in the careful adherence to God's blueprint for the Tabernacle. The Lord's detailed instructions for every part and piece of the Tabernacle were given line by line (Exodus 25:40). The house or Tabernacle was faithfully built, the work completed, and the blessing of the Lord was evident (Exodus 35-40). Moses was faithful in his house. The Lord powerfully reminded Aaron and Miriam of this (Numbers 12:6-8).

What a remarkable "house" Moses built as a witness in Egypt and to Pharaoh. Think of the "house" he built in the lives of God's people, the children of Israel, and the construction of the Tabernacle. Moses faithfully obeyed. Despite the many complainers and accusers, Moses faithfully obeyed the instructions of the Lord except for the day he lost his anger and disobeyed (Numbers 20:9-11).

However, the Lord Jesus Christ is superior! Moses was faithful in the house as a servant. Christ is faithful in the house as a son. The Lord Jesus never experienced a day of failure or disobedience.

Verse 3

As wonderful as Moses was, the spotlight is turned on the one who is far superior and much, much better than Moses. He is worthy of more glory. See Christ in his perfection. **For this man was counted worthy** *axioo* (ax-ee-O-o) which is to be judged fitting, deemed deserving of **more glory** *doxa* (DOX-ah) majesty, exaltation.

The construction illustration continues with **he who hath builded the house hath more honor than the house** (v3b). Regardless of how amazing a building might be, whoever designed and then constructed the actual building is worthy of more appreciation, honor, respect, and even glory than the building itself. The supremacy and superiority of Christ are stunning and unmistakable in the text.

Verse 4

The construction illustration is explained. **For every house is builded** *kataskeuazo* (kat-ask-yoo-AD-zo) speaks of the work of a builder, one who constructs, makes a building, and furnishes it **by some man.** No, friend, the house doesn't suddenly evolve from the ground accidentally. Someone planned, purchased, and produced the building. **But he that built all things is God.** Think highly of the Lord Jesus. He created all things (John 1:3; Colossians 1:16). He is the sustainer of all things (Colossians 1:17) by his powerful Word (Hebrews 1:3). He is highly exalted, and before him every knee will bow (Philippians 2:9-11). He alone is the builder of his household, his family. He is God, expressing the radiance of his glory and the exact imprint of his nature (Hebrews 1:3).

Verse 5

Now the big distinction is made in verses 5 and 6 between Moses and the Lord Jesus. **Moses verily was faithful** *pistos* (pis-TOS) fully trustworthy, reliable, **in all his house, as a servant** *therapon* (ther-AP-ohn) an attendant. It is noteworthy to observe that the word *servant* is not the typical word for slave or bondservant. The writer selected the word used only here as one who willingly serves as an attendant, who willingly discharges his duties with a sense of dignity and freedom. **For a testimony** *martyrion* (mar-TOO-ree-on) witness or declaration **of those things which were to be spoken after.** Everything about Moses and his ministry was a foreshadowing of that which the Lord would later reveal and establish. The Tabernacle and its ministry were strictly erected by the servant Moses. The instruction of the Law was faithfully delivered by the servant Moses. The leading of the people to the land of promise was accomplished by the Lord through his attendant Moses. All of these duties point to Christ and his perfect fulfillment of them.

Throughout his lifetime of building into the lives of the children of Israel, Moses put up with hostility, complainers, doubters, disputers, and discouragements of every kind. Yet the generations of people that would follow held Moses in the highest respect and regard. Wonderfully the writer of Hebrews acknowledges the faithful ministry of Moses while demonstrating the superiority of Jesus.

Verse 6

Everything changes with the words **But** *de* (deh) used for emphasis, signifying a distinguishment between Moses and **Christ** *Christos* (Khris-TOS), the anointed one, the Messiah, the Son of God. A far greater one than Moses is to be loved, cherished, trusted, and listened to!

Christ is greater in every way. Specifically, Moses is a servant but Christ **as a son** *huios (hwee-OS)* is the offspring of God. Moses held a high position; however, he could never come close to the cherished and unique position of a son: *The servant abideth not in the house for ever: but the Son abideth ever. If the Son therefore shall make you free, ye shall be free indeed* (John 8:35-36). Speaking to Philip and the rest of the disciples, Jesus said: *Have I been so long time with you, and yet hast thou not known me, Philip? He that hath seen me hath seen the Father; and how sayest thou then, show us the Father. Believest thou not that I am in the Father, and the Father in me? The words that I speak unto you I speak not of myself: but the Father that dwelleth in me, he doeth the works. Believe me that I am in the Father, and the Father in me: or else believe me for the very works' sake* (John 14:9-11). **Over his own house whose house we are:** What a privilege of being numbered with the Lord's people who belong to him.

1. We by the grace of God are raised up and seated with him already.
   But God, who is rich in mercy, for his great love wherewith he loved us, even when we were dead in sins, hath quickened us together with Christ, (by grace ye are saved;) and hath raised us up together, and made us sit together in heavenly places in Christ Jesus (Ephesians 2:4-6).

2. We are no more strangers and foreigners. We are family!
   Now therefore ye are no more strangers and foreigners, but fellow citizens with the saints, and of the household of God (Ephesians 2:19).

3. We are a spiritual building constructed by our awesome Lord Jesus.
    And are built upon the foundation of the apostles and prophets, Jesus Christ himself being the chief corner stone; in whom all the building fitly framed together groweth unto an holy temple in the Lord: In whom ye also are builded together for an habitation of God through the Spirit (Ephesians 2:20-22).

4. We are a living building because of Christ.
    Ye also, as lively stones, are built up a spiritual house, an holy priesthood, to offer up spiritual sacrifices, acceptable to God by Jesus Christ (1 Peter 2:5).

If we hold fast *katecho* (kat-EKH-o) to possess, keep secure, to be in firm possession of **the confidence** *parresia* (par-rhay-SEE-ah) fearless courage, boldness, assurance (See also 4:16; 10:19, 35). **And the rejoicing** *kauchema* (KOW-khay-mah) which is the ground of glorying **of the hope** *elpis* (el-PECE) which throughout the New Testament generally speaks of the confident expectation of that which is yet unseen but will be realized in the future. **Until the end** *telos* (TEL-os) is that completion of the purpose.

Understand that a genuinely converted, redeemed person of the Lord will indeed continue. This is the test of genuine faith. Those who do not hold fast but rather make the decision to turn away were never really part of the family of the Lord. This holding fast is proof of genuine faith. Those who return to the Levitical system under Moses demonstrate they were never part of the family. John very powerfully describes such a one by saying: *They went out from us, but they were not of us; for if they had been of us, they would no doubt have continued with us: but they went out, that they might be made manifest that they were not all of us* (1 John 2:19).

> **A genuinely converted, redeemed person of the Lord will indeed continue. This is the test of genuine faith. Holding fast is the proof of genuine or true faith.**

Reflection

Think highly of Christ. Read through the Gospel of John and see the "I Am's" and read the miracles he performed. Read through the Epistles and read of the glories of His grace and kindness to his people. See him as Redeemer, Savior, Lord, Advocate, and Builder of his house.

Verses 7-11
Listen to His Voice! Think of the Counsel (v7-11)

It is a matter of the heart to follow him! Having presented the better or superior Christ who is the Apostle, High Priest, Messiah-Savior, and Son who is building his house of his followers, the writer now introduces an incredibly powerful warning. The next several sections will fully develop the idea of **harden** *skieryno* (sklay-ROO-no) to render obstinate, to become stubborn **not your hearts** (v7) and **They shall not enter my rest** (v11).

This section is a direct quote of Psalm 95:7-11. There are at least five warning sections in the book of Hebrews (2:1-4; 3:7-4:13; 5:11-6:12; 10:19-39; and 12:14-29). The first was to consider the danger of drifting (2:1). Now the writer speaks of the danger of doubt and disbelief. God incredibly and miraculously brought Israel out of Egypt and demonstrated his power in awesome ways. Yet their hearts hardened and once again they rebelled against him (Numbers 13-14). Refusing to enter Canaan to conquer and possess it, they forfeited the rest of the joy of living in the land promised to them, the blessings they could have enjoyed because of their obedience, and the gladness that comes with pleasing the Lord. All this was forfeited because of the hardness of their hearts. They came to the very edge of the land that God promised them, and instead of seeing how big their God was, they focused on how big the inhabitants were. Of all things, they refused to listen to the report of Joshua and Caleb and instead listened to the other spies. Upon hearing their report, they hardened their hearts against their leadership and even worse, against the Lord (Numbers 13, 14). They refused to accept the joy of their inheritance, their rest.

Rest (11) will be more fully explained in the sections to follow. The most basic of meanings focuses upon the believer's indescribable joy and blessings that he or she possesses right now in the inheritance of the Lord. This is because of his/her salvation in Christ. Christ himself is our inheritance and God shares everything with us as joint heirs. In the future, we will see the wondrous inheritance with our own eyes (Romans 8:16-17; Ephesians 1:3, 11, 15-23) as we are with him in glory (John 14:1-3).

In spite of the wonderful blessings of our rest, there is great danger lurking in the heart of the believer that is left unguarded: *Keep thy heart with all diligence; for out of it are the issues of life* (Proverbs 4:23). It can become hard, stubborn, and resistant to the Lord. How blessed is the believer whose heart is tender, soft, and seeking the Lord's ways. What is the remedy? Develop a tender heart toward the Lord. This tender heart toward the Lord will be demonstrated in at least four ways.

1. The believer's DESIRE ("I am loving You, Lord" Revelation 2:1-4).

2. The believer's DEVOTION ("I am worshipping You, Lord" Psalm 95:1-7).

3. The believer's DISPLAY ("I am showing Your fruit, Lord" Galatians 5:22-23).

4. The believer's DETERMINATION ("I know how to start and conclude my day with You, Lord" Psalm 92:1-2).

When we consider all this, the conclusion of the matter in this section is found in the words **hear his voice** (v7). There is urgency in this statement. There is finality of authority in this statement. There is obedience and rest in this statement.

God speaks to us through his son. Earlier the writer of Hebrews proclaimed: *God, who at sundry times and in divers manners spoke in time past unto the fathers by the prophets, Hath in these last days spoken unto us by his Son, whom he hath appointed heir of all things, by whom also he made the worlds* (Hebrews 1:1-2).

God speaks to us through his Scriptures: *All scripture is given by inspiration of God, and is profitable for doctrine, for reproof, for correction, for instruction in righteousness: that the man of God may be perfect, thoroughly furnished unto all good works* (2 Timothy 3:16-17).

Listen to him!

ADDITIONAL COMMENTS

Perhaps one of the most well-known illustrations of listening in the Old Testament is demonstrated in the life of young Samuel, who later served as priest (1 Sam 7:8), judge (1 Sam 7:6, 15-17), and prophet (1 Sam 3:20-4:1; Acts 3:24; 13:20). In 1 Samuel 3, the text reveals that Samuel was awoken in the middle of the night by the voice of God. Initially, he was confused and mistook the voice for Eli, but after receiving instruction and hearing the voice again, he responded with the now-famous words, *Speak, for your servant hears* (ESV). God revealed to Samuel his intent to punish the house of Eli for the family's ongoing sins. Then, verse 19 reiterates the result: *Samuel grew, and the LORD was with him and let none of his words fall to the ground* (ESV). In other words, God was faithful to his promise.

In the New Testament, the words of James make a clear connection between listening and doing: *Do not merely listen to the word, and so deceive yourselves. Do what it says. Anyone who listens to the word but does not do what it says is like someone who looks at his face in a mirror and, after looking at himself, goes away and immediately forgets what he looks like* (1:22-24, ESV).

What these two passages have in common is that listening is not meant to merely transfer information from one person to another—it isn't knowledge for the sake of knowledge. Rather, listening to God's voice moves us to action. (Neipp)

STUDY GUIDE QUESTIONS

As outlined in this passage, who is subject to Jesus' supremacy?

Imagine you were tasked with crafting a eulogy for Moses. What qualities and accomplishments would you emphasize? Which achievements would make it into the top 10 list? Given the profound esteem the Israelites had for Moses, what significance does his presence in this chapter hold?

In 3:2-5, Moses' faithfulness to his household is referenced. What does "house" represent in this context? In 3:6, the attention shifts to Jesus' faithfulness over his house. What does "house" signify in this scenario, and why is its significance notable?

In verses 6 and 7, there is an observation of an "if" statement containing a condition. What does this signify?

What set apart the rebellion of Israel in verses 7-9? What were the consequences of their actions?

5

LISTENING TO HIS VOICE (PART 2)

Hebrews 3:12-4:13

Gary L. Anderson

Introduction

God will not be ignored. Turning your back on the living God has severe consequences. The Israelites whom God delivered from Egypt made that fatal error and their carcasses fell in the wilderness (3:17; Num. 14:29-33). The writer of Hebrews cautions his readers to be doubly sure none of them make the same mistake.

This first-century community of Hebrew believers was under pressure from non-believing Jews to abandon their Christian faith and return to Judaism. Jewish dogma contended that salvation was integral to the Abrahamic Covenant and the Levitical system. Being told they had forfeited heaven by professing faith in Christ was designed to alarm these Hebrew believers. An additional incentive to revert was that life as practicing Jews had not brought the suffering and persecution that came with identifying with Christ (10:32-34).

The author of the book of Hebrews pleads with his readers to allow the voice of God (3:7, 15; 4:7) to counter the din of their detractors. To that end, he lavishes them with the Word of God as delivered in the Old Testament. Hebrews contains at least 35 quotations or allusions to the Old Testament. The passage between 3:12 and 4:13 quotes Psalm 95:7 twice (3:15; 4:7) and alludes to the creation account in Genesis 2:2 (4:4) as well as the rebellion of the Israelites at the threshold of the Promised Land recorded in Numbers 14 (3:15-19). Steve Lawson says, "The true nature of preaching is the man of God opening the Word of God and expounding its truths so that the voice of God may be heard... explaining the true meaning of Scripture in a way that conveys divine judgment if it is refused and divine grace if received" (p. 18). That mixture of God-conceived and God-breathed warning and blessing describes the book of Hebrews.

The opening imperative of this passage, **take heed**, strikes a chord of warning. It is translated from the Greek term which means "to see." Those on the verge of abandoning their profession of faith are implored to take a hard look at their hearts to determine whether they are genuine believers. It is there that our consideration of the passage begins.

Is This Warning Aimed at Believers or Unbelievers? (3:12-14)

Hebrews is a written sermon and bears a decidedly pastoral tone. The author craves assurance that every recipient of his letter is a true believer. The use of **brethren** in the greeting in 3:12 is not conclusive evidence that all within the fellowship were believers. It is most likely the cordial address of a pastor to his congregation, similar to the way congregations are currently acknowledged on Sunday mornings. Even though it can be expected that some in the gathering are unsaved, they are not singled out when the pastor welcomes the congregation collectively as "church family" or some equivalent salutation. To have used *holy brethren* here, as the author did in 3:1, would have contradicted his stated concern that some could be harboring **an evil heart of unbelief**. The use of **brethren** amiably assured those needing this solemn warning that the author had their best interest at heart.

Understanding the phrase **made partakers of Christ** (3:14) is key to understanding the author's concern. To be a **partaker** (*metoxos*) is to be a sharer or partner. The term is used outside of Hebrews only in Luke 5:7 where it is translated *partners*. The writer of Hebrews uses it five times and it is translated *partakers* four of those five times (3:1; 3:14; 6:4; 12:8). It should be conceded that **partakers of Christ** are believers.

The issue is whether all being addressed had truly been **made partakers of Christ**. The operative term in 3:14 is the verb **made** (*ginomai*) which means "come or become." It occurs in the perfect tense which conveys action completed in the past producing results continuing to the present. The verse can be properly translated **for we have become partakers of Christ if we hold the beginning of our confidence steadfast to the end** (NKJV). **[Having] become**

partakers of Christ is the completed action in the past and **[holding] our confidence steadfast** is the continuing result. It is a statement of cause and effect with having been made a partaker being the cause and remaining steadfast being the effect. Christians are not saved by persevering. They persevere because they are saved. Consequently, anyone deciding to **depart from the living God** should **take heed** or take a hard look at whether they had ever been **made partakers of Christ**.

> Christians are not saved by persevering. They persevere because they are saved.

1 John 2:19 sheds light on this. John assured his *little children* that the early Gnostics who had abandoned the community of believers had proved their lost estate by their choice to leave: *They went out from us, but they were not of us; for if they had been of us, they would no doubt have continued with us: but they went out, that they might be made manifest that they were not all of us.* The defectors accused those who remained in the fellowship of holding to a misguided faith. If that had been correct it would have meant John's *little children* were lost. He wasn't about to allow those claims to go unchallenged. As if the labels *seducers* (2:26), *deceivers* (2 Jn. 7), and *false prophets* (4:1) weren't reprehensible enough, John assigns the titles *liar* (2:4, 22; 4:20) and *antichrist* (2:22; 4:3; 2 Jn 7) to these critics. He deemed their choice to separate from the fellowship as *manifest* evidence of their real spiritual status. Walking away confirmed their lost estate.

The writer of Hebrews is not as explicit when he warns his readers that a retreat to Judaism could signal they had professed Christ without having possessed Christ. The author does not name names. He singles no one out for being on the brink of turning back, but the possibility of defection was a fearful prospect (3:12; 4:1-3). The word **lest** can mean "just in case" or "if by chance." The phrase could read **take heed** just in case or if by chance **there be in any of you an evil heart of unbelief** (3:12). The four appearances of the term **today** in these few verses (3:7; 13; 15 and twice in 4:7) form a mounting sense of urgency. **Today** speaks of the day of opportunity, the day of salvation, the day of grace. The readers are told emphatically that if any should **come short of the promise** (4:1), it would be on them. The Greek term translated **come short** means to "arrive late" and is used again in 12:15: *looking carefully lest anyone fall short of the grace of God* (NKJV). If the day of grace passes and you are late, there is no redo. Turning your back on the living God has eternal consequences.

Is Departing from the Living God Apostasy? (3:12)

The English word *apostasy* is a transliteration of the Greek term *apostasia* which means "to forsake or fall away." The term occurs twice in the New Testament (Acts 21:21; 2 Thess. 2:3), but never in Hebrews. The book does, however, have much to say about the subject of apostasy (3;12; 4;1; 6:6; 10:35, 39; 12:15). **Departing** in 3:12 is translated from *aphistemi. Aphistemi* is formed by adding a negative prefix to the verb which means "to stand" (*histemi*). It means "to no longer stand where you once stood... to withdraw; to desist or desert." When applied to a total renunciation of one's profession of faith in Christ, as it does here (3:12; 4:2), it defines apostasy.

To be an apostate, one must have at least nominally embraced the gospel and then disavowed it. There may only be a fine line of difference between an apostate and a heretic, or a false teacher, or a reprobate. But there is a distinction; namely that the apostate at one time gave a credible, public profession of faith. Their radical change of allegiance puts them in a category different from other opponents of the gospel. R. Kent Hughes says, "The ignorant cannot commit this sin. It can't be committed inadvertently. It is a sin only church people can commit" (TGC sermon). Where the truth has never been declared, it can be expected that unbelief will abound. But the apostate's unbelief occurs despite full and intimate knowledge of the truth. These Hebrews were sufficiently informed that they should have been teachers (5:11). For any to depart now would turn them into avowed apostates.

Wikipedia says, "Apostasy is the antonym of conversion; it is deconversion." That is a catchy but flawed definition if it means apostates are former Christians who lost their salvation. That would make Jesus a liar. Christ said: *I give unto them eternal life; and they shall never perish, neither shall any man pluck them out of my hand. My Father, which gave them me, is greater than all; and no man is able to pluck them out of my Father's hand. I and my Father are one* (Jn. 10:28-30). To be saved one day and lost the next would refute the

> **To be saved one day and lost the next would refute the incomparable promise of Romans 8:1.**

incomparable promise of Romans 8:1: *There is therefore now no condemnation to them which are in Christ Jesus*! Nothing threatens the souls of those who are safe in Jesus... not now, not ever! And nothing in this passage or any passage in Hebrews teaches the contrary.

What is the Essence of Unbelief? (3:12, 19; 4:6, 11)

An evil heart of unbelief is the intolerable condition described here (3:12). **Unbelief** (*apistos*) is an absence of faith in God; a refusal to take God at his word. This was the seminal sin. Satan corrupted Eve's confidence in God (Gen. 3:1-7). With her perfect surroundings testifying to the contrary, she was persuaded to think of God as a depriver rather than a provider. She concluded God could have and should have done better.

The Israelites who died in the wilderness were guilty of this same faulty thinking. Just two and a half months into their wilderness trek they complained: *Would to God we had died by the hand of the Lord in the land of Egypt, when we sat by the flesh pots, and when we did eat bread to the full; for ye have brought us forth into this wilderness, to kill this whole assembly with hunger* (Ex 16:3). They indicted God for not having done better. God responded by graciously giving them manna. Roughly two years into their wandering, the people began to sing again their sad song of God having wronged them. It is recorded in Num 11:5, 6: *We remember the fish, which we did eat in Egypt freely; the cucumbers, and the melons, and the leeks, and the onions, and the garlic; but now our soul is dried away; there is nothing at all, beside this manna, before our eyes.* God should have done better! God graciously gave them quail (Num. 11:31). By the time they reached Kadesh Barnea as recorded in Num 14:2,3 they had their little melody of woe well-rehearsed: *Would God that we had died in the land of Egypt! Or would God we had died in this wilderness! And wherefore hath the Lord brought us unto this land, to fall by the sword, that our wives and our children should be a prey? Were it not better for us to return into Egypt*! There it is in their own words: "Were it not better?" Shouldn't God have done better? They finally conspired to elect a replacement for Moses to take them back to Egypt. They spoke of stoning Joshua and Caleb and possibly Moses and Aaron except that the *glory of the Lord* appeared before all of Israel to intervene for his servants (Num 14:10).

That is disturbing! The leader they wished to oust was Moses—one of the greatest men among mere men to ever live. A. C. Gaebelein is credited with saying, "There is in all of scripture no person apart from Christ in whose life the supernatural is as prominent as in the life of Moses, the servant of God." It was known that he had been the object of God's supernatural intervention when as a 3-month-old baby he was rescued by Pharaoh's daughter from certain death and given back to his birth mother to nurse him through childhood. He was called by God through the burning bush and met alone with God on Mt. Sinai twice for 40 days each time. He was the instrument of God in the administration of 10 plagues upon Egypt—an epic contest that ultimately left the magnificent throne of the mightiest force on earth vacant, the Pharaoh dead, all of Egypt mourning, and the Hebrew slaves free and rich. God split the Red Sea and two million Jews crossed to freedom on dry ground only to have the Egyptian army drown when God allowed Israel's escape route to fill again with water. For forty years, they had shoes that never wore out, manna every morning, quail every evening, and water from a rock. The guiding cloud was there every day and the pillar of fire every night. And yet, the Israelites who were witnesses and beneficiaries of all that, could not bring themselves to take God at his word. "God should have done better" was their faithless lament!

Coincidentally, the author of Hebrews employs the word "better" 13 times as he describes Jesus. He is declared better than the angels, the prophets, and Moses. His priesthood is better than Aaron's. His new covenant is better than the old one and his sacrifice is better than bulls or goats. Lewis Sperry Chafer says, "In salvation, God has wrought to the extreme limit of his might in sparing not his Son but delivering him up for us all... God could do no more!" (Chafer, p. 23, 52). The writer of Hebrews contends God could do no better!

> **The author of Hebrews employs the word "better" 13 times as he describes Jesus.**

The Hebrews reading this letter didn't lack knowledge. They knew the promised Messiah had come. They were aware of the *miracles, wonders and signs* Jesus had performed (Acts 2:22). They knew he had suffered, died, and risen from the dead (1:1-4). Some were likely eyewitnesses of the wonder-working power entrusted to those 12 whom Christ commissioned to launch the building of his church. The Hebrews contemplating turning back had mixed and mingled with true believers. They had tasted the sweetness of fellowship within a community of those whose sins had been forgiven; those whose lives had taken on new purpose and direction when their center of gravity changed, and their compasses were recalibrated by the new birth (2 Cor 5:17). What the law and the Levitical system had only symbolized had become reality—incarnate before their eyes. And still, some were tempted to turn back. The writer poignantly reminds them of what unbelief earned the Israelites who arrived at the threshold of the Promised Land and then decided God could not be trusted to take them in. Death relentlessly stalked Israel in their wilderness wandering as a grim reminder of the judgment they brought upon themselves. The demise of over six hundred thousand Israelites in 38 years meant an average of over forty deaths per day... every day. The wilderness turned into a massive graveyard. From the history of their own nation, these Hebrews are warned that refusing to **hear his voice** is no way to respond to God.

What is the Rest Offered? (4:4-10)

While divine judgment awaits those who turn a deaf ear to God, divine grace awaits those who listen. In this case, **rest** awaits those who will claim it by faith (4:3). Rest is referenced no fewer than ten times in this passage. There is God's rest which was initiated on the **seventh day** of creation (4:4, 10). There is Canaan-rest into which **Joshua** (Jesus in KJV) eventually led the Israelites (4:8). There is a rest which remained for the **people of God** in David's day (4:7-9). And there is the eternal rest promised to every true believer when he has **ceased from his own works, as God did from his** (4:9, 10).

> **Divine grace awaits those who listen.**

By definition, rest is the suspension of work. Seventh-day rest was initiated by God when on that day he ceased *from all his work which he had made* (Gen. 2:2). His work of creation was finished, and he rested in the satisfaction of it being *very good* (Gen. 1:31). That became the model for a weekly sabbath and the archetype of heavenly rest. From creation forward, God has welcomed his people into his rest at the end of their earthly labor (Rev 14:13).

Canaan would have been rest from oppression, danger, labor, and wandering. But Canaan was never meant to be the final rest for the Israelites. Canaan was temporal rest which illustrated eternal rest. Since it was only a symbol of eternal rest, the loss of Canaan only symbolized the loss of heaven. It cannot be assumed that everyone who died in the wilderness was sentenced to hell. Heaven is gained by grace through faith (Eph. 2:8). Repentant faith which God responds to with forgiveness of sin is an individual, personal matter: *For whosoever shall call upon the name of the Lord shall be saved* (Rom. 10:13). If those Israelites who could not trust God to give them the Promised Land died without faith in the promised Messiah then they forfeited heaven just as they forfeited Canaan. But each Israelite banished to the wilderness would have had to settle those issues in his own heart. The wilderness wandering was time graciously extended so the Israelites could reconsider their faith in God's promise of a Savior. They had Moses the Deliverer as a type of Christ (Deut. 18:15, 18; Heb. 3:1-6). The Law was in place, serving as a *schoolmaster [bringing them] unto Christ, that [they] might be justified by faith* (Gal. 3:24). The Tabernacle was the center of life in the wilderness, and Aaron's role as high priest foreshadowed Christ becoming *a merciful and faithful high priest in things pertaining to God, to make reconciliation for the sins of the people* (Heb. 2:17; 8:1). Each of the countless animals sacrificed over those years of wandering reinforced the absolute necessity of blood being shed for the remission of sin (Heb. 9:22). And annually, the Day of Atonement was celebrated in the wilderness with the sacrificial lamb representing the Lamb of God who one day would *by his own blood... obtain eternal redemption* (Heb. 9:12; Jn. 1:29).

Even though the loss of Canaan did not equate to loss of eternal life, it was a profound judgment against unbelief. It typified the eternal loss that the Hebrews would suffer if their faith was not real. Five hundred years after Joshua led Israel into Canaan, David cautioned his generation not to miss out on the rest which was still available to them (Ps. 95:7-11). He could not have been speaking of Canaan rest because his generation was living in Canaan; rather, he spoke of heaven. One-thousand years after David, the writer of Hebrews said, **there remains therefore a rest for the people of God** (4:9) and he cautioned his readers not to allow **an evil heart of unbelief... hardened through the deceitfulness of sin** to cause them to miss out on it (3:7, 15; 4:7). The promised rest offered in the book of Hebrews is still available for all who believe (4:3), even for Israel (Acts 5:31; 10:35, 36). The age of grace holds the door of heaven wide open to all whose faith is in Jesus Christ and his vicarious atonement for our sins (Jn. 3:16; Rom. 10:9, 10; 2 Cor. 5:21).

Christ offered rest which was both temporal and eternal when he said, *Come unto me, all ye that labour and are heavy laden, and I will give you rest. Take my yoke upon you and learn of me; for I am meek and lowly in heart; and ye shall find rest for your souls* (Matt. 11:28, 29). Christ promises relief now from sin's guilt and every desperate attempt to gain heaven by our own effort. That is temporal rest. The pledge of his presence likewise brings calm now in a world of trouble, frenzy, and anxiety. But the rest that is ours now only hints of the rest to come in glory (Col. 2:16, 17; Rom. 8:17, 18; 1 Jn. 3:2). This is reflected in the use of the term *sabbatismos* for **rest** in 4:9. *Sabbatismos* is used only here in the New Testament and is an entirely different Greek term from the one rendered **rest** (*katapausis*) everywhere else in this passage. Matthew Poole's commentary says this exceptional term speaks of an exceptional rest: "a state and season of most glorious rest, enjoyed by sincere believers, the true Israel of God" (Gal. 3:29). The **people of God** (4:9) in the Old Testament were exclusively Israel, but that exclusivity was repealed in the New Testament (Gal. 3:29). Jesus promised his disciples that he was preparing a place for them so that where he was they would be also (Jn. 14:1-3). "A state and season of most glorious rest" awaits all those *redeemed out of every tribe and tongue and people and nation* (Rev 5:9). The writer of Hebrews wanted each of his readers to be in that number.

What Was the Gospel Preached in the Old Testament? (4:2-3)

This passage threatens judgment for those who refuse to listen to the voice of God, but blessing is promised to those who listen, believe, and obey. The **promise** (*epangelia*) which was preached in both the Old and New Testaments is here called the **gospel** (*euangelizo*). *Euangelizo* is better rendered **good tidings** (ASV) or **good news** (NIV, ESV) since Christ having come and redemption having been completed could not have been preached in Moses' day. But the **good news** that God would make a way for believing Israelites to spend eternity with him certainly was preached (Gal. 3:24-27). The Levitical sacrifices pictured the substitutionary atonement which was to be provided by the promised Messiah and Jesus confirmed that he was the one about whom Moses spoke (Jn. 5:45-47). **Faith** in that yet-to-be-finished work of Christ was the Old Testament saints' claim to salvation (4:2).

Faith (*pistis*) is used 32 times in Hebrews, exceeded only by Romans in which it appears 40 times. Faith generates obedience. Unbelief begets disobedience. When this passage speaks of **unbelief** it uses the term *apistia* which means "without faith" (3:12; 3:19; 4:6;

4:11). And when it speaks of those who **believed** (4:3) it uses the verb *pisteuo* which means "to have faith." It was their lack of faith that triggered the disobedience of the Israelites. The author paints a vivid image when he says **the word preached did not profit them, not being mixed with faith in them that heard it** (4:2). **Mixed** means "to commingle or assimilate" as when saliva mixes with food. The mixing of saliva with food makes the food useful to the body. The good news delivered to Israel never became useful to them because it was not **mixed with faith**.

To delay doing what needed to be done was a fearful proposition (4:1). The Israelites learned that disobedience provokes God's judgment (3:8, 15). He swore that those who declared him unworthy of their trust would never enter Canaan (3:11). An entire generation spent their last days and years toiling in the desert when they should have been resting in the land of milk and honey (Num. 13:27). Their **carcasses fell in the wilderness** (3:17; Num. 14:29-33). The doom which they brought upon themselves by **unbelief** awaits all who **today** refuse to take God at his word.

The Israelites should have known from Pharoah's experience not to linger in **unbelief**. Pharoah was given way more than enough evidence that God was God and that he was to be responded to in belief and obedience. Chuck Swindoll says, "For all of time and eternity, Pharaoh will be an example of what it means to resist and reject the goodness of God" (p. 175). When the Scripture says God hardened Pharoah's heart (Ex. 9:12; 10:1) it should be thought of as God giving him up to the sin which he preferred just as God gave unregenerate men up to *the lusts of their own hearts* when they *changed the truth of God into a lie* (Rom. 1:24, 25). Pharoah entered the drama of the Ten Plagues with a blasphemous declaration that he did not know God and had no interest in knowing him (Ex 5:2). Opportunity after opportunity to recant was scoffed until finally, God gave Pharoah up to his own hard heart. Persisting in **unbelief** is perilous!

The author of Hebrews insists belief equals rest; unbelief equals no rest. It's categorical. It's climactic. C. S. Lewis, in his sermon "The Weight of Glory," referred to the phrase *I never knew you; depart from me* in Matthew 7:23 as "appalling words... to be banished from the presence of him who is present everywhere and erased from the knowledge of him who knows all... left utterly and absolutely outside... unspeakably ignored" (p. 6). To be unspeakably ignored by the one whose attention nothing escapes is the very risk one takes for himself by ignoring God's offer of salvation. The judgment of God will be perfectly equitable. No one will be in hell because God rejected their appeal for grace and forgiveness. The atoning/propitiating work of Christ is offered to all who believe. Reject it at your own peril!

Why is the Classic Passage on the Living Word Here? (4:12-13)

It may seem that verses 12 and 13 of Chapter Four introduce an abrupt change of subject. They do not. They are a declaration of the sufficiency of Scripture to save and to sanctify. Whether from his lips or his pen, the author aspired to be a mouthpiece for the Word of God "expounding its truths so that the voice of God may be heard, the glory of God seen, and the will of God obeyed" (Lawson, p. 18). In true apostolic fashion, his message is grounded in the Old Testament. Peter, on the Day of Pentecost, preached Christ from Joel 2, Psalm 16, and Psalm 10 (Acts 2:14-36). Stephen's sermon delivered to the Sanhedrin referenced no fewer than a dozen Old Testament passages as he recounted Jewish history leading up to *the coming of the Just One, of whom you now have become the betrayers and murderers* (Acts 7:52). Philip confidently *preached Jesus* to the Ethiopian eunuch when asked to interpret Isaiah 53:7-8 (Acts 8:34, 35). And when Paul composed Romans, a repository of New Testament doctrine, he employed as many as 70 Old Testament citations or allusions.

The Apostles patterned their preaching and teaching after the example of Christ. It has been estimated that one-tenth of the words of Jesus recorded in the Gospels are excerpts from the Old Testament. In his post-resurrection ministry, he consoled the two disciples on the road to Emmaus when *beginning at Moses and all the prophets, he expounded unto them in all the scriptures the things concerning himself* (Lk. 24:27). And when meeting with the Disciples in the upper room, Christ *opened their understanding, that they might understand the scriptures* which included *all things... written in the law of Moses, and in the prophets, and in the psalms, concerning [him]* (Lk. 24:44, 45).

So, whether the author of Hebrews is issuing warnings or reiterating promises, he speaks on the authority of Scripture. He considered the Word sufficient to address every need. His great concern expressed in this passage was the potential that some within the fellowship could be harboring **an evil heart of unbelief**. They are reminded that **all things are naked and opened unto the**

eyes of him with whom we have to do (4:13). **Opened unto the eyes** comes from *trachelizo* which means "to lay the neck bare." The term is used only here in the New Testament. The context of a **sword dividing asunder** suggests a sacrifice having its chin lifted to expose its throat to the knife. But the context more closely ties *trachelizo* to the phrase **him with whom we have to do**, suggesting the practice of pulling an accused man's head back to force him to look his judge in the eye. It is the Word of God that brings men to terms with the one to whom we will ultimately give account (Rev. 20:11-15; 2 Cor. 5:10). Hebrews 4:12, 13 has been paraphrased this way:

> There is a dynamic quality to God's every utterance. His Word does things! It uniquely makes things happen. It works within the deepest recesses of our being—searching, exposing, convicting, and healing. We cannot bluff God. Nothing is hidden from him. There is no such thing as keeping anything to ourselves. Whatever a man holds in the darkest corners of his conscience will be exposed and judged by God's Word. Not a single created being can keep a single thing secret from God.

If a man's heart is to be searched, let it be the Word that does the searching. If a man's sin is to be judged, let it be the Word which judges. If grace is to be applied, let the Word administer grace. If strength and courage are waning, let it be the Word which strengthens and emboldens. If old things are to be put off and all things made new, let it be the Word that transforms. God's Word is sufficient.

Conclusion

The book of Hebrews is a sermon. The author/preacher explains the truth of Scripture in order to convey divine judgment if it is refused and divine grace if accepted. In every congregation, the potential exists for some to enjoy the warmth of the community of believers without being true believers. They could be misled and presume to be saved when they are not. Or they may be living a lie, feigning faith in Christ. The same remedy is prescribed for both—generous doses of the Word delivered with a sense of urgency. God

> **The author explains the truth of Scripture to convey divine judgment if it is refused and divine grace if accepted.**

still uses the foolishness of preaching to save the lost (1 Cor. 1:18-25). *Faith comes from hearing, and hearing by the word of Christ* (Rom. 10:17 NASB).

Central to this passage is concern over any who are still outside of Christ, but the passage addresses belabored believers as well. **Exhort one another daily** (3:13) is meant as much to console the despondent as it is to correct the disobedient. **Exhort** is translated from *parakaleo* which means "called alongside." It is the root word for *Comforter* (*parakletos*), the title given to the Holy Spirit (Jn. 14:16, 26; 15:26; 16:7). **Exhort one another daily** is not a mandate for members of the congregation to stand over one another in judgment based on what they see or don't see or what they hear or don't hear. We cannot see into another man's heart. We can barely know our own since it is *deceitful above all things, and desperately wicked* (Jer 17:9). Everyone arbitrarily judging one another is a prescription for meddling rather than mutual edification. The mandate here is to administer a daily dose of the truth of God's Word. It alone is sufficient to save. It alone is sufficient to sanctify. It will *reprove, rebuke...* and *exhort* (2 Tim. 4:2).

The living God has declared himself, his glory, and his eternal purposes nowhere else but in his living Word. Listening to his voice is both our grandest privilege and our gravest duty.

ADDITIONAL COMMENTS

As mentioned within the prelude of this commentary, several positions exist regarding whether the warnings in the book of Hebrews were written with believers or unbelievers in mind. Chapter Five serves as a good example of a valid position, even though it differs from the General Editor's analysis (see the book Prelude). While we encourage readers to carefully analyze both points of view and reach their own conclusions, keep in mind that the authors share more commonalities than differences. Of primary emphasis, note clear agreement on the Doctrine of Eternal Security—meaning that genuine believers cannot lose their salvation. Thus, the question becomes one that is more about the seriousness of one's faith. Unbelievers are called to repentance and believers are called to fully surrender to the one who died for their sins. (Neipp)

STUDY GUIDE QUESTIONS

In 3:13 and 3:15, the term "today" is emphasized, stressing the significance of taking prompt action. Why do we often defer tasks to tomorrow that should be tackled today? What does this inclination disclose about the priority we give to Christ in our lives?

The sin of the Israelites was characterized by a hardening of the heart. How did this show in their daily lives? How does it reflect in our own lives? What are the consequences of such behavior?

Considering the portrayal of events and the language tone in the chapter, what comparison is being made between God's rest in 3:18-4:11? What implication does this comparison carry? How does Matthew 11:28-29 enhance your understanding of this concept?

In verse 4:12, the word "for" connects to the previous verse. How is the idea of rest connected to the operation and purpose of Scripture?

What are the five attributes that describe the Word of God in 4:12? How can we interpret each of these qualities? In what manner should these descriptions shape our viewpoint and method of studying the Bible?

6

PERFECT PRIEST

Hebrews 4:14-5:10

Jon Jenks

Introduction
This section highlights the ultimate priest, needed by sinful and weak mankind. He provides reconciliation, redemption, and ongoing help with total compassion. But for those growing up in a fundamental church environment and witnessing the prayers of the saints being lifted to God with boldness, it might not have occurred to them that a high priest is present or needed. For that matter, those reared outside of church might not have ever considered that they needed a priest or what the role of a priest might be. Allow this passage to introduce this ultimate priest's function, standing, and character, which at the same time will reveal mankind's need and the benefits gained through him. Ultimately, believers receive this humble priesthood so that they might pray with mercy on behalf of themselves and one another.

God the Father rooted the idea of Jesus as high priest in words of prophecy which he now makes plain throughout the book of Hebrews. It begins as an implication in Chapter One where Psalm 110:1 is applied to this begotten Son, the anointed king, who shall be worshipped because he is the glory of God. This same Psalm will be quoted twice in this section, designating Jesus a high priest after the order of Melchizedek (v10; Psalm 110:4). Specifically, this Son of God under whom the whole world was put in subjection became flesh so that he might become a merciful and faithful high priest who dies for the offspring of Abraham to pay for their sin and helps those in the flesh as one who has been in the flesh (2:17). Finally, this high priest, Jesus, who understands the flesh, supersedes the faithfulness and glory of Moses (3:1). Having this high priest superior to Moses beckons believers to hold fast their confession and enter the rest that is from God (4:11,14). This section will now establish how Christ qualifies as a superior priest. He is perfect both positionally and practically; thus, he is the great high priest.

A Great High Priest (4:14-16)

This section begins with a bridge verse (4:14) which repeats the believer's necessary response to **hold fast our profession** that brings rest because Jesus has entered the heavens as a high priest who is superior to Moses. Then a second response to having a great high priest comes to light: **come boldly unto the throne of grace**. These responses are only necessary and possible if Jesus is the ultimate, perfect priest. This section concludes with proof that Jesus is such a priest called by God, like Aaron, yet superior.

Response #1 (v14)

The believer literally possesses **(we have a great high priest)**. This possession does not imply control but rather availability. This priest on one's behalf is, therefore, not a distant idea or person but, as in days of old, he is like a priest willingly living in a household at the disposal of the family. It reveals a personal connection but not with just a standard priest. This priest is a **high priest** or literally a "first" priest, first in authority or standing. In addition, in the lineup of first priests he stands above the rest as the **great** one. For this priest to be great above all human priests he would need to be divine. Thus, the writer clarifies that he is **Jesus, the Son of God**. Chapter One laid out the standing of this Son, the Appointed One, who sat down at the right hand of the Majesty on High. This priest who personally connected to the believer is on location in the throne room or sanctuary of God as he has passed through the heavens (Rienecker, p. 677). He is not just a veil; thus, one can approach almighty God. He is literally both God and priest, mediating on a believer's behalf and present in the heavens with lasting impact. The force of this impact is not a command. Rather, the possessing of this heavenly great high priest nurtures the believer to **hold fast** or literally be in control of their **profession**. In this action of continually holding fast, the high priest and believer unite (this is the essence of the present subjunctive) which assures the believer that he will remain in this profession.

Reflection

Jesus, Immanuel, *God With Us* as great high priest, provides one of the most complete stabilizing pictures of God for the believer. Wrapped up in this picture is his ultimate power as God the Son, his sacrifice for us as Jesus the Savior from sins, his working on our behalf, and his presence with us to sustain and understand us. All of this will be unfolded in the coming verses. When one believes that Christ is this one, he then has Christ working on his behalf. This, as the Hebrews context speaks, brings an active rest. *Rest* because he is this and *activeness* because this rest strengthens one's hold on this gospel truth, compelling one to join with him as a believer priest. He as priest brings one into reconciliation and ongoing interaction with the Father which then becomes one's mandate to worship him and draw others to this worship.

> **He as priest brings one into reconciliation with the Father which then becomes one's mandate to worship him and draw others to this worship.**

An Understanding High Priest (v15)

The **For** indicates the ground or why the believer can **hold fast our profession.** The believer would not be able to hold fast without a great high priest, for just possessing a high priest relationship would not suffice. This priest must possess certain characteristics. Using the double negative to add force, the writer highlights that Jesus understands the feeling of our fleshly weakness. He was **touched with the feeling** or literally shared in the experience of temptation and felt it like every person. He was tempted or tested like us or literally according to our likeness. This word *temptation* has the idea of maliciousness tied to it. He felt this temptation, just like us, for in his flesh he had **infirmities** or weaknesses like every person. In the perfect tense, this temptation has an ongoing impact. He constantly felt the impact of these temptations. The forces of evil were testing him without respite. But the result in the perfect high priest was no sin.

One might say Christ cannot understand the temptation that comes from the impact of a previous sin one has committed. But it is the same root weakness that capitulates to sin the first time as the second or the seventh. Further, how great was the pressure upon Christ in the flesh because he never satisfied the cravings of his weakness! Having the same weaknesses means he had the same temptations, which means he had the same understanding. But in Christ, the same result was not found. Mankind sins, but Christ is **without sin.**

Reflection

Mankind cannot deny the inherent weaknesses of the flesh. When one feels overwhelmed and alone in these weaknesses, how great it is to have a Savior who understands the hardships of these infirmities, is near during temptation, and has removed the power of sin. This brings hope. It is also a model for the believer as "priest" to reveal to one's disciples that he understands their weaknesses because he has the same ones, to walk with them through their temptations while encouraging one another, and to connect them to Christ who is always with them as priest and can deliver. This hope for the believer of always having a priest who understands and who is in the throne room of the Father brings a second response where the believer joins in with the priest.

Response #2 (v16)

Possessing a great high priest who understands our weaknesses and temptations causes the response of holding fast to one's profession and now a second response of coming **boldly unto the throne of grace**. Our personal priest who is both with us and working on our behalf causes us to profess and pray. Again, this is not a command but an ongoing response that connects the believer to Christ as priest. This connection is to the throne room where the great High Priest has passed through the heavens to distribute mercy and grace on behalf of the Father. The believer comes near with confidence to this priest who understands. This boldness means *with every saying*. The believer comes like a child who talks and talks, explaining everything and trying to solve the problem out loud. The believer has confidence that their priest will want to hear them and help because the throne room is characterized by grace (Lane, p. 188). How appropriate that the sinful believer who is being tempted comes to the priest to obtain or receive mercy and grace. One expects that he comes for mercy because of sin that has occurred or for mercy that might remove the temptation. In either case, he finds grace after searching. This grace brings **help** which is a word with the root idea of *crying out*. One cries out when the need is great. This is a cry that comes because now is the time. This cry of faith happens first for salvation, then in times of temptation, and in times when a believer's weakness brings hindrance to obedience. Aaron, as the most respected high priest to this point for the Jews, did not provide such immediate and understanding help. He could not remain at the ready before the Lord for mercy and help as he had to sleep and at times had to deal with his own sin. He could not know all people intimately. Though he was before the Lord, he was not in the very presence of the throne of grace but at a representation before the Ark's Mercy Seat. This Jesus is the ultimate high priest as Son of God who is always with us and in the throne room and always understanding us.

Reflection

It is essential to know and trust this truth that as a believer one has a personal great high priest who stands at the ready to give help in the form of mercy and grace. He wants the believer to ask in the moment even with wordiness. Keep asking and receiving. The test of one's belief will be how bold and immediately one communicates in prayer. If prayer is missing, understanding or belief is missing, or one is not seeing his weakness and vulnerability in temptation. Maybe prayerlessness indicates sin has begun. Or in the case of the Jewish person of the original audience, maybe the prayerless believer is questioning how Christ became a priest. One needs a real priest, not just a metaphor. When one knows this priest is perfect, praying will begin in earnest.

> **One needs a real priest, not a metaphor.**

Called to Be a Perfect High Priest (5:1-10)

For a believer's confidence to be in Christ as the ultimate first among priests, the substance of who he is, how he became a priest, and how all of this makes the complete priest greater than all others needs to be established. This section provides the basis for the high priest ideas from the previous section. The writer unfolds the similarities between Aaron and other high priests to highlight the essentialness of humility and the uniqueness of the high priest who is the author of salvation. In Hebraic fashion, this section appears to be in a chiastic structure (Lane, p. 111):

> A The old office of high priest (v1)
>
>> B The solidarity of the high priest with the people (v2-3)
>
>>> C The humility of the high priest (v4)
>
>>> C' The humility of Christ (v5-6)
>
>> B' The solidarity of Christ with the people (v7-8)
>
> A' The new office of high priest (v9-10)

Every Priest Appointed for the People (v1)

In God's economy, priests are taken from among mankind. God does not send angels to be priests. Rather, he appoints or ordains men to serve mankind. The priests serve people concerning things that matter **to God.** This serving involves offering gifts and sacrifices. These words aptly represent the two types of Old Testament offerings. One represents the grain-type offerings as gifts to God. The sacrifices, because the passage says **for sins,** certainly make one think of the atonement blood sacrifice by the high priest sprinkled upon the altar and in the Holy and the Most Holy Place. Nineteen times in Hebrews the word **offer** will be used as a key theological marker (Lane, p. 108). Three of these uses are in this little section.

Reflection

These basic facts about a priest who is human or in the flesh give importance for why Christ had to come in the flesh on mankind's behalf. Every priest comes from among men and so Christ as man can be **taken** as priest by God. A priest is needed by each person to gain access to God. Is this still true today? If so, who now is a present-day person's priest? Can each person be their own priest?

Every Priest Can be Compassionate (v2)

These human priests **taken** by God are capable of being compassionate or sympathetic. This is sympathy in *a measured way* (Wuest). This sympathy makes the priest function in a caring way but not in a way that might override truth or the need for sacrifice. The priest's humanness makes him know infirmity or weakness. This infirmity is the same word used of Christ (4:15) which is evidence of how verses 14-16 fit with the explanation of them here in Chapter Five. The priest is **compassed** or surrounded by this **infirmity.** The repetition of the pronoun emphatically states his weak position. This imagery reminds one of the deep surrounding poor Jonah as he helplessly sinks into the sea with weeds wrapped around his head (Jonah 2:5). Like Jonah, the sacrifices are for those who have been caused to go astray. Temptation upon the weak has brought them to this sin, as ignorant people walking away from the God of mercy. In the grammar, these are not two different people but two descriptions of the one who sins.

Reflection
Christ, surrounded by weakness, like us, serves as a priest in the flesh with great compassion. The human priest, however, must be measured in his compassion, because his own personal sin must receive atonement. Oh, how wonderful the measure of Christ's compassion on a believer's weakness that then breaks forth in his sacrifice for my sin! Even before this passage is completed these thoughts cause the reader to begin rejoicing in the gifts bestowed upon him.

A Priest's Compulsion (v3)
Because of a priest's infirmities which lead to sin, he owes it to the people he has been ordained to serve before God to offer sacrifices for sin. Further, he is under this moral obligation to offer sacrifices for his own sin (Reinecker, p. 678; Westcott, p. 120). The original Jewish audience reader would hear the instruction of the Pentateuch in this as Aaron, even in his ordaining ceremony, had to offer sacrifice for his own sin which was then repeated before any offering for the people of God (Leviticus 9:7; 16:6). The priest can claim no superiority to the people but must be his own priest for the same needs as his people. The priest offered these sacrifices knowing they were incomplete and just a foreshadowing to the one whose heel would be bruised (Genesis 3:15); to the offspring of Abraham who would bless all the nations as the provided Lamb

> **The Old Testament priest was offering for sins but also waiting for a Messiah to be the superior sacrifice and the superior priest to complete what he as a priest could not.**

(Genesis 22); to the Servant who would one day offer himself as sacrifice for sin. Thus, the Old Testament priest was offering for sins but also waiting for a Messiah to be the superior sacrifice and the superior priest to complete what he as a priest could not.

A Priest Must be Called (v4)

A priest, by nature of this assignment, is humble. He must offer sacrifice for his own sin, and he came into this office because he was **taken** from among men for this task. The task, as the text says, is of great honor, but he cannot achieve this honor. It is **taken** for him in his calling by God. Regarding Jewish priesthood from Aaron's line, as a Levite, he is born to the priesthood and by family and birth order born to the position, then anointed as high priest by God and before God (Exodus 28). He can only claim God's providence. Aaron was the first but still called out of this same sinful position.

Reflection

Like the Old Testament priest awaiting a better sacrifice and a better priest, this passage having been set up by the end of Chapter Four has the reader's mind racing for how Christ became priest.

- How is it similar yet greater than Aaron and other human priests?

- The Father must call him but when?

- Christ has no sin so how does this change the sacrifice he offers?

Christ was Begotten a Priest (v5-6)

In yet another demonstration of his servant humility, Christ who was in the form of God did not grasp hold of the role of the Father (Philippians 2:6-7) who ordains priests from among men. He did not glorify himself as priest but, like Aaron, was called such by the Father. The author here calls him by this anointed name, Christ. This occurred in the timelessness of the Godhead on display in Psalm 2:4-7 where from his throne the Father sends forth a king, a Son that he has **begotten.** In the context of Hebrews the Jewish reader no doubt finishes the phrase, **today have I begotten thee** with "as a priest." The writer then confirms this by quoting Psalm 110:4 which is applied to Christ as the Lord of David ordained as **a priest forever**

after the order of Melchizedek (Hebrews 5:10; 6:20; 7:17). Melchizedek was the priest who blessed Abraham. This **order** or rank of priesthood will be built upon in Hebrews. The **order of Melchizedek** means Christ was called as a priest apart from the Law, apart from heredity, and for a specific purpose. But in the case of Christ, this was no temporary calling like Melchizedek's. Jesus the Son of God has this as a **forever** calling (v6; Hebrews 7:3) as the true king of righteousness and peace. He serves in fulfillment of the Law as a priest who surpasses this law on behalf of every gospel believer forever. He serves as the perfect representative of a priest after the order of Melchizedek.

Reflection
What beauty to see the deity and humanness of Christ in perfect harmony in the godhead. At the same time, he displays the humble position of being chosen just as all human priests are chosen. They are not chosen by merit, but by God's grace. But Christ is greater than Aaron because he comes from the order of Melchizedek, and beyond this, his priesthood is forever, and he is perfect. This means the believer's relationship can be complete forever in Christ who serves forever.

Christ's Offering Received (v7-8)
For Christ to be the great high priest there are two remaining necessary proofs. His offerings and prayers must be heard at the throne of grace on mankind's behalf, and he must be perfect or finish anything lacking by way of sacrifice for sins. Priests are called to offer, so Christ as priest offered up prayers. These prayers, prayed while Christ was fully human (**in the days of His flesh**), contained a progression of intensities from entreaties to crying out and finally with tears. We know in his praying Christ sweat drops of blood which conveys this intensity of offering to the Father. This offering was met with an answer, for he worshipped the glory of the Father to be revealed in himself risen from the dead. He prayed to the Father who could save him *out from under* death. He prayed not in fear or dread, as the common word for *fear* here is replaced by a word meaning *to act cautiously*. This portrays the idea of reverence. This literal translation captures nicely that Christ prayed, and, in his resurrection, the believer embraces the efficacy of this high priest, the Son whom the Father heard and raised from the dead by the Spirit (Acts 2:24; Romans 1:4). But Christ was even more than Son

begotten by the Father. He was a proven Son. He who knows all things **learned** or experienced **obedience** in the flesh with its infirmities and temptations, proving his perfection. He obeyed not just himself but the Father who had purposed for him to suffer. The tense of this verb *suffer* points especially to the cross as the point in time that obedience was completed. More completely, Christ also suffered and obeyed by coming in the flesh and living among men.

Reflection

As Paul speaks, all is vain if Christ is not risen from the dead. But in this resurrection are so many gifts to the believer. Among others, death is conquered; the forever high priest is proven as the highest; sin is conquered by one in the flesh. The believer in this has a personal priest who by example and by perfect sacrifice can overcome sin. This priest stands in the throne room with grace in his hand so that believers might be overcomers. What hope and what love has been revealed in the flesh so that only a small mustard seed of faith will be needed with such proof to receive this gospel! This gospel is not a point-in-time impact but an ongoing relationship with this priest forever.

The Author Priest (v9-10)

This eternal priest became for all time **the author of eternal salvation** as predicted by Isaiah (45:17). He literally authors or causes this by completing the goal set by God that the perfect Son of God might become flesh, endure temptation, live perfectly, learn obedience in the suffering of the cross and offer a prayer that is heard. The proof answer was his resurrection which is what the believer must obey for everlasting life. This required obedience that now must be learned by mankind is "to believe." For all who believe have eternal salvation. No one is beyond what Christ has authored. The final punctuation of the passage is that all of this proves Christ is **called of God an high priest after the order of Melchizedek.** Hold this thought as the writer will pick it back up in Chapters Six and Seven.

Concluding Thoughts

This section began with the reminder that the believer has a high priest in the heavens, Jesus, Son of God in the flesh. This causes two responses that are completed with him: **Holding one's profession** and **coming boldly before the throne of God for mercy and grace** to help in temptations experienced while surrounded with weakness. The author spends ten verses (5:1-10) proving that the great high priest is the perfect priest. He is perfectly called, and he perfectly suffers with compassion for our weaknesses (Reinecker 677). As the perfect priest, he provides eternal salvation for all who believe.

Now believers, with a perfect priest acting on their behalf, interact with him as a kingdom of priests (1 Peter 2:9). The Israelites were a light to the nations with earthly priests and earthly sacrifices that were incomplete. But now completed in Christ, we as his ambassadors direct all people to this perfect priest who can save them when they obey with faith in His eternal salvation. In addition, believers now do not need an earthly priest to serve on their behalf but rather have direct access to the Father through their great high priest who is always available and always heard.

ADDITIONAL COMMENTS

I. **THE AUTHORITY OF OUR MEDIATOR (v14)**
   A. "A Great High Priest"
   B. The Greatest High Priest – "that is passed into the heavens"
   C. The God-Man – "the Son of God"

II. **THE AFFINITY OF OUR MEDIATOR (v15)**
   A. Human Sympathy – "touched with feeling of our infirmities"
   B. Honorable Sympathy – tempted "in all points" like us
   C. Holy Sympathy – "yet without sin"

III. **THE AVAILABILITY OF OUR MEDIATOR (v16) – We May:**
   A. "Come Boldly"
   B. "Obtain Mercy"
   C. "Find Grace to Help" (Spink)

Hebrews 5:1-4
Priests are:
- Human Representatives (v1) – "taken from among men"
- Humane Representatives (v2) – "who can have compassion"
- Holy Representatives (v3) – to "offer for sins"
- Honored Representatives (v4) – "called of God" (Spink)

Hebrews 5:7
Christ was a man of prayer! We find him praying at his baptism (Luke 3:21). Then he retreated into the wilderness for 40 days of prayer and fasting. He would often withdraw into a quiet place to pray early in the morning or late at night (Mark 1:35; Luke 5:16). He spent an entire night praying before selecting his 12 disciples (Luke 6:12, 13). His disciples were so impressed with his prayer life that they asked him to teach them to pray! His transfiguration occurred as he was praying (Luke 9:29). He prayed at the tomb of Lazarus (Jn. 11:41, 42). He prayed at the Last Supper. Luke tells us that the Garden of Gethsemane was a solitary place where Jesus frequented for prayer and it is there where we find him agonizing in prayer on the night before his death (Jn. 17; Luke 22:39-46). And he is still praying – for you and me (Heb. 7:25)! If Christ prayed that much, we should pray even more! (Spink)

STUDY GUIDE QUESTIONS

In what ways do we attempt to represent ourselves before God?

Consider Jesus' life and compile a list of occasions where he was, or could have been, tempted in manners akin to our own experiences.

Given the Old Testament passages portraying the fear of the Lord, does it seem unexpected to be encouraged to boldly approach God's throne? How can we reconcile the notion of fearing God with the concept of confidently approaching him? When you come before God, do you tend more towards excessive fear or an overly casual attitude?

As mentioned in 5:1, what is the function of a priest? What distinguished Jesus from other priests?

Hebrews 5:9 mentions that Christ became the source of eternal salvation. How does this portrayal distinguish Christ from traditional priests?

In Hebrews 5:9, the conditional phrase "unto all them that obey him" is present. Considering salvation is granted by God as a gift, how does obedience connect to the notion of salvation?

7

CHOOSING WHAT IS BETTER

Hebrews 5:11-6:12

Kurt Alber

Introduction
One of the characteristics of champions is that they make different choices than their competitors. Champions show up early, study films, condition their bodies, choose what they eat, listen to their coaches and mentors, and give everything that they have. They also make sacrifices—giving up time with family, relaxation, and pursuing other passions or interests. They intentionally invest themselves in what they believe to be the best use of their time and energy to pursue the greatest ends possible.

This kind of focus doesn't just happen in sports. You will find this kind of effort in many areas of life as people seek to build businesses, master skills, prove their value, earn degrees, care for other people, seek to entertain, or whatever it is that drives their lives. In each case, choices are being made, and people are hoping to achieve something that they believe is important.

How do you find yourself investing your time? What outcomes are you seeing? As we continue walking through Hebrews, we have come to a section where the writers are calling people up. The glory of Christ above all calls for a lifestyle change. It calls us to live better.

This kind of lifestyle requires choices. It requires diligence and effort. But there is something unique about the charge that is given in these verses. The charge to choose what is better given in this text comes with a guarantee—those who demonstrate diligence can do so with full assurance of hope, knowing that others who have followed these instructions have inherited the promises. This is much different from the way the outcomes in this world work. When we set our mind to win a championship or launch a successful business, we may end up being successful, or we may not. Choosing what is better, then, is not only about investing yourself in what is truly significant, but it also comes with outcomes that go beyond temporary pleasure to eternal outcomes.

This call to choose what is better is rooted in the truth that is laid out so clearly in the first half of Chapter Five. Jesus makes salvation available for humanity. How a Christian lives must be appropriate in light of the cross and the saving work of Christ.

Salvation is indeed a gift. Paul makes this clear in his letter to the Romans when he says that *the gift of God is eternal life through Jesus Christ our Lord* (Rom. 6:23). This gift is no ordinary gift, however. The gift of salvation changes us: *Therefore if any man be in Christ, he is a new creature: old things are passed away; behold, all things are become new* (2 Cor. 5:17).

A new person has a new way of life. This is what the text describes. I encourage you to lean in as you pay attention to what this letter to the Hebrews says here. It is a challenge. It is a call that will change all who will listen for the better.

Verse 11

The first thing that appears here is a problem. Those who are receiving this letter have become **dull of hearing**. The Greek word translated **dull** is *nōthros,* which means *sluggish*—think couch potato. We have all had those experiences where we were trying to get someone's attention, but they weren't responding at all. They were too busy doing (or not doing) what they wanted to do, thinking only of themselves and not paying attention to the people around them. Even if they have goodwill inside of them, the couch-induced stupor is preventing them from being helpful.

This is a characteristic of a **child**. Children pay attention to themselves and what they want, but they need to be taught to listen. Unfortunately, many people grow up never learning to listen. They look like adults on the outside, but they've never learned the discipline of paying attention and following directions.

Verse 12

When my oldest son was a young teen, he was focused only on what he wanted. We talked about his desire to do things his own way. As much as I wanted to change that desire in him, I could not.

Finally, we came up with a plan. I told him that since we all lived in the same house, we had to figure out a way to live together that worked for all of us. That made sense to him. I believe it was part of him growing up and understanding the needs of others around him.

At this point in my son's life, he knew enough Scripture that he **ought to be** one of the **teachers** of the Word. Instead, he **need**ed someone to **teach** him **the first principles of the oracles of God**. As he started to think about each member of the family, our discussions went from being combative to being cooperative and practical. I was no longer trying to convince him that his worldview was broken, only to have him react defensively. He became receptive again to some of the Biblical ideals that make living together a joy rather than a burden. He had not been listening to me, but as we began problem-solving together, I had an opportunity to teach him how to listen by listening to him.

Notice that as frustrated as the author is in verse 11 with the fact that the readers are not living like mature followers of Jesus, he does not write them off. He is not throwing the baby out with the bath water. He describes what is necessary for their faith development, even though in his mind it is a step backward. They had **need of milk, and not of strong meat**.

Verse 13

There are many differences between milk and meat, not the least of which is how the nutrition is delivered. A child drinks milk from the mother's breast. Much attention is given from the mother to the child. She pays attention to any problems her child is having and helps to figure out solutions. Nobody blames the one drinking the milk, the responsibility lies with the one feeding the child.

Eating meat comes about in very different ways. Either the animal is taken from the flock and slaughtered or the animal is hunted. Either way, those eating are preparing their own meals, from living animals to meals on the plate, eating meat is a mature process that takes skill and understanding.

Here this distinction is clearly defined when it says that **every one that useth milk is unskilful in the word of righteousness,** but that **strong meat belongeth to them that are of full age**. The good news is that there is a process and a plan intrinsic to the author's illustration. Those who are not listening can be cared for, instructed, nurtured, and taught how to come to the point of being able to take care of themselves.

Verse 14

All children are designed to grow up. Simply through the natural processes of eating, drinking, sleeping, moving, and doing, children become bigger and stronger. They increase their knowledge and understanding. Intentional teaching normally makes that development process work a little more efficiently and with less pain. There is an expectation of development.

The last verse of Chapter Five identifies what maturity looks like. A spiritually mature person has **exercised** their knowledge of the truth **by reason of use**, which simply means by developing habits. This practice helps the child to become a mature adult. That maturity is demonstrated by the fact that they can **discern both good and evil**. Maturity is marked by a lifestyle that understands and chooses to do good, and at the same time recognizes and avoids evil (1 Pet. 3:10-11). Even beyond that, when Christ is above all in our lives, God empowers us to *be not overcome of evil, but overcome evil with good* (Rom. 12:21).

> **Maturity is marked by a lifestyle that understands and chooses to do good, and at the same time recognizes and avoids evil.**

Reflection

I grew up in Iowa, which, at the time, was the premier wrestling state in the nation. Wrestlers are known for mental toughness, wearing trash bags to help them sweat so that they could cut weight for an upcoming meet, and practicing in extreme heat. One of the ways wrestlers would practice is that they would repeat the same move over and over and over again. Normally they would start with a practice dummy or a partner who would not put up much resistance. Over time the wrestler would perfect his technique and his wrestling partner would increase his effort in preventing the execution of the move. The idea behind this practice technique is that the wrestler becomes an expert at the move, knowing when to try it and how to overcome any resistance or evasive maneuvers.

This type of expertise is the result of choosing what is better. A mature believer will be an expert in doing good and in fending off or avoiding evil. None of this happens by laying around on the couch and thinking about winning a state championship. It takes a deliberate investment of time to become a master of the things that bring glory to God. I can become mature by choosing what is better.

2 Peter 1:5-8 lays out a training path for developing this type of spiritual maturity. Like anything it begins with faith. Later in the book of Hebrews, we are reminded that *without faith it is impossible to please* God (Heb. 11:6), but this is just the starting point. What we are called to do is to build on that faith foundation. So, *add to your faith virtue; and to virtue knowledge; And to knowledge temperance; and to temperance patience; and to patience godliness; And to godliness brotherly kindness; and to brotherly kindness charity* (2 Pet. 1:5-7). The Greek word here that's translated as charity is *agape*, which means *love*. Jesus is the ultimate example of spiritual maturity which is demonstrated in his great love for us.

Chapter Six, Verse 1

When I was in college, I got to work with a contractor building houses. My first day on the job was unforgettable. The contractor was building a house for his best friend. The foundation was complete and much of the framing of the house was complete. What hadn't been done was waterproofing the basement. I spent almost my whole day in the trench that surrounded the house painting thick, black tar on the outside of the basement wall with a heavy bristle brush. I left that day filthy, sticky, and sweaty.

Day two was a completely different story. I spent that day helping to finish the rafters and beginning the process of putting the decking on the roof. I had done a good job the day before. Why didn't I just go back and do the same thing again on day two? The answer is obvious and simple, that work was completed. It did not need to be done again. In fact, it would be a waste of time and resources.

Chapter Six opens with a similar type of statement. The **foundations** of faith don't need to be laid again every day, just like you don't just keep building foundations on top of foundations to build a house. **Therefore leaving the principles of the doctrine of Christ** describes the building of a mature life of faith on the foundation of the critical truth that Jesus is the Messiah, the one who came to save. The idea of leaving here is that this part is complete, now it's time to **go on unto perfection**. This

> **Christ describes the building of a mature life of faith on the foundation of the critical truth that Jesus is the Messiah.**

word for perfection, *teleiotes,* means *to be brought to its appropriate finish.* Much like building a house, you lay the foundation, but you don't just leave it and move on. You leave the foundation and complete the house that was designed to be built on that foundation.

The only way to truly bring appropriate glory to Christ is to see Jesus for who he is, and then allow him to finish that work in you. The passive tense of the verb translated to **go on unto** indicates how God's plan functions. He does the work of completing the build. We are carried by him. This idea is repeated by Paul, when he says, *Being confident of this very thing, that he which hath begun a good work in you will perform it until the day of Jesus Christ* (Phil. 1:6).

Several foundational truths are mentioned here. The first of these truths are essential truths regarding salvation—**repentance from dead works, and of faith toward God**. This is the Gospel put in simple terms. When I turn from my sin and trust that only God can save me, my life is forever changed. This is the essential truth that all people are invited to experience.

Verse 2

The next two foundational truths are ecclesiastical, beginning with **the doctrine of baptisms**. The Greek word *baptismos* "refers to Jewish ceremonial washings whenever it occurs in the New Testament" (Constable, p. 104). Outward expressions of God's cleansing work are part of the fellowship we share in faith. So, too, the doctrine **of laying on of hands** is a symbol of fellowship with a ministry partner. It celebrates God's work not only in other believers, but through them, and a commitment to working together in bringing the Gospel to the world.

The final two truths stated here are those directly related to eternity. First is the **resurrection of the dead**. In Paul's letter to the Thessalonians, he goes into more detail as he provides comfort for the believer (1 Thess. 4:13-18). This important truth reminds us that growing to maturity in this life is only a small part of a much larger plan. The other truth mentioned regarding eternity is that **of eternal judgment**. Jesus's teaching on this is summarized in Matthew 25:31-46. Eternal judgment also points to the way our lives today affect the future. People don't like to think about eternal judgment but put in its proper context it provides great peace. We will always ache in this life when injustice goes unchecked. This is only a temporary problem. Justice will prevail in every situation. This final foundational truth provides another reminder of how undeserving the believer is of God's grace, as well as the great price Jesus paid for each of us.

Verse 3
Everything we do falls into the category of **if God permit**s. The good news about the pursuit of spiritual maturity is that we know it is his desire.

Verse 4
What a bold and powerful word—**impossible**. This is the first of four times in the book of Hebrews that you will find the word impossible (see also 6:17-18; 10:4; 11:6). Each time it goes in a different direction. This mention in Hebrews 6 is probably the most talked (and argued) about by theologians. Many of those arguments are rooted in the individual's conviction about the doctrine of eternal security and its implications.

Simply stated the doctrine of eternal security holds that our relationship with God is secure as a "result of God keeping us, not us maintaining our own salvation" (GotQuestions). Those who hold to eternal security point to verses like John 10:27-30, Rom. 8:31-39, Eph. 4:30, and Jude 24. Others believe that a believer can be separated from God by their sinful choices. 2 Tim. 2:11-12, Heb. 10:26-28, Jam. 2:14-17, 5:19-20, and 2 Pet. 2:20-22 are some of the verses that are used to support this position. Quite candidly these next few verses are a problem for both of the main theological camps around eternal security. People often spend too much time being enthralled by their doctrinal statements and not enough time just simply believing what the Word of God actually says.

Let's remember the topic of the text before taking the time to look at these verses. This passage is calling the believers to choose what is better, to grow to spiritual maturity—to become an expert in doing good and resisting evil. This is how we are to represent our faith in the death, burial, and resurrection of Jesus to the world around us. It's all about honoring Jesus and his sacrificial work.

There are six prerequisites for the person being described in this text. If these six things are true, then something is impossible for them. We will get to what is impossible and the reason for that when we get down to verse six. Here are the six experiences that are described:

1) They **were once enlightened**. This phrase is in the passive tense, so it describes what happened to the people. Jesus is identified as *the true Light, which lighteth every man* (Jn. 1:9).

2) These people have also **tasted of the heavenly gift**. Some claim that the word tasting refers to an experience with God but not fully experiencing the heavenly gift. Those people should be reminded that Jesus *should taste death for every man* (Heb. 2:9). Clearly this is not a euphemism for something less than a full experience.

3) The third prerequisite clarifies that experience even further by describing them as people who **were made partakers of the Holy Ghost**. This describes a sharing in the Holy Spirit that was characteristic of new believers from the very first days of the Church described in Acts 4.

Verse 5

4) The fourth description involves another tasting, but this is focused on the **good word of God**. The Greek translated word here is the word *rhema*, not the familiar *logos* (John 1:1), and refers to what is spoken.

5) The fifth prerequisite also shares the verb tasted, this time referring to **the powers of the world to come**. The word for powers, *dynamis*, refers to the mighty works of God, specifically his miracles (Constable, p. 109).

Verse 6

6) Having experienced the previous five things, there is one more prerequisite for the impossible. The text says **if they shall fall away**. The Greek word for *if* here is the word *kai*, which is normally translated "and." This makes the most sense in this text as the sixth of the experiences for the individuals described in this passage. If people experience all of this and turn aside from the truth, then they face an impossibility.

The six prerequisites break up the statement of what is impossible. **It is impossible for those** who experience these six things **to renew them again unto repentance**. The Greek word for **renew** is *anakainizo*. This is the only time it is used in the New Testament, but that doesn't make the word difficult to understand. What cannot be renewed? The answer to that question is repentance, which means a change of mind. A rejection of the apostasy that these people have pursued produces a mind that cannot be changed.

Notice this statement does not say that anything is impossible for God, the impossibility lies with the person who rejected the miraculous work of God. Denying God's Word is always a dangerous path to follow. The author has already warned the readers of the book of Hebrews three times not to harden their hearts (3:8; 3:15; 4:7). The focus of this text, however, is not the impossibility. The why is much more important than the what.

Blasphemy is not a word that is used often in today's world. Most of the time it refers to disrespectful words spoken to or about God, but God can also be blasphemed through a person's actions. This is the why behind the impossibility of repentance described in verse six. So how do they blaspheme God? By rejecting the truth of what they have seen and heard, these people **crucify to themselves the Son of God afresh, and put him to an open shame.** (To be clear, the word blaspheme is not found in this text, but this why statement describes one of the ways people blaspheme God's glorious work.)

Jesus cannot be crucified again. The sanctifying work of Christ was accomplished *once for all* when Jesus completed his Father's will on the cross (10:9-10). Making a mockery of the redemptive work of Christ, the greatest event in all of human history reveals why that is so critical to this text. Philippians 2 reminds us that because of Christ's humility and death, *God also hath highly exalted him, and given him a name which is above every name: That at the name of Jesus every knee should bow, of things in heaven, and things in earth, and things under the earth; And that every tongue should confess that Jesus Christ is Lord, to the glory of God the Father* (Phil. 2:9-11).

God is all about the honor of his name. First and foremost, he is, in his nature, worthy of it, but God also deserves glory because of his actions. From the human perspective, we were designed by God to be worshippers of him. In other words, we will not find true fulfillment in our lives apart from total abandonment for the praise of his name. The inappropriateness of a life that falls away from the glorious work of the cross is incomprehensible. This is the point of these impossible verses. *Be not deceived; God is not mocked: for whatsoever a man soweth, that shall he also reap* (Gal. 6:7).

Verse 7

These next few verses continue the thoughts about God's glory through the use of an illustration. Picture a freshly planted garden on a warm spring day with the rain falling. We know what is supposed to grow in that garden. When I was a kid, my parents would put the seed packets on the end of each row on a stick, so that we could all remember what had been planted there. The expectations are great.

The **earth** is designed to receive water when the **rain** falls **upon it.** That rain, along with the warmth of the sun, and the rich nutrients from the soil causes the seed to germinate, grow roots, and bear fruit. It **bringeth forth herbs meet for them by whom it is dressed**. What grows is what was planted. This is the **blessing from God**. When you plant basil, basil grows, that is his design.

Verse 8

Sometimes other things grow in the garden. The **thorns and briers** are **rejected** by the gardener. How does that happen? It's not because of what was put there by the gardener. No, it is what was already in the soil. The arrogance of humanity, the heart that is set against God produces what is worthless.

This illustration takes us back to Genesis 2 and 3 where God had created the perfect garden—beautiful, abundant in provision, and designed to be enjoyed by humanity. Adam and Eve chose to follow their own ideas, rather than listening to God resulting in the weed seed of sin being present in the soil of each person's heart. But it doesn't just grow in our hearts because of the fall, it literally grows in the soil as well. God cursed the ground because of sin. This **cursing** is appropriate, and so is the **end** of that curse, which **is to be burned**.

Reflection

Just as it is appropriate for the gardener to expect what is planted in the ground to grow and provide fruit, so it is appropriate for God's glorious work to produce in each of us what is better: *For this cause we also, since the day we heard it, do not cease to pray for you, and to desire that ye might be filled with the knowledge of his will in all wisdom and spiritual understanding; That ye might walk worthy of the Lord unto all pleasing, being fruitful in every good work, and increasing in the knowledge of God* (Col. 1:9-10).

If you claim faith in Jesus, this illustration should remind you that the people around you are looking at your garden. This is what a believer looks like. This is what a godly marriage looks like, this is what Christlike leadership looks like. This is how important evangelism is. Choosing what is better is critical for every one of us because it reflects our Gardener.

Verse 9

The weightiness of verses four through eight could be paralyzing to people, especially to those who have not been listening, and who have been unresponsive. Remember these people should be mature in their faith, but they are not. They have been acting like children. I am thankful for these next several verses that help to encourage, set high expectations, and even remind them that they are not the only people to ever need to make the difficult choices necessary to live a life honoring God.

There is a quick shift in tone at the beginning of verse nine as the authors address the Hebrews as **beloved**. They want to remind them that the difficult truths that they are speaking are because they care for them. They consider the audience as part of the good work that God is doing. Then they explain what this is to look like—the better way that they need to choose. This is done, in part, by laying out appropriate expectations.

What do you expect when you go to a baseball game? Is it different from attending an art gallery? What about grocery shopping or a day at the beach? You may feel like your brain has been taken in four opposite directions with each of these examples. In each case, you probably have clear expectations of what those events would be like for you. You probably also have some expectations of what you would wear for each activity. You may take a change of clothes to the beach, but you probably would not take one to the grocery store. You could also anticipate how much time you would spend with each, who might go with you, how much money you would plan to spend, and when would be the best time to go. Certainly, you would not plan to attend a baseball game in Detroit, Michigan on January 3. You would be the only person in the stadium—and you'd be cold!

The writers want **better things** for their friends, but this is not just a desire. In fact, they are **persuaded** of **better things** for them.

They have confidence in what is to come. They are anticipating a positive response by the Hebrews to this letter. Then they go on to categorize what they expect—**things that accompany salvation**. Just like you take cold water and a hat to the beach or dress up for an art exhibition, or make sure you have your wallet when you go to the grocery store, certain things are appropriate for salvation. You can picture in your head what it looks like to choose what is better.

These encouraging words feel needed by the writers. They realized the gravitas for the previous verses could prove discouraging as they qualify what they are saying with the phrase **though we thus speak**. These words are contrasted with the opening line **we are persuaded of better things for you**. Having someone who has confidence in my ability to do what is excellent is certainly encouraging for me. I think this is another important part of the intentional care that is illustrated in verses 12 and 13 of Chapter Five.

Verse 10

As the actions of the people who have experienced the grace of God are described, they are framed within the character of God. This is a powerful reminder that God sees and knows everything and always judges rightly. **God is not unrighteous**. What a critical truth. If God could do something other than what was good and fair, then nothing done by humanity would really matter. We could have no expectations or confidence. But God's righteousness is always evident. He will not **forget your work and labor of love**.

> **God sees and knows everything and always judges rightly.**

1 John reminds us: *Herein is love, not that we loved God, but that he loved us, and sent his Son to be the propitiation for our sins. Beloved, if God so loved us, we ought also to love one another* (4:10-11). The works being done in love are a reflection of and a response to God's work of love in their lives. God's character is manifested in the world around us by what we do. This was affirmed by Jesus when he prayed for all believers: *I in them, and thou in me, that they may be made perfect in one; and that the world may know that thou hast sent me, and hast loved them, as thou hast loved me* (Jn. 17:23). The works done by **which ye have shown toward his name** bring glory to God because they are an appropriate reflection of his great love.

These acts of love have been seen in the past. It was clearly seen that they **have ministered to the saints**. But this kind of love is not shown in a one-time work. Their love continues to abound as they **do** and continue to **minister** consistently.

Verses 11 and 12

I was a slow eater when I was a child. I remember many times sitting at the dinner table and eating by myself. At one point, the rest of the family had been sitting around the table with me, but they had all finished their meals and were off doing other things. My parents had cleaned up the kitchen, put away leftovers, and loaded the dishwasher, except of course for my plate and fork. It's not that they all rushed through dinner, it's that I was that slow.

There were times, however, when I was looking forward to something like a television show (this was before the VCR days) or the family was going to go out for ice cream, or to something that I considered fun. Those days I ate more quickly. There was something I was looking forward to that somehow changed the speed of my ability to eat.

Hope is anticipation. In Scripture it refers to looking forward to something sure, something you know will happen. Most of the time it refers to the future when God deposes the rulers of this world and he rules in righteousness—a time of true peace where things function as they were designed to function. We can have **full assurance of hope**. We can know what is to come, maybe not every detail, but knowing that our good God is in charge means the future will be greater than we anticipate.

So, what do we do in light of that hope? Do we kick back and relax? Do we hide from people who would seem to harm and look for the return of Christ? Jesus answered these questions with a parable. Two slightly different versions can be found in the gospels, one in Matthew 25:14-30, and the other in Luke 19:11-27. In both parables, Jesus is bringing out the same point. God has given each of his followers a job to do and the resources to accomplish them. He is coming back. **Every one of** us **must show the same diligence** to prepare for his return. We must each choose what is better because the Master is worthy of it.

The word translated diligence here is translated *haste* when describing Mary's journey to see Elizabeth after learning that she would be the mother of the Messiah, and that her past childbearing years relative, Elizabeth, was also expecting (Luke 1:39). In other words, the hope that we have for the future should motivate us to move quickly, not just to sit at the table chewing slowly, but getting things done because the Master is returning. In case there is any question about this, it is also spelled out in the negative, **that ye be not slothful**. Choosing what is better requires diligence.

> **Choosing what is better requires diligence.**

But diligence is not the only description of the life that honors the hope that we have in Christ in these verses. There are two other key words laid out here; they are **faith and patience**. While faith is an intangible sort of term, it is demonstrated clearly in its partner, patience. In modern language, the term patience is much more passive than the Greek word *makrothymia*. Perseverance is probably a better description in today's English. It's the idea of digging deep and pressing on no matter how difficult things become. Knowing the end is coming and knowing that Christ is returning should keep us choosing what is better in order to represent his Kingdom well.

In this charge to persevere with diligence, the writers already encouraged the readers that they have confidence in God to do this great work in them and through them. Still, these last verses also point to a reminder that they are **followers of them** who have already endured and have **inherited the promises**.

If you've ever tried to do something that has never been accomplished, it can seem overwhelming. Roger Bannister famously became the first person to run a mile in under four minutes on May 6, 1954. For years people had been trying to break that four-minute barrier. Once the barrier was broken many people followed in his footsteps within the next year.

There is something profound about having examples who have shown the way in the past. This reminder that to honor the cross people must be diligent **unto the end** is made more accessible knowing that others have done this before. Hebrews Chapter 11 overviews the stories of many different people throughout history who have honored God with their faith that enabled them to persevere to the end. Verse 12 here looks ahead to that list.

We all do better when we have examples to follow. Not every example needs to be a person whose story we find in Scripture. Titus 2 lays out that God's plan is for older believers to lead the way for those who are younger. The older believers do this by their example as well as by what they say. It's always encouraging to look around and find those people who are ahead of you in the human experience, people who are bringing honor to God by how they live, and spend time with them, listening to them and learning from them. This is a critical part of the fellowship of a local church. We all benefit from each other as we choose what is better together.

Concluding Thoughts

The Hebrews were stuck. They had been drinking milk for far too long. Maybe you feel stuck in your faith. Maybe you've been going through the same routine for decades and do not seem to be making any progress.

In my experience as a pastor, I have seen people kick themselves over and over again because they are upset with their failure or lack of growth. That is exactly the opposite of what God wants for each of us. The other thing I have seen people do is try to go from infant to adult overnight. They end up getting frustrated because they don't accomplish their goals, and often get discouraged and fall back into the same immature routines.

Choosing what is better is not a goal to be achieved. It's a new way of living life. If it is time for you to grow up, I'd encourage you to make one small manageable change. It could be one of many different things. There is a list of ideas below for you to explore. This list is not comprehensive, but it can be helpful as you take your next step.

I also encourage you to find someone whose faith you respect to serve as an encourager to you. Maybe just reading that last sentence put someone's name in your head. It may feel awkward to reach out to a person and say that you want to choose what is better and that you've seen good things in that person's life that encourage you. If you don't have someone in mind, pray for God to bring someone your way. It's also a great idea to reach out to a pastor to assist you with that.

These simple things will help you to move in the right direction. But there is one last piece of advice that I'd like to offer, and that's this: Look for someone to invite to follow you as you follow Christ. You may feel unworthy. That may seem overwhelming, but it's one of the most important things you can do. This whole section of Hebrews is about how we live in light of the cross of Christ. The cross was all about Jesus seeing our need, and humbly serving in love to provide what we needed to restore our relationship with God. The more you pay attention to the needs of others, and seek to serve them, the more your maturity in Christ will grow.

Points of Application

Please don't try to do all of this at once—that would be overwhelming. My prayer is that this list can serve as a catalyst for your thinking and help you to take a step in the right direction. These are choices for the better that you can do.

1. Go to a church worship service.

2. Pray a verse from the Bible. Here are some great verses to pray: Psalm 19:14; Matthew 6:9-13; Ephesians 3:14-19.

3. Leave the car radio off when you drive alone and spend time being thankful to God.

4. Write a favorite verse on a card and read it every morning when you wake up and every night when you go to bed.

5. Call a friend and ask them how you can pray for them.

6. Listen to only Christian music for a day.

7. Find a Bible reading plan and start reading... just a few verses a day can help you grow.

8. Volunteer to serve an hour a week at church or with a local non-profit group.

9. Give to meet a need.

10. Ask some people you respect about how they grow their faith.

11. Write a paragraph prayer in a journal.

12. Go for a walk outside and remind yourself that God sustains all life.

13. Visit someone who is sick.

14. Be kind even when the people around you are not.

15. Ask God for strength to do what honors the cross.

16. Never give up. If you try something and fail, forget, or fade away, keep starting again.

I want to let you know that if you make an intentional effort to grow in your maturity, you will face opposition. Don't be discouraged if things get hard for you. Let that encourage you because you're doing something good, and God is on your side.

ADDITIONAL COMMENTS

Hebrews 5:11-14
Spiritual Discernement
  I. The Dearth of Spiritual Discernment (v11, 12)
  II. The Dangers Without Spiritual Discernment (v13)
  III. The Development of Spiritual Discernment (v14)

Some Christians are still in kindergarten when they should be graduates already. They have remained as spiritual babies still being spoon-fed and sipping milk from a bottle. They are more likely to be attracted to a church or ministry that feeds them candy. Children love candy. They want a sermonette that tastes good. "Give me something uplifting and entertaining – Bible-flavored, of course, but something that is easy to swallow." This kind of candy can be addicting and people like it. It is found in sermons which tend to be more of human skillful oratory and entertaining rhetoric than solid exposition of Scripture. It is man's word—not God's Word. This text warns of the dangers of child-like lack of discernment. It makes a plea for believers to mature in their faith; to grow up becoming skillful in the Word. (Spink)

STUDY GUIDE QUESTIONS

Think of an individual who has departed from their faith. What observations can you make about their journey? What factors contributed to their actions? Did it involve a deliberate decision or a gradual progression?

Regarding spirituality, what sets apart "milk" from "meat"? Can you give examples of each in a believer's journey? Considering 5:13-14, which skills correspond to "milk," and which ones to "meat"? What dangers arise from a lack of progress?

What understanding does 6:1 offer regarding the author's motivation behind the content to be discussed in the subsequent verses?

What key message is communicated in 6:4-8? How should the warning in these verses shape our view of sin?

What understanding does 6:10 provide regarding God's position when someone abandons their faith?

What strategies for progressing in one's faith are suggested in 6:9-12?

8

SOUL ANCHOR

Hebrews 6:13-20

Cory Prosowski

Introduction
    I grew up near the wondrous sandy shores of Lake Erie. Like many people who live near a large body of water, we spent many hot summer days cooling down at the beaches. However, that is not the only thing our family would do on the lake. My father owned a motorboat. It was not spectacular, but big enough to fit five adults and fast enough to do water skiing and tubing, although if it did have five adults, the small motor would struggle to get up to speed to make tubing or skiing fun. When it was just my four-person family, it felt like the water turned to glass, and we would skim across the surface effortlessly. Those were wonderful days spent as a family.
    In the bow (front) of the boat, we had a large metal anchor. Normally, we would only use it when we decided to go fishing or swimming because even when the lake seemed still, a current would cause the boat to drift, most of the time without detection. The anchor would ensure that we stayed in the same spot, which was crucial so that you did not drift into the break-walls or so the boat would not drift away from us when we were swimming. But the anchor served another purpose in storms. My father would check the weather whenever we were taking out the boat. Not just the temperature but the wind speed and direction and whether there were storms in the forecast. Some days seemed beautiful, with the sun in the sky and only a few clouds, but between the weather reports and my dad's keen eye and intuition, we would either not go

out or start heading toward the shore far sooner than we planned. And sure enough, the storms and winds would come. Thankfully, because my father respected the sea, our family was never caught in a storm while on the water. If we were caught in a storm, we would drop the anchor, which was placed so the boat would face the waves and help prevent the boat from capsizing.

Sailors have confidence in their anchors when the storms come. What will you do when the storms of life come? The modern hymn writers Matt Boswell and Matt Papa wrote these lyrics in their aptly named hymn *Christ the Sure and Steady Anchor:*

> Christ, the sure and steady Anchor
> In the fury of the storm
> When the winds of doubt blow through me
> And my sails have all been torn
> In the suffering, in the sorrow
> When my sinking hopes are few
> I will hold fast to the Anchor
> It shall never be removed

V19 is the glorious climax of our passage in which the author speaks of our hope **as an anchor of the soul, both sure and stedfast.** As we have been reading through the book of Hebrews, the author consistently points us back to Christ. So let us take a look at how we arrived here and why Christ is the anchor of our souls.

Verses 13-17

The author begins this section with the word **For**. This conjunction indicates that he will be connecting something new to a point he just made previously. The beginning of Chapter Six is one of the warning passages in the book of Hebrews. Beginning in verse 9, the author encourages the faithful believers, *though we speak in this way, yet in YOUR case, BELOVED, we feel sure of better things--things that belong to salvation* (Hebrews 6:9 ESV emphasis added). And he encourages the believers to continue doing good works in love. He wants them to show *earnestness* and/or *diligence* so they would have *full assurance of hope until the end* (Hebrews 6:11 ESV). He says the believer's life will not always be easy, but we must press on. It's not a sprint but a marathon, so run with endurance and do not get *sluggish*. We should look to those before us and be *imitators of those who through faith and patience, inherit the promises* (Hebrews 6:12

ESV).

(V13a) For when God made promise to Abraham... There have been many times in my life when I have made promises. I have made promises to friends, family, coworkers, etc., big and small; I have made them all. But never have I made more promises than now as a father of young children. If I tell my children that we will go to their grandparents for dinner, get them something from the store, or get them some presents, I am met with a common phrase, "Do you promise?" They want to have the assurance that what their mother or I have said will come to pass. Even when we are little, we understand the uncertainty of the future. Children learn early on that just because their parents say something will happen, that is not a certainty. Why? Some things are out of our control: someone may get sick, the car may break down, a storm may prevent air travel, etc. By the power of your word, you have told your children something will happen, which is a promise in and of itself. Ironically, in modern English, when we refer to a promise, we interchange it with an oath or a swear, which are different things. My word or promise is only as good as my character, knowledge, wisdom, and power. Am I being honest or using it to control a situation or my children's behavior disingenuously? Am I able to make this promise happen? Do I know that this thing can happen? Do I know that this thing is a wise thing to do? Many variables are in place that can prevent my word from occurring. However, the promises of God are not analogous to man's, in that God knows the end from the beginning, not merely because he can see the future, but because he *declared* it (Isaiah 46:9-10). There is power in the words of God. Through the power of his word, he created the universe and the fullness therein. This includes time. There is no situation outside of his knowledge, wisdom, and power to prevent his promises from coming to pass. The author clearly states later in verse 18 that **it was impossible for God to lie,** thereby removing any question on the integrity of God, if that were even necessary.

> **My word or promise is only as good as my character, knowledge, wisdom, and power.**

What I find comforting about God is that he meets us where we are, both in understanding and, ultimately, by becoming a man himself. In Genesis 12, God tells Abraham all his promises for him.

Repeatedly, God says, *I will,* clearly laying the responsibility on himself. Abraham does what the Lord commands, but after some time of not having a son, he asks God for more assurance: *Sovereign Lord, how can I know that I will gain possession of it (Gen. 15:8 NIV)?* I appreciate this question. I love God's response. Two verses prior say Abraham believed in the Lord, *and he counted it to him for righteousness (Gen.15:6),* so we know it was not a matter of confidence or sincerity on the part of Abraham. God could have said, "My word is enough for you," and in saying that he would have been completely just. This idea or mindset is reflected in the words of the father of the boy with an unclean spirit to Jesus when he declares, *Lord, I believe; help my unbelief (Mark 9:24)!* But God does not do that with Abraham and meets Abraham where he was emotionally and intellectually and decided in his abounding mercy and grace to swear an oath. This works in perfect harmony and reflects what the author described as the character of our Lord and Great High Priest in 4:15 when he says Christ *sympathizes with our weaknesses.*

(V13b) Because he could swear by no greater, he swore by himself... I remember being a kid on the playground swearing that a story I was saying was true, and we would say, "On my mother's grave" or "I swear to God," trying to convince others that what we were saying was true. In the same way, our court system has people stand before a judge and are sworn in, historically with their right hand on a Bible, and are asked something to the effect of, "Do you solemnly swear that you will tell the truth, the whole truth, and nothing but the truth, so help you God?" The integrity of man is always in question. It does not matter who you are or your occupation; even pastors, judges, and officers who testify in court must swear an oath. In verse 16, the author takes it to man's perspective: **For men verily swear by the greater: and an oath for confirmation is to them an end of all strife**. Essentially, what you are doing is attaching the integrity of God onto yourself, which is a very weighty thing to do. You do not want to be found misrepresenting God by lying. Knowing this is how men assure each other; God swears an oath with Abram. This is why verse 17 says God is **willing more abundantly to show.** God wanted to use this custom to give more confidence to Abraham, not only to Abraham but **unto the heirs of promise.** The oath with Abraham happens in Genesis 15; Abraham takes a heifer, a female goat, a ram, a turtledove, and a young pigeon as a sacrifice for the oath and cuts them each in half, but he does not cut the birds in half. The custom is for both parties to make the oath and pass through the halves of the sacrificed animals as a symbol that if either party breaks the oath, they will end up like the animals. God then makes Abraham fall into a deep sleep and makes an oath with Abraham **by himself** because this oath was done by the power of God, not Abraham. This is commonly known as the Abrahamic Covenant.

The quotation of God from verse 13 **swore by himself** and then in verse 14 **Surely blessing I will bless thee, and multiplying I will multiply thee,** is taken from Genesis 22. This is the account of the sacrifice of Isaac. Here, we have God testing Abraham. Abraham knew that God would keep his promises and oath, but how was the thing that Abraham did not fully comprehended? How could God possibly keep promises without Isaac? Abraham probably thought something along the lines of, "Was God going to raise him from the dead?" But he obeyed, and God stopped him before he had killed his son. When reading this account, many questions arise, several of which come from the perspective of Abraham and Isaac. How old was Isaac at this point? Clearly old enough to walk a great distance with supplies, old enough to help in the altar preparations, and old enough to know what is done on the altar. At what point did Isaac realize what his father was doing? There is no mention of a struggle between the boy and his father. We see a father who has raised and discipled his son deeply in the things of the Lord, and Isaac, like his father, is willing to do whatever God asks of him, even when that thing is hard and does not make sense. Marcus Dods sums up the encounter nicely, saying,

> God met him on the platform of knowledge and of morality to which he had attained, and by requiring him to sacrifice his son taught him and all his descendants in what sense alone such sacrifice can be acceptable. God meant Abraham to sacrifice his son, but not in the coarse material sense. God meant him to yield the lad truly to him; to arrive at the consciousness that Isaac more truly belonged to God than to him, his father. It was needful that Abraham and Isaac should be in perfect harmony with the Divine will. Only by being really and absolutely in God's hand could they, or can anyone, reach the whole and full good designed for them by God.

Why did God test Abraham in this way? Primarily, this account points towards Christ, specifically in the words of God: *By myself, I have sworn, declares the Lord, because you have done this and have not withheld your son, YOUR ONLY SON I will surely bless you, and I will surely multiply your offspring...* (Genesis 22:16-17a ESV emphasis added). God the Father gave up his only son, Jesus, for us. But who is Jesus? That may seem like a silly question, but Jesus is the promised offspring of Abraham, whom God mentions here in this verse. Paul clearly states it in Galatians 3:16: *Now the promises were made to Abraham and to his offspring.* It does not say, "And to offsprings," referring to many, but referring to one, "And to your offspring," WHO IS CHRIST (ESV emphasis added). So, in a very real sense, God meant for the promised offspring of Abraham to be sacrificed, and, like Isaac, Jesus would willingly lay down his life.

(V15) And so, after he had patiently endured, he obtained the promise. What were the promises that God made to Abraham? He is promised land, a nation, and an offspring. He is promised that his descendants will be more numerous than the stars in the sky. Did Abraham see all of that? Well, not in his earthly life. Abraham was able to have a son and see the birth of his first two grandchildren, Jacob and Esau. **He patiently endured,** in that he was seventy-five and childless when God first gave him the promise and was one hundred when Sarah gave birth to Isaac. To God, twenty-five years is nothing, but to man, even someone like Abraham, who lived to be one hundred seventy-five, it is a long time: *The Lord is not slow to fulfill his promise as some count slowness, but is patient toward you, not wishing that any should perish, but that all should reach repentance* (2 Peter 3:9 ESV). Sometimes, we can lose sight of the big picture in our impatience. Thankfully, we have a God who cannot be sidetracked and works with us graciously and patiently while we work through our life and the struggles that come with it.

> **We can lose sight of the big picture in our impatience.**

V17-20

Do not forget why the author has been discussing Abraham, God, and God's promises and oath. It serves as an example for us to be *imitators of those who inherit the promises through faith and patience (6:12).* He now transitions back from the example to the application for his primary audience, **the heirs of the promise (V17).** This means that he is speaking not only to the church in Jerusalem but to all Christians everywhere, for all time, including us. Though we are nearly 2000 years removed, we are still **heirs of the promise.** As we said, God desired to give us even more confidence in these promises than we would have had without it. He wanted to show us **the immutability of his counsel** or, as the ESV says, *the unchangeable character of his purpose.* God wants us to realize that no matter what will happen or how long it may take, he will achieve everything he said. We can get so lost in the things of this life; as the saying goes, we cannot see the forest through the trees. God never loses sight of his purpose, even when we cannot see or understand it. He continually *works all things together for good, for those who love him and are called according to his purposes (Romans 8:28 ESV).* If you believe in Jesus, you are an **heir of the promises** and *are called according to his purposes.* Therefore, you can be comforted or **have a strong consolation, who have fled for refuge to lay hold upon the hope set before us.**

Why can we have encouragement? Verse 18 begins speaking of **two immutable things.** What are these unchanging things? They are God's *promise* and his *oath.* Why are these things **immutable?** The author gives us the answer: **it was impossible for God to lie.** That is one of the most comforting truths. God cannot lie to us as this verse says, **it was impossible for God to lie.** Often, you will encounter people, commonly new believers or children, wrestling with the attributes of God. As part of my job, I lead the music for our Sunday morning service. One of the great ways to learn theology is through music. We teach young children simple songs that teach deep truths. Yet sometimes, the songs, because they are simple, lack nuance, and once the child is older and starts thinking deeper about the truth, they will start asking questions. A great example is the song "My God is so Big." Let us briefly examine the lyrics, "My God is so big, so strong, and so mighty. There is nothing my God cannot do." Do you see the claim? There is NOTHING that God cannot do. I've gotten a version of this claim numerous times from people of all ages, not just kids. Most commonly, it takes a form or something to the effect of, "Could God create something so heavy he could not lift it?" Firstly, God can do anything that is not a logical contradiction. So, this question in and of itself is a non sequitur. Secondly, this song clearly speaks of the attribute of God's omnipotence, him being all-powerful, not speaking of his character or nature. We know through verse 18 that there is something that God cannot do: lie. He can't sin; therefore, it is **impossible for God to lie** because lying is a sin. This may seem weird to beings whose nature is totally stained by sin not to have the ability to sin. God cannot sin because it is not in his nature.

So, what, or rather, who is **our hope set before us** that which we hold onto? Who is the **refuge** to which we have **fled?** Who is the **anchor of the soul, both sure and steadfast**? Who is the priest that **entereth into that within the veil?** Who is the great **high priest forever after the order of Melchizedek?** The answers to all those questions are the same person, which has become the stereotypical Sunday School answer: Jesus! Yes, Jesus! For those of us who have **fled for refuge** into the arms of Jesus our Savior, we can have confidence in all of God's promises. The Apostle Paul says in 2 Corinthians 1:19-22, *For the Son of God, Jesus Christ, whom we proclaimed among you, Silvanus and Timothy and I, was not Yes and No, but in him it is always Yes. For all the promises of God find their Yes in him. That is why it is through him that we utter our Amen to God for his glory. And it is God who establishes us with you in Christ, and has anointed us, and who has also put his seal on us and given us his Spirit in our hearts as a guarantee* (ESV). All the promises of God are yes and amen in Jesus! This is why he is our Soul Anchor. When the storms of this life are strong, the waves are huge, and the ship seems all but lost, Jesus is the anchor to which we can have assurance. We can have assurance because it is **impossible for God to lie.**

Our Soul Anchor protects us in the storm but also the calm. Sometimes, it is in the stillness, or seemingly stillness, that is when we most need our Soul Anchor. Even when the water seems still, we can drift, and the drifting will send us from peace and calm into the possible calamity of nearby rocks. Drift is nearly impossible to notice until you drop the anchor and have a fixed position on which to focus. Drifting spiritually is just as insidious. When we allow ourselves to permit the near occasion of sin or allow sin around us, we can be desensitized to it, and before we know it, we can start affirming it. As an example from our current culture, this is what has happened to a lot of churches and individuals who accept and affirm homosexuality and the other letters, LBGT plus.

> **Drift is nearly impossible to notice until you drop the anchor and have a fixed position on which to focus.**

They take something clearly called sin in Scripture, and through a long process of compromising, they have drifted to the opposite conclusion that it is not sin but rather good and holy. This is why we need our *soul anchor* in Christ so that we are fixed on him, by him, and his Word so that he holds us fast and we will not drift away.

Jesus **entereth into that within the veil.** This refers to the high priest's role on the Day of Atonement when he would enter the Most Holy place, also known as the Holy of Holies, in the temple to make sacrifices on behalf of the people. At the death of Jesus, we know that the veil itself was torn from top to bottom (Matthew 27:51-28:20). Now, since Jesus is the perfect sacrifice and Great High Priest, this entering through the veil is further revealed in Hebrews, 10:19-21 as through the flesh of Jesus. That is to say that because of the atoning work on the cross, we now have access to all the heavenly places in Christ Jesus. As the author said in 4:16, we can now approach *boldly upon the throne of grace.* Entering into the Holy of Holies would not be a thing that would ever have been conceivable without Jesus. He has to be our **forerunner; that is,** he had to go before us as our great high priest and perfect sacrifice so that the people could follow him. Doing this has made him a **high priest for ever after the order of Melchizedec.** This is a quotation of the prophecy and a description of the promised Messiah given by David in Psalm 110:4. **After the order of Melchizedek,** describes the dual role that Melchizedek had that was different from Aaron's. Melchizedek was both a King and a priest; therefore, Jesus is both a king and a priest and reigns forever because all other priests die; Jesus is risen and reigning on high at the Father's right hand, continuously interceding for us.

ADDITIONAL COMMENTS

An anchor that is too light will skim across the seabed carried by currents and the boat's mass above. An anchor that is not durable will break when placed under tension. And, an anchor that is not tethered securely will leave the vessel adrift, at the mercy of wind, wave, and current. If an anchor is to be effective, it must be three things: weighty, durable, and tethered. The Christian has such an anchor. It is our confidence in Christ. This hope is secure in the weight of his unchangeable word. It is secured by the strength of his immutable character. And it holds fast because it is tethered to him who is our Great High Priest. Hebrews begs the question, "Are you held fast in the security of Christ, your divine anchor, or is your soul adrift on the perilous waves that crash upon the shoals and lead to spiritual shipwreck?" (Gardiner)

STUDY GUIDE QUESTIONS

In verse 6:13, the author references the promises made to Abraham. What core concept is being communicated through this allusion?

According to verse 16, what is the purpose of taking an oath? Have you ever experienced that making a promise helped you follow through on your commitment?

Based on verses 13-17, what are the two unchangeable elements mentioned in verse 18?

In verse 19, the term "anchor for the soul" is employed. How does our faith in Christ function as a stabilizing anchor?

Could you offer examples of promises from the Bible that God has fulfilled? Additionally, can you share instances of promises in your life that God has kept? How do these experiences of fulfilled promises shape your outlook on God's future deeds?

9

KING AND HIGH PRIEST

Hebrews 7:1-28

Alex VanCuran

Introduction

Hebrews Chapter Seven is one of the more difficult sections of this letter to understand. Many of its elements are tied to Old Testament types and texts, which the most learned of Jesus' day failed to comprehend. This should offer all of us some comfort! If you find yourself struggling to understand the relationship between Christ and Melchizedek, you will find yourself in good company with the original audience of the letter. The superior nature of Christ's priesthood was a matter of much importance and material, yet these people had become **dull** *of it* (Heb. 5:11). The radiant glory of this doctrine appeared to be flooding out of the author (as it seems to be the most distinctive idea of the letter), yet their souls were hard of hearing.

Such dullness was a grave threat to their assurance of hope in Christ, which the author equates with faith in Christ (11:1). Without that hope they might *shrink back... or turn away... to destruction* (Heb. 10:38-39 NASB). Therefore, it appears that the whole of Chapter Seven is a detailed exposition of the author's desire for their better hope (Heb. 6:9-20). He previously noted how he longed that the seed of their love and faith would go on to bear fruit. What was the desired fruit? That they would *show the same earnestness to have the full assurance of hope until the end* (Heb. 6:11 ESV). The goal was a long and hot pursuit of hope in God's invincible promises—especially as they climax in Christ (Heb 3:6, 6:20, 7:19, 10:23). Thus, if one takes greater hold of the hope offered in the Savior—even while still failing to grasp the nuances of Chapter Seven—they do incomparably better than those who miss it entirely. As James exhorts, applied understanding is far better than illustrious self-deception (Jas. 1:22). Better still is deep thinking and earnest application.

> **Applied understanding is far better than illustrious self-deception.**

To that end, the author begins with the example of Abraham, which is a natural place to start with these people. He argues that two unchangeable things solidify the Christian's hope in Christ:

(1) God has made an oath—which is final for confirmation.

(2) God cannot lie. When one takes hold of Christ, he takes hold of the unbreakable promises of God.

Yet what about this Jesus? These Jewish believers were confronted with the accusation that they were abandoning, nay destroying, the Law and customs of Moses. They faced many difficult questions: If Christ was their great high priest, why was he not born of the line of Levi? How is he both priest and king if the Law forbids it? If the temple system and Levitical priesthood could be superseded, what would keep God from loosening the sure and steady anchor of Christ at a later time?

The answer to these questions is that the covenant mediation of Jesus is an eternal appointment, after a superior priesthood, established by a superior oath. God has promised, he cannot lie, and the perfect guarantee and mediator of that promise has been established forever (Heb. 6:20). That idea, and its implications, are the foundation of Hebrews Chapter Seven, and it is a foundation for invincible hope.

The author opens the chapter with a commentary on the end of Genesis 14, wherein he highlights the superiority of Melchizedek to Abraham. This simple yet significant truth is then used to argue *a fortiori* that Jesus's priesthood—being superior to that of Melchizedek—is vastly superior to that of the Levites. Using the messianic prophecy of Psalm 110:4 as his theological key, the author demonstrates this superiority in terms of Christ's **origin**, **oath**, and **office**.

Christ's Superior Origin (Hebrews 7:1-10)

The priesthood of the Messiah is far better than that of Levi, and one can see this looking in any direction. The backward glance settles upon a strange cameo in the narrative of Genesis. A priest-king by the name of Melchizedek emerges, seemingly out of thin air, following the rescue of Lot from the forces of Chedorlaomer. He receives tithes from Abraham, blesses him, and then disappears from the storyline altogether. This three-verse account in English raises more questions than it answers. Had not the Holy Spirit later revealed its messianic significance, the story of Melchizedek might remain an element of Jewish mythology. Psalm 110:4 reads thus: *The LORD has sworn and will not change His mind, "You are a priest forever after the order of Melchizedek"* (ESV).

Hebrews 7:1-4: What does it mean that the Messiah would be a priest *according to the order* of Melchizedek?

The answer is found in the first four verses of Chapter Seven, which constitute one run-on sentence. The first three verses are concerned with describing the object of that sentence, and it is not until verse four that one is given the subject and main verb. It is a command given to the reader: (You all) **consider how great this man was** (v.4). This is the only imperative of the whole chapter.

It appears that the author had taken his own advice and he presented them with a succinct description in verses 2-3. It is worth noting that he fails to mention that Melchizedek offered Abram bread and wine. This is the only detail omitted from the Genesis account. Why was this parallel left out? Did he take it for granted that his readers would make the connection? Some scholars guess that since this was a common ritual of priests in ancient times, it was not meant to be typological in Genesis. To say that he offered bread and wine as a priest would have been redundant. Yet such begs the question: If it would have been redundant, why mention it in the first place?

Interestingly, several early church fathers ignore the omission altogether. Cyprian pursues a connection of the bread and wine of Melchizedek with the doctrine of the Eucharist (Roberts, et al., Vol. 5., p. 359), as does Ambrose (*A Select Library of Nicene and Post-Nicene Fathers of the Christian Church*, Vol. 10., p. 323) and Jerome (Roberts, et al., Vol. 7., p. 543). Such has been the bias of the Roman Catholic and Eastern churches ever since. John Calvin, who wrote extensively on the Lord's Supper, opposed this view from the same text. He notes that the glaring omission of bread and wine is either a matter of great forgetfulness on behalf of the Holy Spirit or, more obviously, a clear condemnation of the doctrine of the Eucharist. Although this seems to be a worthwhile use of the argument from silence, Calvin does not venture to guess as to the reason for the silence. A fair guess might be that the author is drawing an exact parallel in verses 2-3 between Melchizedek and Christ's fulfillment of Psalm 110. Like Melchizedek, Jesus is a priest of the most high God, King of Righteousness and of Peace, and possesses an eternal priesthood based on his eternal nature. Since the psalm omits bread and wine, the writer of Hebrews follows suit. Certainly, this does not make the parallel unimportant. The author spends the next two chapters highlighting that Christ himself has become the new and final substance of atonement.

Verse 1 mentions that Melchizedek was **king of Salem**, often thought to be Jerusalem, and a **priest of the most high God, who met Abraham returning from the slaughter of the kings, and blessed him;** To whom also Abraham gave a tenth part of all. Turning to Psalm 110 one sees a number of parallels. The messianic priest-king will also come from Zion (v.2); he will slaughter the enemies of God's people (v. 1-2, 5-6), and he will receive their offerings or pledge (v.3). A compelling case can be made that this will be fulfilled in Revelation 19. The people of God, dressed in holy garments, will freely offer themselves, or give pledges, to the Messiah who treads down his enemies.

Verse 2 highlights that **Abraham gave a tenth part of all** (meaning the spoil of war) to Melchizedek. This tithe was given before his warriors were granted their per diem and his allies were given their share (Gen. 14:24). All the spoil was tithed on, and this point is repeated in verse 4 to stress the superiority of Melchizedek in receiving it.

He goes on to explain the Hebrew meaning of Melchizedek, which is **King of Righteousness** or as the rabbinic traditions translated: "The Justifier of those who dwell in him." It was popular in Jewish midrash for Rabbis to attribute righteousness as belonging to Jerusalem, saying that the city justified its inhabitants. Such is hard to conceive from the writings of Moses or the Prophets. Instead, this is a type of the priesthood of Christ, which allows for God to be the *Just and Justifier of him who believes in Jesus* (Rom. 3:26). It is this justifying righteousness that highlights his role as **King of Peace**, which the author gets from relating the city of **Salem** to the Hebrew word *shalom*. Righteousness and peace go together in God's economy (Ps. 119:165; 37:37; Isa. 32:17; Rom. 5:1), and it is fitting to highlight this as a characteristic of Melchizedek's order.

Verse 3 speaks of Melchizedek's superior origin to Abraham by virtue of his lack of genealogy. This is an argument from silence, which is generally weak; however, it becomes stronger when the silence interrupts a normal pattern. Such is the case of Melchizedek in the thematic structure of Genesis. One of the strongest themes uniting the book is the conflict between righteous and unrighteous offspring (Gen. 3:15). This is set within ten divisions ordered around the Hebrew word *toledoth* (generations), and the suspense of the growing narrative is the question of whether the righteous seed will succeed in returning to the holy rest of God's mountain sanctuary.

For this reason, the narrative meticulously traces the genealogy of the righteous seed of woman from Seth to Joshua and beyond. Similarly, the records of those born of the priestly line of Levi were meticulously kept in the temple. If one's Levitical lineage could not be accounted for, then he could not serve in the office of priest (Ez. 2:62). The requirements to be the high priest were even more stringent. Certainly, a first-century Jew could not conceive of a high priest that was not of the line of Abraham, let alone of Levi; however, Melchizedek proved to be an exemplary one with no relation to either man.

This is the typological sense in which the author writes that he was **without father, without mother, and without descent, having neither beginning of days, nor end of life**. The gentle whisper of Scripture about Melchizedek is an inspired whisper, and so is its silence thereafter. Bruce captured this well when he wrote, "Historically Melchizedek appears to have belonged to a dynasty of priest-kings in which he had both predecessors and successors. If this point had been put to our author, he would have agreed at once, no doubt; but this consideration was foreign to his purpose. The important consideration was the account given of Melchizedek in holy writ" (p. 137). He had a father and mother; he was born, and he died. It is not to be believed, as some do, that Melchizedek is an eternal being; for if he were, who else could he possibly be than Christ himself?

But that idea has major flaws. The first is that the Scriptures say Melchizedek was **made like unto the Son of God**. The Greek word translated as **made like unto** is rare but used in Xenophon and Plato to refer to something modeled after something else. To say that something is like another is to imply that it is not the same thing; otherwise, how can a comparison be made at all? This is seen even when someone is compared to himself. In an apology he might say, "I have not been myself lately." He is not therein denying the law of identity; he is not saying that he is, and is not, all at once two different people. Instead, he is saying that his attitudes and actions have not been in line with how he normally characterizes himself. He is holding up the real as compared to the ideal. This is the same reasoning that allows the Christian to say that he is being made holy like God, despite the fact that this cannot be in the same exact sense in which God is holy. Pressing the language of verse three as hyper-literal is to commit the fallacy of equivocation; and as one will see, it creates more problems than it solves.

A second problem with identifying Melchizedek as Christ concerns simplicity. Moses demonstrated fine skill in identifying a theophany (Gen 18:1-3; 32:24-30), and so did the apostles (compare Ex 3:4-15 with Jn 8:58; Ps 23:1 and Jn 10:11). If the author of Hebrews believed Abraham had tithed to Christ in Genesis 14, why would he not say so? Would this not eliminate much confusion? Certainly, it would if they were the same person; however, because they are not, conflating them causes further difficulties. If Melchizedek had no father or mother, then he could not be Christ, since Christ had an earthly mother and heavenly Father. If he had no biological lineage, he could not be Christ, for the Lord was born of the line of Judah (v.14), and his genealogy is clearly cataloged in Scripture (Matt. 1:1-17). The author of the epistle is not confused.

Instead, remembering the significant difference between Melchizedek and Christ—namely, that Christ is the eternal God—the author writes that Melchizedek was **made like** the Son of God. He was not preexistent with Christ but was presented in Scripture as a thematic type of the eternal priesthood Christ would embody.

> **Melchizedek was not preexistent with Christ but was presented in Scripture as a thematic type of the eternal priesthood Christ would embody.**

Although in the story of redemption, he lived before the incarnate

Son, he was fashioned by Christ as a servant and sign of himself (Col 1:16). In this regard, the origin of Christ is easily superior to Melchizedek.

Verses 4-10 reveal that this is important because Melchizedek is superior to Abraham and his descendants. Thus, if Christ is superior to Melchizedek, then he is far superior to Levi, to whose priesthood the audience was tempted to return. This reasoning might have been difficult for the Jewish reader to grasp since most regarded the patriarch Abraham as the foremost of religious devotion. The rabbinic tradition presented him as a righteous and sanctifying figure.

How could Melchizedek be greater than Abraham?
The author of Hebrews gives two proofs:

> (1) **The patriarch Abraham gave** a **tenth of the spoils** to him (v.4). The Greek word for spoils is a compound word whose meaning parallels its translation. It means *top of (the) heap*, and this comes from the Greek practice of piling up the spoils of war and then devoting a portion off of the top to the gods. This practice was as old as the world, and it can be seen in many of the ancient Near Eastern texts. Its significance in terms of the Genesis narrative is to highlight the greatness of Melchizedek. Abraham had previously made offerings to God, and he himself had the right to consecrate the first fruits of his spoils to God. Instead, he offered them to the Lord through one whom he recognized as having a higher religious office than himself.
>
> This superiority is further highlighted by the fact that Abraham gave his tenth as a freewill offering. The Levites receive their tithe as a matter of compulsion, whereas Melchizedek received his out of natural reverence. This brings to mind the story of Joseph. The murderous Levi was eventually compelled to honor his brother Joseph through force of law (Gen 43:26), yet how much greater was his reverence when it was given without fear of threat (Gen. 50:21)?

Such is the argument of verse 5, which is a preview of his later argument about Christ's superior oath in verses 11-22. He writes that **the sons of Levi, who receive the office of the priesthood, have a commandment to take tithes of the people according to the law**. They were honored **of their brethren** with tithes made obligatory through the Law; Melchizedek was honored by the free giving of their father Abraham. The superior nature of the giver, with the freeness of the tithe, showcased the greater honor of the one who received it.

(2) Melchizedek was also greater than Abraham in that he **blessed him that had the promises. And without all contradiction the less is blessed of the better** (v.6-7). In the genealogical ordering of Genesis, the blessing of the Patriarchs is greatly emphasized. He who blessed was the greater, and every patriarchal blessing would be carried out in light of the covenant of blessing that God promised *through* Abraham (Gen. 12:1-3). Yet here we see this suspended, and it is Abraham who is blessed of God by Melchizedek. The writer of Hebrews takes this thematic interruption as a simple yet significant proof of his argument. By these two signs, what Jewish reader could maintain that Abraham was still superior?

From this, two subsequent proofs are then offered for the superiority of Melchizedek to Levi:

(1) The term of Melchizedek's priesthood was of superior value. He says, **And here men that die receive tithes; but there he receiveth them, of whom it is witnessed that he liveth.** Presently, his audience revered a mortal priesthood, yet the origin of Christ's priesthood is confirmed by Scripture to be perpetual. The one to whom Abraham gave tithes, so far as the record goes, *still liveth*. The practical effects of this are further applied in verses 23-25.

(2) Levi gave tithes to Melchizedek **in the loins** of Abraham. The beginning of verse nine reads **And as I may so say** but would be better translated as ***and so to speak***. This

acknowledges that what he would say next might seem excessive; however, he said it nonetheless, because it is true. A surprising support for Melchizedek's superior origin is that Levi gave tithes to him while in Abraham's loins. Thus, his order was inferior on both federal and seminal grounds, since he was both represented by his great-grandfather and present in him.

How is this so? The Scriptures commonly present one's forefather as having his descendants already within him. The Lord makes this argument in Malachi 1:2 by way of Genesis 25:23. The people of Israel in Malachi's day were loved in Jacob before he was born. To what degree? The imagery is biological. Similarly, it was not simply that Abraham represented Levi in the tithe, but Levi was physically present somehow at the offering. Although foreign to common theological discourse, this truth has a much broader significance. For instance, it carries very easily into the debate over Adam's headship in Romans 5:12—and subsequently into the debate over the nature of original sin, yet such is outside the purview of this study.

Although it could be perceived by some as a stretch, the seminal headship of Abraham over Levi is leveraged to show that Levi gave tithes in his forefather—thus showing the superiority of the order of Melchizedek. This is done as an implication of the previous (and stronger) arguments. It also functions as a rhetorical shift in terms of temporal mood. He is moving his focus from the past to the present. The original audience was tempted to return to the Mosaic Law and Levitical Priesthood. How did that stack up compared to the priesthood offered to them in Christ?

Without a doubt, his origin was far superior. Now one shall see the same is true of his oath.

Christ's Superior Oath (Hebrews 7:11-22)

Verse 11 begins with a second-class conditional statement. This is when a false hypothetical is presented in order to refute it. The premise was that **perfection** came **by the Levitical priesthood**, because **under it the people received the law**. This was a thought that the audience found to some degree appealing. Their families and neighbors were urging them to return to temple worship, to forsake what they perceived to be a messianic cult. The pressure to apostatize from Christ was great, and it was being forwarded in the name of the Word of God. Their counterargument to verses 1-10 might have been that the Aaronic priesthood superseded the earlier order of Melchizedek, as it had with the order of Adam or Noah. The priesthood of Levi was established under the covenant of Abraham, and it mediated God's holy law. The problem of their present imperfection, they might have said, was not in the priestly order but in the faithfulness of the people.

The author—gripping tight the linchpin of Psalm 110:4—will not let this happen. He poses a question: If this priesthood was capable of bringing **perfection** (complete shalom between God and his people), whereby they walked freely with him, then what need would there be of **another priest...after the order of Melchizedek**? Or in other words, why did God give his people Psalm 110:4; and more importantly, what do you do with it now that he has? It should be noted that the word **another** in verse 11 might be better translated as ***different***. Christ was not another priest of similar substance; he was a vastly different and superior priest.

> Christ was not another priest of similar substance; he was a vastly different and superior priest.

This is not to say that his priesthood is dissimilar to that of Aaron. Aaron and his high priestly work typified that which Christ would fulfill. There is no incongruence between the requirements of the Law and the work of Christ. Yet one might have readily objected that Jesus could not fulfill the letter of the law concerning the high priest, since he did not descend from Aaron. He was born of Judah. This objection is presented in verse 14, and it appears that verses 12-13 anticipate it.

Verse 12 states that the change of the priesthood established by Psalm 110:4 necessitates **a change also of the law**. The Messiah's priesthood would be after the order of Melchizedek, which means that he could not come from the line of Levi. How can one be so sure? First, the line of Melchizedek had no physical lineage. Second, it is clear from Scripture that the Messiah would be of the line of Judah (Gen 49:10; 2 Sam. 7:16; Jer. 23:5; Mic. 5:2).

Verses 13-14 explain the ground for this change in law: **For he of whom these things are spoken** (the Messiah) **pertaineth to another tribe, of which no man gave attendance at the altar**. As the Scriptures predicted, the Messiah was born of the tribe of Judah. Jesus met the requirement in a way that was **evident** to them all, and at once he was disqualified from the Levitical priesthood. This does not trouble the author. Aaron's order, like the Law, served a temporary purpose. It was a shadow of the real substance to come (Heb. 10:1). As the Apostle Paul encouraged the Galatians, the author encourages his audience that the law and its provisions were meant to lead them to Christ (Gal.3:24).

Verses 15-18 further highlight the *carnality, weakness, and unprofitability* of the law. Those are strong words aimed at a Jewish audience who revered God's Word. They appear so blunt that on the face one might think the author of Hebrews was renouncing the Law. This should not surprise those who are familiar with the ministry of Jesus and his Apostles. Jesus taught the Scriptures in such a way that he was often accused of breaking and wanting to abolish the Law. Understanding this tendency, he began the sermon on the mount by warning, *Do not think that I came to abolish the Law or the Prophets; I did not come to abolish but to fulfill* (Matt 5:17 NASB). The common mind of the time struggled to distinguish between those two outcomes.

Years later, Stephen confounded his opponents concerning Christ and the Law. When those who belonged to the synagogue of the Freedmen argued with him, and they could not withstand the wisdom of the Spirit any longer, they instigated men against him. Their testimony, although false, was certainly believable to the Jewish mob that put Stephen on trial. What was this testimony? They said, *This man never ceases to speak words against this holy place and the law, for we have heard him say that this Jesus of Nazareth will destroy this place and will change the customs that Moses delivered to us* (Acts 6:13-14 NASB).

When asked for his rebuttal, Stephen argued from the Torah that they had rejected its promised fulfillment in Christ, and they did so just as the people in the wilderness had rejected Moses who gave it to them. He did not oppose the Law; they did, from beginning to end. At this, the crowd stopped up their ears and rushed upon him. They murdered him for speaking of Christ, just like the high priests of old had murdered the prophets who foretold of him (Acts 7:52). Their honor of the Law was a rejection of the Law.

This is, so to speak, the theological equivalent of putting plastic over one's furniture. The most common goal of a couch, unless I am mistaken, is to provide a relaxing place to sit or lay. Thus, when it is entombed in a thick coat of polyethylene, one thoroughly sacrifices the purpose of the couch in order to preserve it. To remove the stiff and sticky film and lay down on the bare cushions would be, in the mind of the owner, a great offense. In the same way, when Christians began to talk to their Jewish brothers about the purpose of the Law, and they began to lean into it and rest, they were accused of great offenses. When they spoke of the fulfillment of the priesthood and temple in Christ, they were perceived as wanting to destroy them. When they honored the Sabbath in their hearts like Jesus, they were accused of breaking it.

Is this not a temptation in the church today? Are not pastors often elevated to this ritualistic status of priest? Are they not tempted to conflate themselves (and their callings) with the actual purposes of God in shepherding? Like the bureaucrat, some believe the church exists to provide them a job. Such discipleship then leads the saints to believe the church exists to give them and their pastors something to do on Sunday. Likewise, the meeting place of the church is too often revered like the temple—entombed in laws and regulations that would make the Pharisees jealous. In all of this, the means of worshiping and serving God become the ends, and the one who calls for reform and return is hailed a *troubler of Israel* (1 Kings 18:17).

The author of Hebrews certainly exposed himself to this possibility of misconception. He speaks of the Law as **a carnal commandment,** yet he is not speaking in the language of sin and worldliness. The Greek word can be translated as *fleshly*, but the context tells us that he is speaking in terms of the physical requirement of bodily descent. This is evidenced by its use in comparison: The superior priest would be appointed, **not after the law of a carnal commandment, but after the power of an endless life.** The power of the Law is being compared to the power of Jesus' resurrection. This was an **even more evident** cause for a change in the Law, which only accounted for the appointment of priests in terms of mortal descent. In this, the Law is referred to as weak and unprofitable (v.18), for it did not provide the conditions necessary to accommodate the priesthood of the Messiah.

Verse 19 reads, **For the law made nothing perfect, but the bringing in of a better hope did; by which we draw nigh unto God.** The word translated as **perfect** is from *teleios*, and here it means something different than how most English speakers use it. When one speaks of something being perfect, it often means that it has no flaws, or that a task was carried out without error. In common biblical usage, however, *teleios* conveys the idea of something being made complete in its intended purpose.

In baseball, a perfect game is where the pitcher finishes the game without any of his opponents reaching the base. Although difficult, this is a fairly loose definition of perfect. He does not have to throw all strikes to achieve a perfect game. The batter can even hit the ball so long as it is fouled or caught out. But even if both teams were to manage to pitch only strikes, one could hardly say that this was the *teleios*, the fullness or completion, of the game. So it is with the Law. It had no power to make the Hebrew blameless, let alone **perfect**; yet even if it could have made one blameless according to the letter of the flesh, it still could not bring him to completion. This is the author's point. The Law was holy, righteous, and good in its purpose before God (Rom. 7:12). This was not to make sinners blameless but to lead them to the one in whom they could **draw nigh unto God.** One needs an eternal *King of Peace* to lead them into the eternal *shalom* of God. Such has been the *teleios* of the elect from before the foundation of the world, and the Law could not accomplish that. On the contrary, the rites and rituals of the law, especially the priesthood, were designed to "keep men at a distance from God (rather) than to bring them near" (Bruce, p. 149).

In the phrase **they draw near** to God (v. 19), the Holy Spirit gives us a succinct definition of those who are true Christians. They are not like the first prodigal son, who drew near to his father only to plunder and leave him (Lk.15:12-13). They are not like those professing people who care nothing for the things of God—his people, his Word, his work, or his worship. Instead, they love and seek all these things. Yet in doing so they are not like the older prodigal son who—although he remained physically near his father—did not regard the man any better than a slave driver (Lk. 15:29). The true Christian is not satisfied with attending corporate worship, or hearing the Word

> **Under the Law, one was forced to stand apart from God, until the *better hope* was introduced.**

explained, or doing his duty to his neighbor. He longs in all these things for something greater: to draw near to God. Yet under the Law, one was forced to stand apart from him, until the **better hope** was introduced.

Verses 20-22 clarify this better hope. The word of the Law could not secure it, but the word that came later has done so *once for all*. Here the author focuses in on the **oath** of God in Psalm 100:4 versus the utter lack of one in the appointment of the Aaronic Priesthood.

The appointment of Aaron was not directly communicated to him. Instead, the word came through Moses. The Lord said, *Bring near to you Aaron your brother, and his sons with him, from among the people of Israel, to serve me as priests* (Exod. 28:1). In this, there is no mention or insinuation of an oath at all. On the other hand, the Lord spoke directly to Jesus in his eternal appointment, and he swears this as an oath. The language of this oath in Psalm 110:4 is so strong that it could hardly be fortified. Thus, he quotes it directly: **The Lord swore and will not repent, Thou art a priest for ever after the order of Melchizedec.**

The wording of this promise only increases the hope offered in the previous chapter. He wrote of the promise through Abraham: *God, desiring even more to demonstrate to the heirs of the promise the fact that His purpose is unchangeable, confirmed it with an oath, so that by two unchangeable things in which it is impossible for God to lie, we who have taken refuge would have strong encouragement to hold firmly to the hope set before us* (Heb. 6:18 ESV).

How strong is the Christian's encouragement? Could it be stronger than that? Indeed! God has sworn an oath by himself, and he cannot lie; furthermore, of his oath he has said, **I will not repent**, meaning that he will not change his mind. The Messiah is a high priest whose appointment is eternal and irrevocable. The **sure and steady anchor** will never be moved. What could cause someone to turn from Christ?

Astonished at the comparison, he exclaimed that **by <u>so much</u> was Jesus made a surety of a better testament** (v.22)! Like the origin of Christ's priesthood, the oath of his appointment is superlatively superior. It is an invincible foundation of hope for those who draw near to him.

The word translated as **surety** (*enguos*) is a hapax legomenon in Scripture. This means it is used only once (*hapax* meaning "once," and *legomenon* meaning "said"). Outside of Scripture, however, it is a common Greek word used in formal and legal documents to describe a guarantor. This guarantor possessed a much more serious obligation than a mediator. Such is readily assumed throughout the rest of the letter (8:6; 9:15; 12:24). In ancient times this guarantor would stand in for someone else and, if necessary, fulfill the obligation to which he had been sworn. If he was presented as part of the bail of a rich defendant, he would sit in prison in his place. Such was the case when Joseph took Simeon as a guarantee that his brothers would return to Egypt with Benjamin (Gen 42:24).

As for Jesus, he is a far superior guarantee than what was found in the Law or Aaronic Priesthood. In truth, there was no **surety** in the Old Covenant—the people were on their own. In response to the requirements of the Law, the people said, *All that the LORD has spoken we will do! And Moses brought back the words of the people to the LORD* (Exod. 19:8 NASB). The Messiah, however, guarantees the fulfillment of both sides of the covenant which he mediates. In him, the Law is held up and fulfilled.

An early church hymn reflects this great hope of the believer. The Apostle Paul quotes it to encourage the Ephesian church. The last line reads thus: *If we are faithless, He remains faithful, for He cannot deny Himself* (2 Tim. 2:13 NASB). The weak and weary Christian, even in the grips of doubt, needs to be greatly strengthened. They can look to their Savior—who having placed himself in their stead—will carry them to completion, according to an eternal and irrevocable oath. This would be, no doubt, sufficient material to consider, but the author of Hebrews goes on to add one more argument concerning this order of Melchizedek. It is without question that Christ possesses a far superior origin and oath. Now he will begin to argue about his superior office.

Christ's Superior Office (Heb. 7:23-28)

Turning from the subject of what *is offered* to his audience in the mortal priesthood and Law, he turns his gaze upon what *might be offered* in comparison to Christ. The temporal mood is shifted toward the future, where Christ is presented as carrying out the everlasting guarantee of salvation.

Verse 23 may have addressed or anticipated some remaining admiration of the Levitical priesthood. Such admiration seemed to be built upon a version of the *ad populum* fallacy, namely, the idea that more is better. He admits that there **truly were many priests**, as there were many sacrifices (v.27), but the problem was not of numbers but of substance. Pointing to the numbers would have been a vast categorical mistake. For instance, if one were to offer a small child a wheelbarrow of pennies or a check for three million dollars, he might be very tempted to take the three-quarter-ton of pennies, despite its rough value of about $3000. Similarly, the number of priests and sacrifices was not an argument for their strength but their weakness. What weakness? Like the *carnal commandment* that they mediated, they were mortal. They all could not, and would not, continue in service due to the reality that bodies would all eventually attain room temperature. Jesus, on the other hand, **hath an unchangeable priesthood.**

The word **unchangeable** would be better translated as *permanent* or *perpetual*. This Greek word is also a *hapax legomenon*, and it conveys (in the least) the idea of being unchangeable. When taken with verse 25, one sees by application that there is no need for a successor, since his saving work is **to the uttermost**. Thus, Christ has not picked up a priesthood that he will ever put down or share with another.

Joseph Smith must have overlooked—and the ensuing cult of the Church Latter Day Saints must continue to overlook—this simple and invincible truth. They maintain that God has appointed an elaborate system of priests after the orders of Aaron and Melchizedek (Smith, p. 350), and many of the young men of their system claim to be of the greater order—having no idea what it means in the Scriptures. In doing so they not only commit error, but they seek to thrust aside the Lord himself and trample *underfoot the Son of God, and... profane the blood of the covenant by which he was sanctified* (Heb. 10:29). Those ministering to them must remember that the believer is to give a *defense for the hope that is* in them (1 Pet. 3:15), and this hope is found in a priest who is the final successor of his order.

It follows from these verses that any sect that calls itself Christian but institutes a further priesthood is a system of false hope and cannot represent Christ. The error of the doctrine of the Eucharist has already been touched upon, but it is worth considering once more. Both the Roman Catholic and Eastern Orthodox traditions assert that their Eucharist *is* the body and blood of Jesus. Roman Catholics believe this is accomplished in *transubstantiation* (Catholic Church, p. 347), and they trace this idea back to the second-century work of Justin Martyr, which is to say it is a long-standing error. The Eastern Orthodox tradition has also maintained that Christ is present in the elements, but this is thought to be mystical.

In both cases the bread and wine are said *to become* at some point the body and blood, and in this, the sacrifice of Christ is carried forward. In response to the accusation that they are sacrificing the Lord over and over again, many claim that they are simply appropriating the *once for all* sacrifice of verse 27. Yet is this not the sole mediatorial work of Christ, who has no successor? Did God not tear the veil of the temple in two (Matt. 27:51)? Did not Caiaphas disavow the mortal priesthood when doing the same of his garments (Matt. 26:65; Lev. 21:10)? Is it not Christ who opened the way of hope by which all God's people can boldly draw near the throne of grace (Heb. 4:16; 7:19)? Let no one doubt it! The Roman Catholic and Eastern Orthodox traditions may be far older than the cult of Joseph Smith, yet they do no less violence to the office and sacrifice of Christ.

Do not be misled: Christ is seated at the right hand of God, who will make his enemies his footstool (Psalm 110:1; Heb. 1:13; 10:13). He is no more on the cross than in the grave. Thus, we are instructed that the token of his mediation is not the re-presentation of calvary from week to week. Instead, **he ever liveth to make intercession for** those he purchased with his blood. The nature of this heavenly intercession is not expounded; however, one can be assured of this: If God *did not spare his own Son, but delivered him up for us all, how will He not also with him freely give us all things* (Rom. 8:32)? Our Master intercedes with all power, sufficiency, and sympathy for all that is necessary to make us complete. Our righteousness and final sanctification are as secure as him who sits at his Father's right hand. This is the glorious hope found in the superior office of Christ.

Verse 28 summarizes this whole last section this way: **For the law maketh men high priests which have infirmity; but the word of the oath, which was since the law, maketh the Son, who is consecrated for evermore.**

The high priest to whom his audience was tempted to return was an infirm sinner. Such is attested to by the Law itself, which called for him to first make a sacrifice for **his own sins** (v. 27). How much greater was the **word of the oath**, coming after the Law, which appointed a Son who is **holy, harmless, undefiled, separate from sinners, and made higher than the heavens** (v.26)? What hope there is in such a Son! Looking backward one sees that his origin was incomparably better; looking around one sees that his oath proves incomparably better, and looking forward one sees that his office remains incomparably better.

Turning to the next chapter, one will see that this is far from the last word on the subject. Having planted a word about a better *covenant* in verse 22, the author will go on in the subsequent chapters to reap a harvest concerning it. It will be, no doubt, a word of hope. And if the Holy Spirit is working in the reader, he will go on to draw near to God in it. I pray that you will do likewise.

> **Looking backward one sees that his origin was incomparably better; looking around one sees that his oath proves incomparably better, and looking forward one sees that his office remains incomparably better.**

ADDITIONAL COMMENTS

Hebrews 7:1-22
On the pages of history there have appeared, from time to time, various enigmatic characters which peak our interest but about whom little is known. Sometimes, stories are told about them but the actual truth is hidden in a cloud of mystery. And it is that mystique which draws more attention. Who was Joan of Arc? What about George Washington chopping down his father's cherry tree? How about Johnny Appleseed, Daniel Boone, Davey Crockett, John Henry, Paul Bunyan, the Lone Ranger, and Robin Hood. These are all historical figures that have enjoyed folklore embellishment and the mystery behind those stories fascinates us.

In Jewish history, there is a mysterious person who appears in their pages very briefly. His appearance is sudden while his actions and exit are all so quick and mysterious, that few seem to have a clue about this man's mission. His name is Melchizedek. The author of Hebrews wants everyone to look at this man for a few moments for a very significant reason: Melchizedek presents a picture of Jesus Christ in his life and appearance. This is called a type. Melchizedek is a type of Christ.

The word "type" comes for the Greek term *typos*, which means "a person, thing, or event that represents or symbolizes another that is to come" (Webster). It is a prefiguration, model, or a foreshadowing. Identifying a type should not be an arbitrary postulation by a creative interpreter. The text should give clear evidence.

Hebrews 6:20 gives a strong clue and 7:15 specifically identifies Melchizedek as a type, using the word "similitude" meaning *like* or *of the same kind*. The author pulls out this mysterious person from Biblical history and explains how he was a type of Christ or perhaps even more precise—he was a picture of Christ. Consider carefully; look at this man Melchizedek with the author of Hebrews and see just how he is a picture of Christ. (Spink)

STUDY GUIDE QUESTIONS

Have you encountered difficulties in recognizing Christ within the Old Testament? How does this chapter establish connections that bridge the gap?

What importance does the perception of Christ as a king hold? And what about his role as a priest? How do these roles impact your life?

What shortcomings existed in the law and priesthood of the Old Testament? How did Christ confront and resolve these deficiencies?

Verse 24 highlights Christ's priesthood as eternal. How does his role as a priest differ from that of Old Testament priests? And how does it contrast with the concept of the priesthood of all believers?

In what way does Jesus' sinless character enhance his effectiveness as a priest?

What does it mean for Jesus to continuously intercede for you in the presence of God? How should you ideally respond to both Christ's sacrifice and his continual advocacy on your behalf?

10

HIGH PRIEST OF A NEW COVENANT

Hebrews 8:1-13

Steve Strong

Introduction

I remember when I purchased my new computer. I had already jumped onto the Apple bandwagon and was replacing my Apple MacBook with a new, updated, and improved one. I didn't have the drawn-out learning curve that previously occupied a week of inefficient productivity attached to making the change from a Windows machine to an Apple one. I was able to jump in and enjoy all the updates, the new novel features, and of course the increased operating speeds. Naturally, though, the newness wore off and this new machine (I'm actually typing on it right now) became my new normal, garnering no longer any bit of excitement each time I lifted it open.

New possessions easily lose their luster and quickly become commonplace and less valued. The worry over scratches and dents on the new car eventually lessens. The apprehension over others borrowing a favored tool diminishes over time. The anguish over pets on the new furniture slowly dwindles. New things always become too familiar. Owners always become too comfortable with their possessions and gradually treat these possessions with growing nonchalance.

The author of Hebrews is thoroughly presenting something that, unlike our new possessions, never loses luster and is ever-growing in its significance. That something is a *someone* and that someone is Jesus. Jesus is better—the better sacrifice, the better priest, the better prophet. The recipients of Hebrews were facing a strong temptation to abandon Christ and move back to Judaism, and the letter to the Hebrews is an ardent appeal to remain faithful to what is new and better—to Jesus! The current passage is central to this appeal and continues a presentation of Jesus as the better high priest. He is **such an high priest** (8:1) who serves in a better temple (8:1-2), who performs a better priesthood (8:3-5), and who mediates a better covenant (6-13).

> **The author of Hebrews is thoroughly presenting something that, unlike our new possessions, never loses luster and is ever-growing in its significance. That something is a *someone* and that someone is Jesus.**

Jesus is Such an High Priest (8:1)

Hebrews 8 serves as a transitional passage. The use of the conjunction **now** joins it to the previous passages in presenting Jesus as the better high priest. And yet, it also carries forward the emphasis on the better, new covenant that his priesthood mediates. This new covenant was introduced in 7:22 and is further expounded upon in the chapters following the current passage.

The transition from his better priesthood is expressed in a summary, or a synopsis statement when he writes, **Now, of the things which we have spoken this is the sum,** or to put it simply, "The main point is this!" The word for **sum** or *main point* is in the emphatic position and can mean "an accumulated, large sum of money." My sons have worked at a local car wash each summer and one of the perks is the tip money they receive for cleaning an individual's car. Each day they come home with a handful of bills and place them on their nightstand. Over the course of a month, they accumulate a large stash of small bills. They find it rewarding, for obvious reasons, to count their accumulated, small fortune and carry it to the bank. Small bills, day by day, accumulate into rewarding, significant sums.

This illustration is also consistent with Luke's usage in Acts 22:28 where he records Paul's conversation with the Roman tribune about their citizenship. The tribune explains that he bought his citizenship with a large sum of money—a large sum of accumulated money for some time.

In the same way, here are the accumulating truths the author has been writing about Jesus' priesthood. The main point, or the sum of those truths, is that Jesus is **such an high priest**. The accumulated truths that make up Jesus being **such an high priest** include:

- Jesus, the better revealer of God (1:1-4)

- Jesus, the incarnate Christ, crowned with glory as the founder of salvation (2:5-18)

- Jesus, the superior prophet and counted worthy of more glory (3:1-11)

- Jesus, the great high priest through whom believers enter the rest (3:12-4:13)

- Jesus, the source of eternal salvation (5:9)

- Jesus, the anchor for the soul (6:13-20)

- Jesus, the guarantor of a better covenant (7:1-28)

- Jesus, the holy, innocent, unstained, separated from sinners, and exalted to the heavens high priest (7:26)

Such a vast sum of greatness and glory is reason for pause and reflective worship—and most certainly reason enough not to abandon Christ for Judaism. But the author is doing more than just looking back on previous descriptions; he is propelled forward into the better ministry **such an high priest** performs.

Such an High Priest Who Serves in a Better Temple (8:1-2)
One of the literary hallmarks utilized by the author of Hebrews, seen especially in this passage, is the pattern of comparison he makes between the old and the new. This pattern demonstrates a correspondence between the old and new, but also a significant difference between the two.

This is seen first here in the location of the high priest's ministry, the Temple. The Temple was the epitome of worship in Judaism, being the very locale of God's presence with his people. Jesus, the better high priest, is **set on the right hand of the throne of the Majesty in the heavens**. He is described as being **set** on the right hand, but more literally understood not in the passive, but active sense of "taking a seat" which harkens the reader back to the psalmist's description of *The LORD says to my Lord: 'Sit thou at my right hand'* (Psalm 110:1). This signifies a position claimed after a work done well and fully.

This position is not in Jerusalem, and not on earth, but rather in the heavens on the throne of majesty. Herein lies the correlation yet significant difference. The Old Testament high priest had a place of ministry, a significant place even. Yet, there is a significant difference; the better high priest's place of ministry is in heaven, on the throne of majesty. This throne of majesty is also the place that inspires awe in Revelation (Chapters 4, 5) and reflects the size, strength, power, and authority of God. Being in the heavens, it is a temple of authority above and over all authorities, even the earthly Temple. Also, a significant difference is seen in the fact that Jesus, the better high priest, takes his seat permanently in the better Temple. The high priest in the earthly Temple would only visit his place of ministry, and even during his visit, there was separation and limitation from the full presence of God.

> **A significant difference is seen in the fact that Jesus, the better high priest, takes his seat permanently in the better Temple.**

Not only does **such an high priest** take a seat on the throne of majesty in the heavens, the author also explains he is a **minister of the sanctuary, and of the true tabernacle, which the Lord pitched, and not man**. He is a minister in the holy place and a minister of the holy things. There is a ministry that he is carrying out, namely expressed in 7:25 as the ministry of intercession. This is a ministry "that covers anything & everything that would prevent us from receiving the final salvation he has won for us on the cross" (O'Brien, p. 278). This ministry happens in the **true tabernacle** (literally, "tent"), the tabernacle that God set up not man. The author is here planting the seeds for his **shadow** reference in verse 5. The point of correlation is continued in that just as there was a tabernacle on earth, there is one in heaven. The significant difference is seen in who erects the tabernacle—**not man**, but God. The earthly tabernacle is built of perishable elements, but the one built by God is composed of imperishable and eternal elements.

Such an High Priest Who Performs a Better Priesthood (8:3-5)

Not only does Jesus, the better high priest, have a temple in which to minister that corresponds to the earthly but is significantly better, but he also performs a better ministry. The author continues by highlighting the corresponding nature of his ministry with what the Levitical high priest is ordained to perform. The first point of correlation is that Jesus the better high priest is appointed to the priesthood just as the Levitical high priest. The high priest was *taken from among men* (5:1) and ordained to act on behalf of men in relation to God. This acting on behalf of men before God required offering **gifts and sacrifices,** which operated in a representative way. This is a direct reference to the Levitical offerings and specifically the Day of Atonement. The way the Levitical priesthood operated is why **it is of necessity that this man have somewhat also to offer.** The Levitical high priest was ordained to offer gifts and sacrifices; in correlation, so also Jesus, the better high priest, had something to offer (his own life as a sacrifice).

There is a significant difference between the two ministries performed, though. First, Jesus' better priesthood strays from the Levitical because if he was "earthly" he would not even have been a priest, since he was not from the line of Aaron. The Aaronic priesthood is established on the earth and **according to the law**; whereas Jesus' priesthood is established in heaven and thus superior.

The second significant difference is seen in that the Levitical priesthood is an **example and shadow of heavenly things**. This is not a new concept for the Hebrew reader, or at least should not have been for it is seen throughout Exodus (25:9, 40; 26:30; 27:8). There was a heavenly standard to which the earthly adhered. The reader would be tempted to think that Jesus is the better high priest because of the Levitical priesthood, especially with the "necessity" language used; however, the reader would be far mistaken. Jesus' better priesthood is not because of the Levitical priesthood; no, the Levitical priesthood is as it is because of Jesus' priesthood. So, as the author writes, the Levitical priesthood *necessarily* pre-shadows Christ's.

This **shadow** concept is important for the reader to grasp, as well as a significant motivation for the reader not to abandon Christ. Think of any shadow we come across today. Take for instance the shadow of a giant oak tree. Standing with the tree to your back and looking out into the shadow, you can see the general shape and size—both significant and both consistent with the tree itself. And, while standing in the shadow provides a respite from the hot sun, no one is in awe of the shadow. There is only awe and wonder when looking at the tree casting the shadow. The branches, leaves, bark patterns, and other wonders of the tree are not seen in the shadow; they are only seen in looking at the actual tree. This is so also when looking at the Levitical priesthood. When looking at the Levitical priesthood, one is looking at the shadow of Jesus Christ, the better high priest. The Levitical priesthood is as it is because Jesus is as he is! The plea for the author is for his reader not to abandon Jesus for his shadow.

> **The Levitical priesthood is as it is because Jesus is as he is!**

A third significant difference, albeit one only slightly referred to, is the nature of what is offered by the priests—the sacrifices themselves. The author doesn't specify anything about the offerings, but he is hinting at what he will more fully develop in subsequent chapters.

Such a High Priest Who Mediates a Better Covenant (8:6-13)

The author now commences on the consideration that covers the bulk of this eighth chapter. Jesus' better priesthood that is performed in a better temple is better because he is mediating a better covenant which itself is founded on better promises. Repetition is used here purposely—for the author cannot use any more superlative language than he has here in verse 6; moreover, each superlative is in the opening, emphatic position in each clause. Jesus' ministry is **more excellent**; the covenant is "much better" (translated simply as "**better**"); and the covenant is founded on **better promises**. The grand theme of the whole letter seems to find expression here in verse 6. Following the shadow motif, this covenant is better than the old one because the old foreshadows the New Covenant—and the New Covenant is better than the Old Covenant in the same way your spouse is better than your spouse's shadow, and you would rather have it this way!

The *corresponding but significant difference pattern* continues in this section. The correlation is seen in that both covenants were enacted on promises. The promises of the Old Covenant don't reach back to Abraham and the patriarchs but rather are found within the covenant:

- The promise of Israel being God's people and Yahweh being their God (Exodus 6:7)

- The promise of Yahweh dwelling amongst the people of Israel and being their God (Exodus 29:45)

- The promise of Yahweh walking amongst them as their God and they as his people (Leviticus 26:12)

- The promises of blessing for obedience (Deuteronomy 28)

In addition, the Old Covenant had a mediator, Moses. Moses was the agent invested with divine authority to deliver, enact, and carry out the covenant.

Within these corresponding elements are significant differences. First, the mediator is better. Jesus has already been argued to be better than Moses (3:1-6), so attention is given to the better promises on which the New Covenant is founded. The Old is said to have been faulty; for if it had been faultless, there would have been no anticipation for the New. The fact that it was faulty gave reason to look for and anticipate the **New Covenant**. Where is the fault found? The author answers with a lengthy quote from Jeremiah 31:31-34, specifically in verse 9. The fault is found in Israel's inability to persevere (**they continued not**) in the Old Covenant. Because they did not remain faithful, the Lord showed them no concern (**I regarded them not**), or in other words, he allowed them to continue in their disobedience. The Old is faulty because it could not do what was needed within sinners. It could not bring anyone to completion and perfection. The Old Covenant could not make any person alive (Ezekiel 11:19-20; 36:26-27). The Old could not do the great work of the Gospel as expressed in Romans Chapters 3-8.

The new and better covenant is significantly different in that it promises vastly better promises, also expressed in Jeremiah's passage:

1. Those under the New will obey from the heart for the law and truth will be written on their minds and hearts.

2. There will be a firmly established and mutual relationship between God and his people, not just in designation only or one-sided faithfulness.

3. There will be direct and personal experience for those under the New Covenant. No one will teach another because everyone will know Yahweh. Nor will they be classed in rank, age, or office, but rather defined as "people who know God" in its fullest and most personal, vibrant sense.

4. There will be efficient and effective dealing with sins and completion of forgiveness, which is the basis for all preceding promises. The Old did not deal with sin, it only reminded those within the covenant of sin and longed for an adequate atonement. In the New Covenant, there will be no reminder of sin, only the reminder of the one who has atoned for sin. Sin has been abolished and can no longer imperil the divine-human relationship!

The author concludes these significant differences with the mediator, by speaking the New into existence, declaring the Old obsolete and growing old (**decayeth and waxeth old, ready to vanish away**). Every human being is learning what it means to grow old when their capacities wear out, lose strength and vitality, and become ineffective. So has become the Old Covenant. It has served its purpose and is giving way to the New. Foolish are the ones who run back to something obsolete, unserviceable, and in need of a replacement.

Here at this point, it is worth taking a moment to briefly explore whether or not believers today are found in this new and better covenant of which the author speaks. There are three main viewpoints in answering this question:

1. Multiple New Covenants: There is one New Covenant for Israel and one for the Church.

2. There is a single New Covenant solely for Israel: The church is separate from the covenants.

3. There is a single New Covenant with multiple participants: The church is one limited participant in the present age, serving in a way to provoke Israel to jealousy (Romans 11).

This author agrees with the third viewpoint as it best explains the work of Christ for which the Old anticipated and to which the Church today clings and from which applications spring (Chapter 12ff). Regardless of one's position, the New Covenant is rooted in Christ's work and was at work in these early New Testament believers.

Conclusion
For the author, Chapter Eight serves as an overflowing summary of the better ministry and work of Jesus Christ, as well as a springboard into the exposition of the better atonement accomplished by Christ. These serve as sufficient reasons for the Hebrew people to persevere in their faith and resist abandoning Christ. The readers find themselves in transition between the great, anticipated promises outlined by Jeremiah and the better ministry of Christ through the New Covenant. The realization of those better promises shapes how they see themselves, how they see each other, how they see God at work in the world, and it solidifies their commitment to Christ. So it should be with today's reader.

ADDITIONAL COMMENTS

One significant quality of the New Covenant is that sins could be completely forgiven. Under the Old Covenant, the sacrifices merely represented the one true sacrifice who could forgive sin. However, these sacrifices were merely copies or imitations. They could not actually forgive sin. Only the sacrifice of the Great High Priest was sufficient to pay the cost of sin. So, the Old Covenant sacrifices were a means of a 'deferred payment,' if you will.

The word 'remember' means "to recall information from memory, but without necessarily the implication that persons have actually forgotten" (Louw & Nida, p. 346). Thus, the idea here does not require God to relinquish his omniscience, either in the eternal state or in a moment in history. Rather, it means that God, in order to be merciful to their iniquities, does not bring them to mind, or recall them. We see throughout the Old Testament that God confronts his people and lists their transgressions. He tells them what they have done wrong, how they have violated the covenant, and what the consequences will be. And yet, they still rebelled.

Under the New Covenant, however, this will not happen. How? This will be detailed later, but basically because the perfect sacrifice was offered, the sins of the people were reassigned to Christ. And when he died, the debt was paid, and the sins of man were assigned to Christ. So, they are no longer ours, and thus he shows us mercy. And so we see the heart of God. He will be merciful toward their sins and remember them no more, not because of a poor memory, but because of a paid price—a price he paid through his perfect son! (Fowler)

STUDY GUIDE QUESTIONS

Because Jesus didn't originate from the tribe of Levi, he couldn't fulfill the role of a priest within the Old Testament framework. As a superior priest, what attributes distinguish this new form of priestly ministry?

What was the significance and intent behind the Law and the Old Covenant?

The Tabernacle held great significance for the Jewish people as the place where they believed God communicated with humanity. What message did the author of Hebrews intend to convey to his readers regarding the relationship between the Tabernacle and heaven?

How does the prophecy from Jeremiah 31:31-34, referenced in 8:8-12, reinforce the author's motif of juxtaposing the imperfect and flawed with the superior alternative?

How much do you typically focus on obeying the Law and keeping a mental tally of behaviors that you believe make you righteous before God? How does this chapter change your outlook?

11

OUR MEDIATOR

Hebrews 9:1-28

David Hixson

Introduction
We eagerly study the book of Hebrews because it is the truth of God revealed in words. We know Christ through his Word and so the letter of Hebrews comes to us with great significance. The book of Hebrews wonderfully brings to our attention that Christ is above all. He is better than angels, better than Moses, better than priests, and better than the Old Testament sacrifices. The superiority of Christ is revealed chapter after chapter. In Hebrews 9 we discover that Christ secured our eternal redemption. Hebrews 9:12 tells us that the work of Christ **obtained eternal redemption for us.**

The Tabernacle
The whole Old Testament points us to the coming Messiah and the Tabernacle in particular points us to the redemptive work of Christ. The Tabernacle was the place where the worship of the one true God was experienced. There the presence of God and the glory of God were on display. Only two chapters in the Bible are devoted to the creation story but fifty chapters are devoted to the tabernacle. The tabernacle is important and demands attention in our study because it is a giant portrait of Jesus Christ. Hebrews 9:1-10 is all about the tabernacle, its arrangement, and its furniture. This traveling earthly tent would eventually be replaced with a more permanent temple built by Solomon. Then there would be Herod's temple. Eventually, both temples would be destroyed. But in

Hebrews 9, we find this traveling tabernacle out in the wilderness. God would use the Tabernacle to meet with His people.

This chapter is divided into two parts that compare and contrast the old covenant with the new covenant. In Chapter 9:1-10, we have the old covenant which is a description of the Tabernacle and all its sacrificial system. Then in Chapter 9:11-28, Jesus is contrasted as better than all the blood sacrifices that were shed. We have the earthly tent compared to the heavenly tent. We see the comparison between the Old Testament high priests and Jesus Christ our great high priest. The high priest entered the Holy of Holies once a year, but Jesus Christ entered once for all. The priest entered with the blood of animals; Jesus entered with his own blood. The high priest offered a sacrifice for his own sin, but Jesus offered himself as a sinless sacrifice. The old covenant could not cleanse the conscience (9:9) but Jesus' sacrifice purifies our conscience from dead works to serve the living God (9:14). The old covenant sacrificial system provided a temporary covering for sin but the new covenant provides eternal redemption from sin.

Compare & Contrast

Old Covenant (9:1-10)	New Covenant (9:11-28)
Earthy tent	Heavenly tent
High priest	Great high priest
Enter once a year	Enter once for all
Enter with blood of animals	Enter with his own blood
Offering for himself as a sinner	Offered himself as sinless
Cannot cleanse the conscience	Can purify the conscience
Temporary covering for sin	Eternal redemption from sin

Chapter Nine presents a snapshot of the Old Testament Tabernacle and how it pictures and points us to Jesus the ultimate fulfillment of it.

The Door

There was a door on the east side of the Tabernacle. This door to the Tabernacle was 35 feet wide. The wall made with curtains was 150 feet long and 75 feet wide. This wide door welcomed all to come into the presence of God and there was one way to come. There were not three doors, there weren't four doors, there weren't many doors but only one door. Jesus said, **I am the way, the truth and the life** (John 14:6). He also said, **I am the door** (John 10:9). Jesus is that door.

> **There weren't many doors but only one door.**

The Altar of Burnt Offering

The first thing people encountered in the Tabernacle was the altar of burnt offering. It was 7½ feet square by 4½ feet tall. Here the animal sacrifice was made. The first obstacle they would encounter was, "How can we enter the Tabernacle?" The answer—by the blood that was spilled. Jesus is the perfect sacrifice for sin. Jesus is the blameless lamb. This bronze-covered altar of the acacia wood used for daily sacrifices points us to Jesus who would give his life for us once for all.

The Bronze Laver

The bronze basin was used by the priests to cleanse their hands of all the sacrifices that were made. This symbolizes the daily cleansing of our sins. Jesus gives us daily cleansing from our sins and restores our fellowship with him (1 John 1:9). That sin price has been paid in full at the cross.

The Holy Place

Our journey through the Tabernacle begins in a holy place and then it gets holier and then it takes us to the holiest place—where the presence of God is on display. The Holy Place was 30 feet long and 15 feet wide. In the Holy Place, we find the golden lampstand. This lampstand symbolizes Jesus lighting our path and guiding our steps by his very word (John 8:12). There is also the Table of Showbread having twelve loaves of sacred bread for the 12 tribes of Israel. This represents how Jesus feeds everyone with the bread of his word (John 6:35). Then the Altar of Incense symbolizes how Jesus intercedes for us as we come to Him in prayer (Heb 7:25).

The Holy of Holies

Now we come to the 15-foot-wide and 15-foot-high cube called the Holy of Holies. This is the holiest place because this was where the presence of God was displayed. Here we find the Mercy Seat: *And he (Jesus) is the propitiation for our sins: and not for ours only, but also for the sins of the whole world* (1 John 2:2). The term "propitiation" (*hilasterion*) is the very same word used in the Septuagint translation of Exodus 25:17 describing the Mercy Seat. Jesus is our true mercy seat.

In Exodus 25:22, the Lord says concerning the Mercy Seat: *and there I will meet with thee, and I will commune with thee from above the mercy seat, from between the two cherubim which are upon the ark of the testimony of all things which I will give thee in commandment unto the children of Israel.*

This is where God meets with man and the only way that's possible is through the blood of the sacrifice. What we are seeing here is that Jesus is that blood sacrifice. He is the one who makes a way for us to come to God. Hebrews 9:7 describes the Mercy Seat: **But into the second went the high priest alone once every year, not without blood, which he offered for himself, and for the errors of the people**. Only the high priest goes into the Holy of Holies once a year on Yom Kippur, the Day of Atonement. He could not go in there by himself; he could only enter with the blood of sacrifice. This sacrifice was offered for himself and the unintentional sins of the people.

The Day of Atonement

The Day of Atonement pictures Christ's work of atonement (Heb 9:7). The work of the high priest in the Holy of Holies on the Day of Atonement pictures Christ perfectly. Whenever an Israelite sinned, his communion with God was broken. Consequently, the sacrifices for sin were never finished and the priest's work was never done. Despite the continual sacrifices made, many unknown or forgotten sins would accumulate, for which no sacrifice had been made. The Day of Atonement was intended to make sacrifices for all those sins that had not yet been covered.

It was a great day for the liberation of the conscience (Lev. 16). The Israelites knew that whatever sins may have been missed in the daily sacrifices would now be covered. The slate would be completely clean, at least symbolically for a while. Yom Kippur was a time of release and relief. The devout Jew longed for the Day of

Christ Above All

Atonement. He could not himself go into God's presence, but the high priest would go in for him and he would be delivered.

Very early on the Day of Atonement, the high priest cleansed himself ritually and put on his elaborate robes. The breastplate, near the heart, signified that he carried the people in his heart. The ephod on the shoulder, signifying that he had power on their behalf, represented the twelve tribes. He then began making sacrifices for his own sin. Unlike Christ who knew no sin, the high priest was required to sacrifice for his own sin. Very likely he would have already slaughtered twenty-two different animals by the time he reached the event known as the Atonement. It was an exceptionally busy and bloody thing that he did on this day.

After finishing all these sacrifices, he took off the robes of glory and beauty. He went and bathed himself again completely. He then put on a white linen garment, with no decoration or ornament at all, and performed the Sacrifice of Atonement. In this ritual, the high priest symbolized Jesus Christ, who, in his true and perfect work of atonement, stripped off all his glory and beauty (Phil 2:7). He became the humblest of the humble. He dressed himself in human flesh, pure, plain, and unadorned. In all his humility he never lost his holiness. In the garment of white linen, the high priest took coals off the bronze altar, where the sacrifice was going to be made.

> **In all his humility, he never lost his holiness.**

He put them in a gold censer with incense and carried it into the Holy of Holies. Here again is a beautiful picture of Christ, interceding for his own before God's presence.

Then the high priest went out and took a bullock purchased with his own money because it was to be offered for his own sin. After slaughtering the bullock and offering the sacrifice, he had another priest assist him in catching the blood as it drained off. He swirled some of it in a small bowl and carried it into the Holy of Holies, where he sprinkled it on the Mercy Seat. The people could hear the bells on his robe as he moved about. He hurried out, and the people breathed a sigh of relief at seeing him. Had he entered the Holy of Holies ceremonially unclean, he would have been struck dead.

When he came out, two goats were waiting for him by the bronze altar. In a small urn were two lots to determine which goat would be used for which purpose. One lot was marked for the Lord and the other for the scapegoat. The goat designated for Jehovah was then killed on the altar. Its blood was caught in the same way as that of the bullock and was swirled in the bowl as it was carried into the Holy of Holies. This blood, too, was sprinkled on the Mercy Seat, but this time for the sins of the people. The high priest again hurried back out.

He then placed his hands on the scapegoat goat that remained. He symbolically placed the sins of the people on the goat's head. That goat was taken far out into the wilderness and turned loose, to be lost and never to return. The first goat represented the satisfaction of God's justice, in that sin had been paid. The second represented the satisfaction of man's conscience because he knew he was freed of the penalty of sin. Still, again we see Christ. In his own death, he paid for man's sin, thereby satisfying God's justice. He also carried our sins far from us, giving us peace of conscience and mind. He satisfied both God and man. The two goats actually are two parts of one offering: *And he shall take from the congregation of the sons of Israel two male goats for a sin offering* (Lev 16:5). They represented propitiation and pardon, two aspects of the one atoning sacrifice (MacArthur, p. 224-226). That is who Jesus is and that is how he relates to the whole of the Old Covenant fulfilled in the New Covenant.

A Perfect Tabernacle

But Christ being come an high priest of good things to come, by a greater and more perfect tabernacle (Heb 9:11). When Christ appeared, he fulfilled God's promise made in the Garden of Eden.

There would be a way that God could be satisfied being in the presence of his people. The Old Testament symbols pictured the Lord Jesus Christ but could not do the work of Christ. When Christ appeared, we moved from the shadow of the Tabernacle to the substance of Christ. We moved from the picture in the Tabernacle to the perfection of Christ. We moved from the symbol in the Tabernacle to the actual Savior, Jesus Christ. **He entered in once into the holy place, having obtained eternal redemption** (Heb 9:12). **How much more shall the blood of Christ, who through the eternal Spirit offered himself without spot to God, purge your conscience from dead works to serve the living God?** (Heb 9:14). With this lovely assertion, the writer of Hebrews involves all three persons of the Godhead in the sacrifice of Christ, which magnifies the greatness of his redemptive offering. When sin entered the human race, sin was passed upon all humans (Rom 5:12). Our actions confirm that sinful nature and we stand condemned before a holy

God. But God promised a way back to the Garden of Eden, a return into his holy presence. How would that be? Through a very long elaborate sacrificial system, God would picture Jesus Christ, the Lamb of God, who came to take away the sins of the world (John 1:29).

Christ appeared as a high priest of the good things (Heb 9:11 ESV). The Redeemer has come. The solution is here. The remedy is available and consequently, we rejoice in Christ. When Christ appeared, he entered into the Holy of Holies having the authority and the office of high priest. He wasn't from that priestly line but from the royal line of Judah. He is the King of Kings and Lords of Lords. His priestly line came from Melchizedek, who represents the eternal line that was better than the Abrahamic line (Heb 7:17). As our great high priest, he had the authority to enter the Holy of Holies. He entered once, not needing to enter repeatedly year after year. He entered with his own blood because he was the spotless, sinless Son of God. His blood is different than anyone else, any other animal or any other person because of the uniqueness of who he is, the God-Man. He is perfect, sinless, and holy. He entered securing eternal redemption for us. He made the payment in full—that is why he is better. That's why he is supreme. That is why he's the door. Our eternal redemption is secure in Christ.

Christ's sacrifice was superior to the former sacrifices because he is the God-Man, not merely a sacrificial animal. No matter how special the animal sacrifice was it was not enough. Christ is perfect and without blemish. Every person has blemishes and is unworthy of paying the price to take away sins, but Christ removes our sins as far as the east is from the west (Psalm 103:12). He can purify the conscience, not just cover it. Every Jew was looking for a way to have a clear conscience before God. Daily sacrifices were made, but it was not enough. Temporary sacrifices for a day were made but then it started all over again. Christ's sacrifice purifies the conscience eternally. He changes our hearts to want to serve him, not just because it is required. There is an internal change not merely an external obligation. Salvation does not depend upon my activity and my good works because Christ paid it all. Jesus provides rest for our souls. We worship him for who he is. He is the Sovereign One. He is the Saving One. He is the perfect sacrifice for our sins and he came to do that because he loves us.

True followers of Christ have been convinced that Jesus is the true Savior of the World. They repent of their sins and rely on Jesus alone to forgive them. They have called on the name of the Lord and are saved eternally. The superiority of Christ in providing our redemption causes us to delight in him. We worship him for who he is. He is the Sovereign One. He is the perfect sacrifice for sin. He is the Saving One and he came to do that because he loves us. We denounce all false rivals. We must reject all false ways that say if your good deeds outweigh your bad deeds you will go to heaven. We need to be the people with the voice to say that is wrong. We need to dedicate ourselves to Him because he is the true Savior of the World. We are compelled by Christ's love to no longer live for ourselves but for him who died for us and rose again (2 Cor 5:14-15).

Our Mediator

Hebrews 9:15 brings us to a pivotal verse. It begins with these words **and for this cause.** In light of everything that has been written up to now, Jesus is **the mediator of a New Testament** (covenant). This is the summary of the entire Bible. In a few words, it summarizes all the drama of redemption. This is who Jesus is and what Jesus has done and if you grasp this you can be saved. Man is on one side and there is this new covenant on the other side made possible by the Lord Jesus Christ himself so that those **who are called might receive the promise of eternal inheritance.** He is the mediator between man on one side and God on the other. **This eternal inheritance** comes not by man's own production but by God's. It comes to us as a gift of the God-Man. Only Jesus Christ, the God-Man could make a way by which sinful man could come into the presence of a holy God (1 Tim 2:5). Here at what might be the pinnacle of the book of Hebrews we see the word **eternal.** Since Christ has accomplished, by his own blood, an **eternal redemption** (Heb 9:12), we can share in this **eternal inheritance** (Heb 9:15). Who receives this eternal redemption? Those **who are called.** Those who hear the call of the truth of the gospel and respond to it with a repentant heart; those who respond to the work of the Holy Spirit in their life. We respond to the truth of this gracious message of salvation because the Holy Spirit quickens us to respond to it (Eph 2:1). We were dead in our sins, but the Holy Spirit makes us alive to repent and receive the true gift of eternal life. Since Christ has

> **Only Jesus Christ, the God-Man could make a way by which sinful man could come into the presence of a holy God.**

accomplished an eternal redemption, we can share in an eternal inheritance.

The Relationship Between Death and Forgiveness
This portion of Hebrews could be outlined in three sections: **A will requires a death (Heb 9:16-17); Forgiveness demands blood (Heb 9:18-26); Judgment demands a substitute (Heb 9:27-28)**. First of all, we consider that a will (testament) requires a death. A will takes effect only at death. When a person who has a will dies, then that will is implemented. Jesus had to come and die so that we could have eternal life. He became our mediator. He had to die to initiate this new covenant. Jesus is our sinless substitute: *And he took bread, and gave thanks, and brake it, and gave unto them, saying, This is my body which is given for you: this do in remembrance of me* (Luke 22:18). As our Mediator, he is the Bread of Life. The price that Jesus our Savior paid in his own sinless body has given us eternal life. Jesus stated: *This cup is the new testament* (covenant) *in my blood, which is shed for you* (Luke 22:20). There are various covenants: the Mosaic Covenant, Abrahamic Covenant, Davidic Covenant and this would be a New Covenant. Christ as the mediator of the new covenant poured his blood for us. He is the fulfillment of all that has been pictured for generations. Jesus is the only sinless substitute needed to satisfy the demands of a righteous God. Jesus is also our purifying substitute. Only he can purify us by his blood. The Old Testament sacrifices could not make us perfect and clear our conscience. The blood of Christ was necessary to purge our conscience from dead works to serve the living God.

Forgiveness demands blood. Some might think it bizarre that we sing "Hallelujah for the Cross" and "Nothing but the Blood of Jesus." Why does the Old Testament require the throats of animals to be slit and their blood collected and sprinkled on the people and throughout the Tabernacle (Heb 9:19-20)? Why did they need to kill all those animals? Why would we celebrate the cruel violent execution and bloody sacrifice of Christ? Here is the reason—sin is serious! We tend to discount and minimize sin. We do not see sin from the perspective of a holy God. "Sin" is a bad word you can't use in polite company. The Bible calls us all sinners: *Wherefore, as by one man sin entered into the world, and death by sin; and so death passed upon all men, for that all have sinned* (Rom 5:12). The wages of sin is death and death required the shedding of blood. The life of a person is in the blood (Lev 17:11). **Without shedding of blood is no** remission (Heb 9:22). The only remedy for our sin is the death of the God-Man. Only His payment could satisfy the demands of a holy God. Jesus offered this better sacrifice. The sacrifices of the Tabernacle were good but Christ's sacrifice is better. Those sacrifices were necessary back then, but they were pictures looking forward to the perfection of Jesus Christ. They were shadows looking forward to the substance of Jesus—the perfect sacrifice for sin. **So Christ was once offered to bear the sins of many** (Heb 9:28). The blood of bulls and goats would picture the need for a blood sacrifice, but the perfect Lamb of God would be the fulfillment of it. **For then must he often have suffered since the foundation of the world: but now once in the end of the world hath he appeared to put away sin by the sacrifice of himself** (Heb 9:26). He appeared—this is his first coming. This is what we celebrate at Christmas. God became man and dwelt among us. He has appeared to put away sin *once for all*. This was the final installment. The high priest repeatedly year after year went in and offered sacrifices. Sin could finally be dealt with. That promised redeemer, who had been anticipated for years, has appeared. Christ put away sin by the sacrifice of himself. Only the God-Man's sacrifice will fulfill this requirement. **For Christ is not entered into the holy places made with hands, which are the figures of the true; but into heaven itself, now to appear in the presence of God for us** (Heb 9:24). He *has appeared* (past tense) and now we can say He *is appearing* (present tense) in the presence of God the Father pleading his blood on our behalf so that we can have a mediator now as our substitute (Heb 7:25).

Judgment demands a substitute. **So Christ was once offered to bear the sins of many; and unto them that look for him shall he appear the second time without sin unto salvation** (Heb 9:28). The whole story of redemption can be summarized in these three statements: He *has* appeared—past (Heb 9:26), he *is* appearing—present (Heb 9:24), and he *shall* appear—future (Heb 9:28). Christ is coming again and what is he going to do when he appears? He will save those who are eagerly waiting for him. We have a glorious, merciful Savior. **And as it is appointed unto men once to die, but**

> The whole story of redemption can be summarized in these three statements: He *has* appeared—past, he *is* appearing—present, and he *shall* appear—future.

after this the judgment (Heb 9:27). Judgment is coming for all of us. Every one of us will die; in fact, you could probably even biologically say we are all dying. One day we will all end up in the same place called a grave, but the grave is not the end. We all have eternal existence somewhere. We will stand before God.

Our Response

God has responded to our greatest need. We have sinned and God has provided his own Son as an offering for many. This is the only remedy for our sin. We must respond. We will be held accountable for what God did to remedy our sin. If you do not receive Christ, you will be condemned forever in hell. God is holy and we are unholy. We cannot bridge that gap between God and man. Christ appeared to save us from our sins. What will you do with Jesus? If you stand before the Lord in your own merit, you will miserably fail, because God is holy and you are not. The only way to go to heaven and be in the presence of God is to be clothed in his holiness. His presence was protected in that Old Testament tabernacle and there was a reason for that. He wanted people to know you don't come into the presence of a holy God without blood. So, the God-Man Jesus Christ gave his own blood so that you could come into his holy presence forever. That's a story of grace, mercy, and redemption. That's the good news of the gospel—the story of Jesus. Those who repent of their sins find forgiveness. Receive him as your Savior and Lord today: *For whosoever shall call upon the name of the Lord shall be saved* (Rom 10:13). *But as many as received him, to them gave he power to become the sons of God, even to them that believe on his name* (John 1:12).

As a believer in Christ, are you eagerly waiting for him by living a godly life? *Beloved, now are we the sons of God, and it doth not yet appear what we shall be: but we know that, when he shall appear, we shall be like him; for we shall see him as he is. And every man that hath this hope in him purifieth himself, even as he is pure* (1 John 3:2,3). When the Lord saves us, we are made positionally holy. This is an immediate gift. It's now our privilege to practically live out holiness to match his holiness. In light of Christ's certain return, let us be on an eager journey toward living a holy life. If the Holy Spirit is convicting you of a particular sin, agree with him and seek forgiveness. We want to walk in newness of life. We want to grow in our walk with the Lord. We want to be a light in this dark world. We want to let our light shine brightly so that others may see our good works and glorify our Father in heaven (Matt 5:16). Let us show them what really happens when a person's life is transformed to match Christ's holiness.

ADDITIONAL COMMENTS

The English word **appear** is found three times in verses 24-28, and these three occurrences summarize Christ's work in the past, present, and future for us. In verse 26, we find the past appearance of Christ to remove our sins. Jesus Christ was made manifest as God the Son in order to pay for and remove our sin. Christ's present appearance is found in verse 24, where he is presently appearing in God's presence to intercede **for us** (see 7:25). His future appearance is found in verse 28, where he returns to bring eternal salvation. We are saved eternally the moment we trust Christ, but one day he will return to complete our salvation and take us to be with him for all eternity. (Alexander)

The New Covenant that Christ instituted is superior because it has results that are final—nothing further is needed. Foundationally, we learn that one offering, the sacrifice of Christ, is sufficient (v25). The blood of Christ is infinitely superior to the blood of animal sacrifices (**blood of others**), and his blood was offered only once, not **often**. Further, his offering of himself **put away sin** (v26). The singular noun refers to the principle of sin, rather than individual sins. Christ's *once-and-for-all* offering abolished sin and settled the sin question *once for all*. Finally, his sacrifice paid our sin debt in full and guaranteed our eternal salvation (v28). Our sins are forgiven because Jesus paid for them, and we are eternally secure. Christ's New Covenant is superior! Its results are final! What more could we need? (Alexander)

STUDY GUIDE QUESTIONS

In the Old Testament system, the high priest had to use the blood of a bull and a goat. With what did Jesus enter the Holy Place?

What function does Christ fulfill in the establishment of the New Covenant? What is the significance of a mediator?

This chapter emphasizes the concept of "once for all." What does this phrase signify? How does it differ from the Old Testament framework? And how does it deviate from the practices of religious systems outside of Christianity?

Precisely, what does Jesus achieve on our behalf through his blood? What does the concept of redemption symbolize?

To what extent did individuals in the Old Testament have access to God? How does the degree of access to God compare between their time and ours?

We often find ourselves in polarizing situations. Have you ever downplayed either the seriousness of your sins or the sacredness of God's holiness? Which of these aspects do you tend to overemphasize in your own life?

12

ONCE FOR ALL

Hebrews 10:1-18

Chuck Pausley

Introduction

Day after day, year after year; repeat. Day after day, year after year; repeat. The Old Testament sacrifices were never finished. Day by day and year by year they were a reminder of sin and never provided full relief from guilt. In contrast, Christ's sacrifice for sin was *once for all*. It never needs to be repeated and nothing additional needs to be done for it to be effective. The finished work of Christ on the cross and his death made it possible for mankind to have a remedy for sin that is final and complete. In this section of verses, we will look at areas that help us see the significance of Jesus Christ's death being *once for all*.

Verses 1-4

(v1) For the law having a shadow of good things to come, and not the very image of the things, can never with those sacrifices which they offer year by year continually make the comers thereunto perfect.

The Law refers "to the Mosaic system, which includes the Levitical system and the priesthood, together with all of the sacrifices and offerings for sin" (Krejcir, p. 1). The details of this system can be read as given to Moses in the first five books of the Old Testament (the Torah). The sacrificial system of the Law was weak. The system was temporary and could not accomplish anything permanent. The repetition of the sacrifices day by day and the Day of

Christ Above All

Atonement year by year communicated the system's weakness.

A shadow portrayed something real, but the shadow in itself was not real. The sacrificial system of the Law was a type or a picture of the work that Christ would accomplish on the cross. As a picture, the Law's purpose was to point to the salvation that was to come, and to make the people look to future promises and blessings. In today's world, it might be compared to the ultrasound picture new parents might receive months before their baby arrives. It is a "shadow" of what is to come, but not the real thing.

Very image emphasizes again that a shadow is not an exact replica. The sacrifices were only a reminder, a promise of what was to come—the promise of a sacrifice to come that would be *once for all*.

Make... perfect is the promise to bring to completion or finish what was to be accomplished through Christ. This terminology is used elsewhere in the New Testament based on a person's faith in the completed work of Christ: *Whom we preach, warning every man, and teaching every man in all wisdom; that we may present every man* **perfect** *in Christ Jesus* (Colossians 1:28). The Old Testament "comers" or worshippers could not achieve this perfection through their sacrifices.

(v2) For then would they not have ceased to be offered? The answer to this rhetorical question is yes. If the old system could have removed sin, the old sacrifices would no longer be necessary. They were a continual reminder that the sacrifices could not take away sin. **Because the worshippers once purged should have had no more conscience of sins.**

Purged—or cleansed, **no more conscience of sins**—suggests man's awareness of doing wrong in his life and sense of guilt. The Old Testament Law and sacrifices could bring no freedom from the awareness of sin and guilt and the conviction it brings.

> If the old system could have removed sin, the old sacrifices would no longer be necessary. They were a continual reminder that the sacrifices could not take away sin.

(v3) But in those sacrifices, there is a remembrance again made of sins every year. Every year there was a continual reminder that these sacrifices could not take away sin. It was constantly before them that the sacrifices were no final solution.

(v4) For it is not possible that the blood of bulls and of goats should take away sins. "Under the Old Covenant, the priests were busy all day long, from dawn to sunset, slaughtering and sacrificing animals. It is estimated at Passover as many as three hundred thousand lambs would be slain within a week. The slaughter was so massive that blood would run out of the Temple ground through specially prepared channels..." (MacArthur, p. 246-247).

The blood of bulls and goats couldn't accomplish man's redemption. That could happen only through the shed blood of Jesus Christ, the *once for all* sacrifice yet to come, and the redemption that he would provide.

Verses 5-10
This section of the chapter makes reference to Psalm 40:6-8 written by David which appears Messianic in nature as verses 5-9 of our text quote Jesus in conversation with his Father.

(v5) Wherefore when he cometh in the world, he saith, sacrifice and offering thou wouldest not, but a body hast thou prepared for me. "Wholehearted obedience is the sacrifice that God really desires, the sacrifice which he received in perfection from his Servant-Son when He came into the world" (Bruce, p. 233). The incarnation of Jesus and his death was the only, *once for all* sacrifice.

(v6) In burnt offerings and sacrifices for sin thou hast had no pleasure. Samuel challenged Saul: *To obey is better than sacrifice* (1 Samuel 15:22). David also said: *The sacrifices of God are a broken spirit; a broken and a contrite heart, O God, thou will not despise* (Psalm 51:17). "It is essential to know that the external ceremonies had an internal requirement to make them acceptable to God. The person who did not sacrifice out of an honest heart was not covered even externally or ceremonially. It is this sort of sacrifice that 'thou hast not desired'" (MacArthur, p. 251). It is also true today that believers can do the externals of worship (church attendance, singing, giving, listening) without focusing on the person of worship and with hearts far from acknowledging his lordship and sovereignty: *True worshipers will worship the Father in spirit and truth; for the Father is seeking such to worship him* (John 4:23 NKJV).

(v7) Then said I, Lo, I come (in the volume of the book it is written of me) to do thy will, O God. God's eternal plan is fulfilled as communicated in the whole of Scripture. "He acknowledged that his own body was to be the sacrifice that would please God... Jesus' supreme mission in coming to earth was to do his Father's will. Over and over in the gospels, Jesus speaks of his having come to do the Father's will and only the Father's will" (MacArthur, p. 252). What a challenge to believers today to view their lives as only to do the Father's will as shown by Christ's example throughout his life (John 5:30, Luke 22:42).

(v8-9) Above when he said, sacrifice and offering and burnt offerings and offering for sin thou wouldst not, neither hadst pleasure therein, which are offered by the law; then said he, Lo, I come to do thy will, O God. He taketh away the first, that he may establish the second. Again, we see an Old Testament quote from Psalm 40:6-8. MacArthur reveals: "God took away the first, that is, the old sacrifices, to make way for the second, the new sacrifice. His point was to show the Jewish readers that the Old Covenant was not then, never had been, and never could be satisfactory. It was not meant to be permanent or truly effective, only temporary and symbolic" (p. 253). The old system has been replaced. The sacrifices were external. They never got to the heart of the problem. Sin is always an internal issue. The old system could not reach inside a person to change them: *For if the blood of bulls and of goats and the ashes of an heifer sprinkling the unclean, sanctifieth to the purifying of the flesh: how much more shall the blood of Christ, who through the eternal Spirit offered himself without spot to God, purge your conscience from dead works to serve the living God?* (Hebrews 9:13, 14).

> "The Old Covenant was not then, never had been, and never could be satisfactory. It was not meant to be permanent or truly effective, only temporary and symbolic."

The terms **sacrifice, offering, burnt offerings**, and **offering for sin** specify the different kinds of sacrifices required under the Old Covenant (Leviticus 1-7). "The word *sacrifice* refers to any of the animal sacrifices. *Offerings* cover the meal offerings and the drink offerings. The burnt offering and sin offering are mentioned

(Hebrews 10:5,8). The trespass offering would be covered in the word *sacrifice* (Hebrews 10:5). Each of these offerings typified the sacrifice of Christ and revealed some aspect of his work on the cross" (McArthur, p. 313).

(v10) By the which will we are sanctified through the offering of the body of Jesus Christ once for all. Believers **are sanctified**. God made us holy. Simply stated, sanctification means he set us apart to himself. This is positional sanctification: *But as he which hath called you is holy, so be ye holy in all manner of conversation; because it is written, be ye holy; for I am holy* (1 Peter 1:15, 16). God has made it possible for each one of us to live a life that pleases him. "The Greek verb form in verse 10 (we have been sanctified) is a perfect participle with a finite verb, which shows in the strongest way the believer's continuing and permanent salvation" (MacArthur, p. 254). It is also an "inward cleansing from sin and being made fit for the presence of God, so that henceforth they can offer him acceptable worship. It is a sanctification that has taken place once for all; in this sense it is as unrepeatable as the sacrifice which effects it" (Bruce, p. 236).

Jesus Christ's **offering of the body** was an atoning and sacrificial death. He paid for the penalty of man's sins in full. His death was sufficient to care for all of mankind's sins and it becomes effective for us individually the moment we receive the truth of the gospel. His death was the one-time, final, and complete payment for sin **once** and **for all**.

Verses 11-18

(v11) And every priest standeth daily ministering and offering oftentimes the same sacrifices, which can never take away sins: It was the priest's daily responsibility to minister and offer the same sacrifices. This sacrificing could have been monotonous at times. It was a constant reminder that these sacrifices could not completely remove sin. The very words, **standeth, daily, oftentimes, same, never take away**, communicate the daily, never-ending responsibility of the priests to make sacrifices that would ultimately not be effective in the taking away of sin.

(v12) But this man, after he had offered one sacrifice for sins forever, sat down on the right hand of God; The believers' sin has been paid for completely. Jesus Christ's (the perfect God-Man) death was once and forever effective, never having to be repeated. His death cared for all of mankind's sins. His death satisfied the righteous demands of a holy God forever: *And he is the propitiation (satisfaction of God) for our sins:... but also the for the sins of the whole world* (1 John 2:2). *But God commendeth his love toward us, in that, while we were yet sinners Christ died for us* (Romans 5:8). His redemptive work was complete, signified by his position sitting at the **right hand of God**. Many theologians have pointed out that the priest's work was never completed as they were continually referred to as "standing." In contrast, Jesus **sat down.** "Christ, then, has taken his seat in token that his sacrificial work is finished; but more the worth of his sacrifice and the dignity of his person are further indicated in that he has taken his seat not merely in the presence of God but at the 'right hand of God.' From the shame of the cross, he has been exalted to the place of highest glory" (Bruce, p. 239).

> **"From the shame of the cross, he has been exalted to the place of highest glory."**

(v13) From henceforth expecting till his enemies be made his footstool. The enemy, Satan, has been destroyed. Jesus Christ's death defeated Satan at the cross and rendered him powerless: *Forasmuch then as the children are partakers of flesh and blood, he also himself likewise took part of the same; that through death he might defeat him that had the power of death, that is, the devil; and deliver them who through fear of death were all their lifetime subject to bondage* (Hebrews 2:14,15). *And you, being dead in your sins and the uncircumcision of your flesh, hath he quickened together with him, having forgiven all trespasses; blotting out the handwriting of ordinances that was against us, which was contrary to us, and took it out of the way, nailing it to his cross; and having spoiled principalities and powers, he made a show of them openly, triumphing over them in it* (Colossians 2:13-15).

The LORD says to my Lord: 'Sit at My right hand until I make Your enemies a footstool for Your feet (Psalm 110:1 NASB). "He (Jesus) is now only waiting until **his enemies be made a footstool,** that is, until they acknowledge his lordship by bowing at his feet" (Phil. 2:10) (MacArthur, p. 255).

"...everything Christ died to accomplish will be accomplished. No enemy can hinder his work in the end. The atonement was utterly complete; the father was utterly satisfied; and all the enemies will fall utterly before the reigning Christ in heaven" (Piper, p. 3).

(v14) For by one offering he hath perfected forever them that are sanctified. The **one offering** refers to the once for all sacrifice of Christ on the cross. His offering gave believers sanctified lives **forever**. God has set them apart **forever** on account of Jesus Christ's death. He has given them a perfect standing before God the Father. The believer's salvation is **forever** secure based upon the salvation that God has provided: *There is therefore now no condemnation to them which are in Christ Jesus* (Romans 8:1).

"The death of Jesus Christ removed sin forever for those who belong to him. We are totally secure in our Savior. We need cleansing when we fall into sin, but we need never fear God's judgment on us because of our sin" (MacArthur, p. 256).

(v15-17) Whereof the Holy Ghost also is a witness to us: for after that he had said before. This is the covenant that I will make with them after those days, saith the Lord, I will put my laws into their hearts, and in their minds will I write them; and their sins and iniquities will I remember no more. The promise of the New Covenant is fulfilled. The reference of the Holy Spirit communicating truth is found in Jeremiah: *But this shall be the covenant that I will make with the house of Israel; After those day, saith the Lord, I will put my law in their inward parts, and write it in their hearts; and will be their God, and they shall be my people. And they shall teach no more every man his neighbor, and every man his brother, saying, Know the Lord: for they shall all know me, from the least of them unto the greatest of them, saith the Lord: for I will forgive their iniquity, and I will remember their sin no more* (Jeremiah 31:33, 34) relating back to Hebrews 8:7-13.

"Finally, the new sacrifice of Christ is effective because it fulfills the promise of a New Covenant. In other words, the new sacrifice had to be made and had to be effective because God promised that it would be. The new sacrifice was central to the new covenant, which God said would **put his laws upon their heart, and upon their mind,** and which would cause him to forget **their sins and their lawless deeds.** The new sacrifice was effective, therefore, because it had to accomplish these things (prophesied in Jeremiah 31:33-34) in order for God to fulfill his promises, which cannot be broken... The promise was not Jeremiah's, but was God's—the very witness of the

Holy Spirit" (MacArthur, p. 256-257).

(v18) Now where remission of these is, there is no more offering of sin. Remission—there is complete forgiveness. Forgiveness is provided and the sacrifice is complete through Jesus Christ. The believer's sin has been totally cared for. The believer has been provided complete forgiveness and his sin will never be mentioned against him again: *As far as the east is from the west, so far hath he removed our transgressions from us* (Psalm 103:12).

"The forgiveness is permanent because the sacrifice is permanent... the work of sacrifice is done. There will be no more. Forgiveness is already provided for those who trust in this one perfect sacrifice" (MacArthur, p. 256-257).

Praise the Lord for his forgiveness, goodness, and grace to us!

How Does Hebrews 10:1-18 Impact Our Lives?

1) We are saved: A salvation that is complete and personal based upon faith in the finished work of Christ, *once for all*.

2) We are sanctified: He has sanctified us through the finished work upon the cross, *once for all*. He has set us apart from sin, self, the system of the world and Satan, and set us apart to God for his purposes.

3) We are secure: Our salvation is forever because of the *once for all* sacrifice of Jesus Christ.

"The cross was not an accident or an unforeseen tragedy that took Jesus by surprise. It was not a temporary setback that God figured out how to turn for good. Rather, the cross was God's predetermined plan, before the beginning of time, to deal with our sin. The Son of God would come into this world, as a man, would fulfill through his obedience the complete Law of God, and then would die as the sacrifice that the justice of God demands as the payment for sin" (Cole, p. 4). ***Once for all!***

ADDITIONAL COMMENTS

Hebrews 10:1-14
  I. **The Prelude Shadow (v1-8) – animal sacrifices**
   A. Unreal (v1)
   B. Unsatisfactory (v1-4)
   C. Unacceptable (v5-8)
  II. **The Perfect Sacrifice (v9-14) – Jesus Christ**
   A. Satisfies Prophecy (v9)
   B. Substitutes the Previous (v9)
   C. Sanctifies Perfectly (v10-14) (Spink)

Hebrews 10:10-14

SIGNIFICANT CONTRASTS

OLD TESTAMENT LAW	CHRIST
Number of priests: Many priests	One priest: Christ "but this man"
Posture: standing	Posture: "sat down"
Number: many sacrificies	Number: "one sacrifice"
Frequency: "daily"	Frequency: "once for all"
Continuous: "the same sacrifices"	Complete: "forever"
Effectiveness: "can never take away sins"	Efficacious: "hath perfected forever"

(Spink)

STUDY GUIDE QUESTIONS

In verses 5-7, the author references Ps. 40:6-8. How does David describe God's perspective of the sacrificial system?

In verses 16-17, the author makes a reference to Jeremiah 31:33-34. While Jeremiah's perspective appears forward-looking, how does the book of Hebrews seem to reflect on the past? Moreover, how does Christ act as the focal point that intersects these two perspectives?

What *better than* comparisons can be seen in this chapter?

What were the drawbacks of the Old Testament system? If sacrifices and offerings did not fully satisfy God, what could have been the rationale behind establishing this system?

How does having an innate moral compass granted by the Spirit exceed dependence on an external one?

What empty rituals and practices (sacrifices and offerings) do you tend to think will be pleasing to God?

13

FAITHFUL LIVING

Hebrews 10:19-39

Tom Alexander

Introduction

Hebrews 10:19 is a key transitional verse, marking a major break in the flow of the book. This letter was written to encourage Jewish believers to go on to maturity, rather than turn back to Judaism in order to escape the persecution they were facing. The author does that by demonstrating that Christ is superior in every way to the Old Testament faith in the Mosaic Law. Christ, in his person, is superior to the prophets, to angels, and to Moses. And his priesthood is superior to that of Aaron. He ministers according to a superior covenant in a superior sanctuary in heaven. The emphasis in the first half of Chapter Ten is that Jesus Christ made a superior sacrifice—the sacrifice of himself.

So now, after proving in so many ways that Christ is superior, the author transitions to practical exhortations. Knowing that Christ is superior in every way should lead the believer to the superior life in Christ, which is the life of faith. He says, "Don't go back to the old ways of Judaism. Christ is superior in every way you can imagine. Don't turn back. Stay with Christ and go on by faith to maturity in him." This practical section begins with two provisions for our superior life in Christ.

THE PROVISIONS FOR OUR SUPERIOR LIFE (v19-21)

Access to God (v19-20)

The Persons with Access to God
The author starts by defining the persons with access, whom he calls **brethren**. He is writing to believers, and he is referring to all believers, not just pastors, missionaries, and *super-spiritual saints*. There are good Bible scholars who see this word simply as a reference to Jewish brethren, who may or may not be truly saved. However, only true believers have **boldness to enter into the holiest by the blood of Jesus**.

As the author speaks to believers, he also portrays them as priests. In Christ, and under the New Covenant, all believers are priests, a fact that is clearly taught in 1 Peter 2:5 & 9, and in Revelation 1:5-6. That means that every believer is invited to enter God's very presence in the **holiest**, the Holy of Holies.

The Privilege of Our Access to God
Under the Old Covenant, only the High Priest was allowed to enter the Holy of Holies once a year on the Day of Atonement. When he entered, he was required to enter with sacrifices for himself, and then for the people. The author reminds us of these Old Testament restrictions in Hebrews 9:6-7.

But every New Testament believer has **boldness**, a word that speaks of confidence and assurance. It refers to freedom in speaking—the ability to speak frankly and openly. The author is saying that we have the privilege to enter into the presence of God, and then we can actually speak with him. Unlike the Old Testament priests, who were forbidden to enter the Holy of Holies, we have confidence and **boldness** to come right into God's presence on a regular basis. In fact, we are encouraged to live daily in the presence of God.

So what changed? What gives us this boldness that even the high priest in the Old Testament did not enjoy? What is the path of access to God?

The Path of Access to God
In verse 19, we find that we have **boldness** to enter God's presence through **the blood of Jesus**. The death of Jesus on the cross opened the way for us. This death involved the shedding of Christ's

precious blood (1 Peter 1:19). The author emphasizes in 9:12-14 that our salvation was not purchased with *the blood of goats and calves*, but with Christ's *own blood*.

In verse 20, we find that the path of access is also through the body of Jesus, **his flesh**. Christ has instituted a **new... way**. This is the only time this particular word **new** is found in the New Testament, and it has the idea of "recent" in this context. This way to God was different from that of the Old Covenant. Jesus has also instituted a **living way**, not based on a dead animal sacrifice, but on the crucified and now resurrected and living Son of God. Jesus himself is our access to God.

Through the veil refers to the curtain that separated the Holy Place from the Holy of Holies in the Temple. We find in Matthew 27 that this veil was torn when Christ died—when **the veil** of his **flesh** was pierced and torn for us. The offering of Christ's body opened **the veil**, allowing us access into God's presence.

We have a superior life in Christ, the life of faith. The author is cautioning his readers, "Don't even consider going back to any former way of life that you may have practiced. What you have in Jesus is far superior." The provisions for this superior life include full access to God, something unheard of under the Old Covenant, as well as acceptance by God.

Acceptance by God (v21)

We are accepted by God as priests because Jesus himself is our **high priest**. God accepts us because of his Son. This truth is proclaimed clearly in Ephesians 1:6, which states that he has *made us accepted in the beloved*. In Christ, we are accepted by God as priests, ministering in his very presence. We also have access to his very throne, because Jesus is our **high priest**, welcoming us into God's presence at any time.

> **We have access to the throne of God because Jesus is our high priest, welcoming us into God's presence at any time.**

The author of the book of Hebrews shares these two provisions for our superior life in Christ. We have access to God, and we are accepted by God because of Jesus. Next, the author turns to the practice of our superior life. He encourages us to do three specific things to put our position into practice. Three times he says **let us**, and all three are in the present tense, meaning that these are things that we should continuously be doing. The first of these exhortations is to **draw near** to God.

THE PRACTICE OF OUR SUPERIOR LIFE (v22-25)

Draw Near to God (v22)

Robert W. Ross wrote in *The Wycliffe Bible Commentary*, "**Draw near**, bears the idea of coming to God frequently, openly, intimately, and unhesitatingly, but always with a cleansed heart…" (p. 1420). The author is encouraging us to consciously and continually dwell in the presence of God. We are able to enjoy our Father. We are able to approach him and be close to him. We are to live our lives in constant awareness of his presence in a continual spirit of communion and prayer with the Father.

We can come to God with a **true** (sincere) **heart**, and **in full assurance of faith**, because Jesus has paid our sin debt. Our sins have been forgiven. God will no longer hold them against us. We do not have to fear. We can come boldly into his presence because of the blood of Christ. Unlike the Old Testament believer, who could not even enter the Holy Place, let alone the presence of God in the Holy of Holies, we have the privilege of coming into God's presence and drawing near to him.

The author goes on to explain two reasons that we are encouraged to **draw near**. In stating each of these reasons, the author uses the Greek perfect tense, indicating that these two cleansings happened when we trusted Christ, and they continue to be true. They allow us to draw near to God. First, we have a cleansed conscience: **having our hearts sprinkled from an evil conscience**.

The Old Testament priest was ceremonially cleansed by the sprinkling of the blood of the sacrifice. Our hearts are cleansed, meaning that our <u>inward</u> guilt is gone, and our fellowship is restored, because of the blood of Christ. There is no guilt when the blood of Christ cleanses us. We are able to draw near to God in fellowship.

We practice the superior life by drawing near to God. We are able to approach him because we have a cleansed conscience, but we are also able to draw near because we have a cleansed life: **having… our bodies washed with pure water**.

In the Old Testament, the priest was cleansed at the laver. There were various washings to deal with daily defilement. This verse informs us today that our **bodies** are **washed**, dealing with <u>outward</u> impurities.

We need to draw near to God, but we must draw near with a pure, clean life. Christians are not perfect—just forgiven. We must never take sin lightly. It is extremely serious in God's eyes; it cost him his son. But our sins can be forgiven. We can approach God with a clean life. When we fail, our sins can be forgiven. Daily defilement can be dealt with when we confess those sins.

Ephesians 5:25-27 proclaims that Christ gave himself for us to cleanse us, purify us, and wash us. He does that daily cleansing through his Word, and through the ministry of his Holy Spirit. When we read and obey the Word of God and submit to the control of the Holy Spirit, we will be in a place where we can draw near to God.

We have a superior life in Christ. How do we put that life into practice? We must draw near to God, and we must also defeat doubt. In verse 23, we find two ways to defeat doubt.

Defeat Doubt (v23)

First, we must **hold fast** to our hope. The word **profession** refers to the public acknowledgment of our **faith**, or hope. **Faith** translates the Greek word _elpis_, normally translated "hope." This noun is found 54 times in the New Testament, with this being the only place where it is translated **faith** in the KJV. We must hold unwaveringly to our hope of salvation and eternal life in heaven.

The author is encouraging these suffering believers, "Don't waver in your hope. Your faith is real. Jesus is coming. Rewards are waiting. Hold unswervingly to your confession of Christ. Don't doubt and go back to the old ways."

We are able to **hold fast** as we rely on God's faithfulness. The word **for** introduces the reason that we are able to hold fast to our hope: we are relying on the fact that God is **faithful**. God always fulfills what He has **promised**: _Faithful is he that calleth you, who also will do it_ (1 Thess 5:24).

The author gives us one more key truth as we think about practicing our superior life in Christ. We must draw near to God. We must defeat doubt. But we must also disciple one another. Verse 24 informs us we must disciple one another personally.

Disciple One Another (v24-25)

We need to **consider one another**, or think about each other, and find ways to **provoke** one another to obedience. The word **provoke** is a strong word. The Greek term is the basis for the English word "paroxysm." It means, "to stir up; to incite; to stimulate; to irritate." But in this context, it is used in a positive sense.

So, in answer to Cain, "Yes, I <u>am</u> my brother's keeper." And he is my keeper. This is a mutual command. We are to be ministering to each other—and we should be willing to accept the ministry of others in our lives.

There are two specific goals in our personal provocation. First, we must **provoke**, or stir up, one another **unto love**. This deals with an inward heart attitude. We must stir up one another in the body of Christ to love God and to love fellow believers in an even greater way. That is one of the purposes of church gatherings.

> **We must provoke, stir up, incite, and stimulate one another to obedience, love, and good works.**

Love for others is commanded in 1 John 4:7, and the fact that God commands it is proof that we can do it. Love is not primarily a feeling—it is a decision to act in the best interests of others. Love for God involves obedience to his commandments (1 Jn 5:2-3). Love for others is practical and active, focused on doing good (1 Jn 3:18).

We are also **to provoke** one another **to good works**. Our good works are an outward demonstration of our love. As believers, we are responsible to, and for, one another. We must minister to one another. Our goal, whenever we are together with another Christian, should be to encourage and challenge that person in such a way that he increases in his love and good works to the glory of God.

We must disciple one another personally, but also corporately. In verse 25, the author shares three truths about our church attendance. The first is that we must attend faithfully. Verse 25 begins with the words, **Not forsaking the assembling of ourselves together**. Apparently, some people had already stopped attending church. They were facing persecution, and they had decided to avoid that persecution by staying away from church. Perhaps they had even gone back to the practices of Judaism. There is also the possibility that they felt Christ was coming back soon, so they did not need church. Whatever the reason, they were wrong.

Unfortunately, we see the same problem among professing Christians today. Some decide that the church is not relevant. Others may have had their feelings hurt by someone in the church. Still others have concluded that they can worship God on their own. Perhaps work, or family priorities, or the busyness of life keeps some away. But once again, whatever the reason, they are wrong. Avoiding church as a pattern of life is one indication of a spiritual heart problem. There must be a regular pattern of church attendance in our lives as Christians. Unfortunately, that element is all too often lacking today.

We must attend faithfully, but we must also attend purposefully. What are we supposed to do when we get to church? The author tells us that we are to be **exhorting one another**. The Greek word used here is a very broad word. It can mean to exhort, to comfort, to beseech, to encourage, to admonish, to instruct, to console, or to strengthen. When we come to church, our attitude should not be, "What can I get out of it?" but "What can I contribute to it? How can I help someone else?" When we go to church, we are there to minister to one another.

We must attend church faithfully and purposefully, but we must also attend expectantly. The author says that we need to assemble **so much the more, as ye see the day approaching**. What day is the author referring to? Some see **the day** as referring to the judgment that would come upon Jerusalem in 70AD when it fell to the Romans. That may have been involved, but the meaning goes much further. The ultimate reference is to the Second Coming of Christ. It is the day of Christ's return, the day of judgment when we will meet our Savior and receive our rewards. And verse 37 supports the view that **the day** speaks of Christ coming and not tarrying.

The day is approaching. What are we doing about it? The author says that we should do **so much the more**. So much the more drawing near to God; so much the more defeating doubt; so much the more discipling one another; so much the more assembling together; so much the more being involved in stirring one another to love and good works and encouraging one another.

Jesus Christ is superior! So, the author encourages his readers to live the superior life of faith and not return to the old patterns of life which are useless. Beginning in verse 26, he abruptly begins to warn his readers of the pitfalls hindering that superior life. These verses constitute the fourth warning section in the book of Hebrews.

John MacArthur explains, "This warning against apostasy is one of the most serious warnings in all of Scripture" (p. 1914). William MacDonald adds an observation, "As has been indicated, there is considerable disagreement among Christians as to the real nature of this sin... No matter which view we hold, there are admitted difficulties" (p. 2192). There are three major views concerning this warning.

THREE VIEWS CONCERNING THE FOURTH WARNING SECTION

The Warning is to True Christians, Warning That They Might Lose Their Salvation

This view obviously goes contrary to the clear teaching of Scripture concerning eternal security. We are *kept by the power of God* (1 Pet 1:5). God, who began *a good work in you will perform it until the day of Christ* (Php 1:6). Jesus promised that he would *never leave thee nor forsake thee* (Heb 13:5). Jesus declared that no one can pluck his sheep out of his hand, or out of the Father's hand (Jn 10:27-30). Jesus clearly stated that our salvation is eternal in John 5:24: *Verily, verily, I say unto you, He that heareth my word, and believeth on him that sent me, hath everlasting life, and shall not come into condemnation; but is passed from death unto life.*

There are many abundantly clear New Testament Scriptures declaring that a true believer can never lose his salvation, so this view must be rejected as false. Two other views have been proposed by good Bible scholars, and either one is possible.

The Warning is to Professing Christians Who are Not Truly Saved

Within the congregation of Jewish believers that received this letter were many true believers. But most churches also have some people who have not yet truly come to faith in Christ. This warning is to those who may be professing Christ, but do not yet possess Christ. They may lose their opportunity to get saved. Some would even say that, once they turned away and apostatized, they would have no opportunity to ever get saved.

This is the most popular view of this passage, but it does have some problems. In verse 19, the author identifies his readers as **brethren** who are able **to enter into the holiest by the blood of Jesus**. That statement can only be true of real believers. He also identifies his readers as priests in verses 19-21. In verses 32-34 he reminds his readers of some of the evidence of their salvation. And in verse 39, he clearly states, **But we are not of them who draw back unto perdition; but of them that believe to the saving of the soul**. The context surrounding the warning strongly indicates that the readers of this letter were truly saved. That brings us to the third possibility.

The Warning is to True Christians Who are Tempted to Turn Back to Judaism

The recipients of this letter were Jewish believers who were suffering from persecution and were considering returning to the safe and familiar faith of Judaism. The author has written to convince them of the superiority of Christ and of Christianity. He wants them to go on to maturity (6:1), rather than turning their backs on Christ. He warns them that, if they did, they would face God's serious discipline, possibly including the loss of their physical lives, but not of their salvation.

Some even see this as a hypothetical warning, designed to help convince true believers that they should not return to Judaism, but instead draw near to Christ, persevere, and go on to maturity. If they turned their backs on Christ, there would be no other hope of salvation. The author is convinced that they are saved, but he uses strong language to show them what would be the result if they did apostatize. Homer A. Kent, former President of Grace Theological Seminary, wrote, "Hence it is proper to see in warnings such as this one in Hebrews the means whereby God achieves the goal of keeping true believers faithful to the end (3:14)" (p. 207).

This third view is the view that will be followed in the remainder of this section. The author has discussed the provisions and practice of the superior life of faith. Next, he turns to the pitfalls hindering the superior life. The message in this section is a warning to believers against choosing the path of sin and unbelief.

THE PITFALLS HINDERING THE SUPERIOR LIFE (v26-31)

Willful Rebellion Brings Judgment (v26-27)

The author warns his readers not to sin willfully. The context of the chapter before and after verses 26-31, along with the fact that the readers **have received the knowledge of the truth**, which is a strong statement, indicates that the author is speaking to true believers. The fact that the author includes himself in the word **we**, along with his closing statement of assurance in verse 39, would also seem to argue that he is speaking to true believers. On the other hand, the warning is very strong. Those who sin willfully will face judgment with no available sacrifice, and that judgment is described as **fiery indignation, which shall devour the adversaries**.

The author is speaking of apostatizing or turning back from Christ. This would be a deliberate, willful choice that the readers could make in order to avoid the persecution they were facing. These true believers were facing severe persecution, and they were beginning to doubt whether they had made the right choice in trusting Christ. They were considering returning to the safety of Judaism. But if they did that, they would be turning their back on the only sacrifice that would save them—the sacrifice of Jesus Christ. There is no other **sacrifice for sin**. The author is warning them that, if they did choose to abandon Christ, they would also be abandoning the true hope of salvation. Scholars on both sides of this discussion agree that the willful sin in verse 26 is apostasy, renouncing their faith in Christ.

Rejecting Christ Brings Judgment (v28-29)

Rejecting Moses' law brought the death penalty (v28). That penalty is found in Deuteronomy 17:2-7. Based on that Old Testament penalty, the author informs his readers that rejecting Christ will bring a worse **punishment** (v29).

The wickedness of turning back from Christ is painted in graphic detail in verse 29. The person guilty of this sin would be trampling **under foot the Son of God**, considering his blood sacrifice to be **an unholy thing**, or worthless. He would be insulting the Holy **Spirit** Who has done the work of applying Christ's payment to the believer. We should note that the word **sanctified** in verse 29 is another indication that the author is speaking to true believers.

The exact punishment for apostatizing is not specified in this verse. Besides the loss of rewards at the Judgment Seat, it could involve various forms of chastening (Heb 12:5-11), including sickness and even death (1 Cor 11:27-32; 1 Jn 5:16). J. Dwight Pentecost explains, "The apostle certainly is not threatening them with loss of salvation, but rather warning them that the physical, temporal judgment that was to come on those who were the adversaries of Christ and his followers would fall upon them as well" (p. 176).

The author goes on to declare that God's judgment is sure in verses 30 and 31. In these verses, the author quotes from two Old Testament passages to remind us of the holy character of God, and the fact that he must judge sin (Dt 32:35-36; Ps 135:14). The word **vengeance** as it applies to God is not to be seen as a personal, vengeful spirit, but instead as meeting out the justice that is deserved. Verse 31 is clear: **It is a fearful thing to fall into the hands of the living God**. William MacDonald comments, "This passage was purposely written in its sharp, searching, challenging style so that all who profess the name of Christ might be warned about the terrible consequences of turning away from Him" (p. 2193).

The author is speaking to true believers who are considering turning their backs on Christ and returning to Judaism due to the persecution they were facing. In this strong warning section, he warns them of severe consequences, including the potential of losing their physical lives and losing rewards in heaven. He may also be stating the hypothetical results of what would happen if they abandoned Christ. He is telling them, as he has throughout this book, that if they turned back from Christ they would be losing any chance of salvation. Strong language is used to convince them to stay with Christ, who is the only hope. The doctrine of eternal security convinces us that a true believer will never apostatize, and verse 39 assures us that these Jewish Christians will not, either.

In the final section of this chapter, the author returns to a positive note. In verses 32-39, he speaks of the perseverance of the superior life. What do we need to do so we can persevere in times of serious trials? The key message is that we need to endure trials with boldness.

THE PERSEVERANCE OF THE SUPERIOR LIFE (v32-39)

Remember Previous Victories (v32-34a)

The word translated **call to remembrance** in verse 32 means to not only remember, but to consider and weigh well what you have remembered. Remembering and learning from how God has dealt with us in the past is a key to facing present and future trials.

> **Consider and weigh well what you have remembered.**

The author challenges them to remember the **former** or earlier days after they had been **illuminated**, or enlightened. He is speaking of a time after their salvation, probably shortly after they trusted Christ. During that previous time, they had **endured a great fight of afflictions**. The noun translated **fight** is only used here in the New Testament. Its verb form is used twice in 2 Tim 2:5, where it is translated *strive*. It is the Greek word from which our English word "athlete" comes. It refers to a difficult struggle. The word **afflictions** refers to suffering. In the past, shortly after their salvation, they had faced a difficult struggle that involved suffering.

In verse 33, the author gets more specific concerning this suffering. Through their personal **reproaches and afflictions**, they had been made a **gazingstock**, or a spectacle. This translates a Greek word from which we get the English word "theater." They were publicly exposed to contempt and were made a spectacle because of their faith.

Others who were not subject to that severe persecution stood with them, and willingly shared in their sufferings. The Greek word translated **became companions** is the word that is typically translated "fellowship." While some suffered, others stood with them in the fellowship of the gospel. Even though it might have caused these believers to face persecution themselves, they supported their suffering brethren.

The persecution was severe enough that it had led to the imprisonment of believers. They also **took joyfully the spoiling of your goods**. They had faced serious trials, including the loss of property, and they had survived these trials victoriously. They needed to remember these previous victories. They should also focus on eternal rewards.

Focus On Eternal Rewards (v34b-36)

The author assures them that losses here on earth will be more than recompensed **in heaven**. In verse 35, the author encourages them, **cast not away your confidence**. They must not throw away their **confidence** as if it had no value. The grammatical form of the verb indicates that they were not doing that. He is warning them to not even consider doing it.

Instead, they must have **patience** and do **the will of God**, because the **reward** is coming. The author is encouraging his readers to stay with Christ and endure the sufferings, because eternal rewards are waiting. Verse 36 leads naturally into verse 37, where the author reminds them to look for Christ's return.

Look For Christ's Return (v37) cf. Isa 26:20-21; Hab 2:3

In this verse, the author loosely quotes from the Old Testament prophets Isaiah and Habakkuk as he encourages his readers with the coming of Christ. Jesus is coming back, and when he does, He **will not tarry**.

These are very loose quotations. Why can he treat the Old Testament as loosely as he does? The answer lies in the fact of the inspiration of Scripture. The Holy Spirit inspired the Old Testament, and he inspired the New Testament, including the book of Hebrews. He has the right to use, explain, or interpret his Word as he chooses. But that does not give us the right to treat Scripture similarly.

The final word of exhortation forms a bridge to Chapter Eleven, as the author challenges these Christians to live by faith.

Live By Faith (v38-39) cf. Hab 2:4

Verse 38 is one of three times, along with Romans 1:17 and Galatians 3:11, that Habakkuk 2:4 is quoted in the New Testament. Each time this Old Testament verse is quoted in the New Testament, it has a slightly different emphasis. In Hebrews Ten, the emphasis is on living **by faith. The just** may experience trials and persecution in this life, but those difficulties must be faced with faith in God's good plan for believers. That principle of living **by faith** has been the emphasis in this passage, which transitions into Chapter Eleven.

In the second half of verse 38, the author expresses his complete displeasure with anyone who might **draw back**. But then in verse 39 he expresses his confidence that the believers receiving this letter would not **draw back**. They are **of them that believe to the saving of the soul**. They will endure their persecution and will one day enjoy their rewards in Heaven.

The life of faith in Christ is superior in every way. Whatever we may be facing, we need to trust in God's faithfulness, refuse to turn back, and live by faith.

ADDITIONAL COMMENTS

Hebrews 10:19-25
Why Go to Church?
  I. To Seek The Lord (v19-22)
 II. To Strengthen Your Faith (v23)
III. To Stimulate the Faith of Others (v24, 25) (Spink)

Hebrews 10:26-31
The Warning:
  I. Is to Saints (v26, 30)
      A. Believers –
          1. The context indicates believers (v19-25)
          2. The author includes himself – "we"
          3. He is identified as "sanctified"
          4. "the Lord shall judge his people" (v30) = the saved
      B. Sinning Believers – "for if we sin"
      C. Deliberately Sinning Believers – "sin willfully"
      D. Habitual Deliberately Sinning Believers – Present tense participle indicates constant or continuous action
  II. Is Serious (v29) – despising Christ and the Holy Spirit
  III. Is Scary (v27-31) – Divine Capital punishment (Spink)

STUDY GUIDE QUESTIONS

The word "Therefore" in verse 19 connects previously discussed principles to the current subject. How does this link between theology and the practical aspects of living as a believer become evident?

Which of the "let us" statements in verses 22-25 do you find easiest to understand and follow? Conversely, which one presents the greatest challenge for you, and what factors contribute to that difficulty?

In modern society, numerous individuals embrace the belief that spiritual advancement can occur independently, without engaging with the church. How do verses 23-25 mirror the author's stance on the importance of the church? Why might this theme be woven into this particular chapter?

How does the text portray individuals who deliberately partake in sin? Which aspects of this depiction resonate with your own experiences?

Witnessing the chaos in the world may result in a loss of faith in God's plan. What actions should we pursue when we sense a decline in our hope?

Verse 32 encourages us to ponder the past. How does reflecting on past experiences help guide our thoughts towards the future? Reflecting on the past week, what are some actions you might have approached differently if given the opportunity to redo them?

14

MARKS OF TRUE FAITH

Hebrews 11:1-40

Larry Nocella

Introduction

Hebrews 11 has been referred to as "The Great Hall of Faith," depicting deeds done over the centuries by the great heroes of the Christian faith. While it does include a list of men and women from the Bible who faithfully served the Lord, it is more about the faithfulness of God than the exploits of man. If that is so, then why does it contain this long list of people along with descriptive phrases attached to each one? The answer to this question is found in what directly precedes and follows Hebrews 11, and it is all about Christ. The second half of Chapter Ten urges the readers not to lose their confidence in Christ resulting in **drawing back** (v39) from him, but rather to **live by faith** (v38) and **believe** (v39) in Christ. Chapter Twelve begins by urging the readers to follow the example of the many who have gone before them and keep their focus on Christ. These saints ran the race of the Christian life with patience, keeping their eyes of faith fixed on Christ the whole way (v1-2). So too, we should have faith in a faithful God who kept his promises to his people by sending his Son who faithfully carried out the will of his Father.

This message of living by faith and remaining faithful to Christ is what the readers of Hebrews needed to hear. They needed to be reminded that theirs was a faith worth holding onto despite persecution or abandonment by others who once professed Christ. They needed faith described and exampled.

Faith Described (v1-3)

Faith Is (v1)

Faith is the substance (assurance) **of things that are hoped for**. The idea is something that has a solidness or a sureness to it. Our faith in Christ is solid enough to take our stand in life and solid enough to hold us up through all eternity. The word **hope** has to do with expectation. The men and women in Hebrews 11 were those who expected the promises God made would come to pass. They believed them and acted on them as though they were real because they were real. **Faith is the evidence** (conviction) **of things not seen**. God the Father, God the Son, and God the Spirit are all unseen, yet believers are convinced they are real. Why? Because there is real evidence that this one God in three persons does exist and is active in our lives.

> **The men and women in Hebrews 11 were those who expected the promises God made would come to pass. They believed them and acted on them as though they were real because they were real.**

Faith Produces (v2)

Faith produces divine approval. Our text reads, **by it** (faith) **the elders obtained a good report**. The many who are cited in this chapter are commended for their faith in God. Hearing "well done, good and faithful servant" from Christ is dependent on the degree to which they follow God's commands, do things his way, and act on his promises (Matthew 25:23).

Faith Gives (v3)

Faith gives understanding about how things came to be. **The world was framed by the Word of God**. Over and over in the first chapter of the Bible we read, "And God said, and it was so" (Genesis 1). We are also reminded that God made all that is out of nothing. This too is what we read in the opening verses of the Bible.

Faith Exampled (v4-40)

The writer of Hebrews takes the time to provide numerous examples from the Biblical record of men and women whose faith rested on the Lord and his promises. The list is not meant to be exhaustive. Prominent men of faith are absent from the list such as Job and various godly kings of Judah. The prophets are simply referenced as a category rather than by name. Notable women of faith are also excluded from the list. Among them are Rebekah, Rachel, Leah, Ruth, Abagail, and Esther. The point is not to provide a catalog of chief servants of the Lord. Rather the writer wants the readers to see a pattern of faith in God from one servant to another throughout history. The faithful servants each take their turn on the stage of history and exercise their faith in him however great or small that faith may be. People come and go but a faithful God remains the constant through it all. Also of note, are the many failings of those who are listed. Whole chapters in the Bible are dedicated to detailing the sinful behavior of most of those who are listed in Hebrews 11. If perfection were the standard, then no one would make the list. Faith is what is required and that is what each of these men and women possessed and put into practice. As a result, the moments of failure of those mentioned are purposely omitted. Just as the list itself is not exhaustive, so too the personal histories of these people are not meant to be exhaustive. The purpose for including them is to remind the readers that God uses the faith of his servants to carry out his will and that the exercise of their faith in him is what pleases him.

> **People come and go but a faithful God remains the constant through it all.**

Pre-Flood Faithfuls (v4-7)

Abel (v4): Abel's faith is commended due to the **more excellent sacrifice** he offered to the Lord. This account is found in Genesis 4 and retells how two brothers, sons of Adam and Eve, came before the Lord to offer sacrifices. Neither the Genesis account nor the Hebrews account specifies why the Lord found Abel's offering acceptable and not Cain's. There are various speculations, including the fact that Abel offered a blood sacrifice while Cain did not. While the Lord accepted non-animal offerings during the Tabernacle and Temple Periods, he also required the blood of animals to atone for one's sins.

It is possible this was why Abel's offering was accepted and Cain's rejected. The main point in this passage, however, is the fact that Abel offered his sacrifice to the Lord in faith while Cain did not. This resulted in **God testifying of his gifts** (Abel's sacrifice), meaning that he accepted them. The writer of Hebrews describes God's assessment of Abel as **righteous,** evidenced by the Lord's acceptance of his sacrifice. The last phrase of the verse tells us that Abel, **being dead, yet speaketh**. The amazing truth is that a man or woman of faith continues to have a voice for the Lord long after his or her life on earth is over. This is possible because they are connected to the one who transcends time and who is not subject to death himself. Cain murdered his brother, yet it is Abel who lives on. The difference is one *lacked faith* in God and the other *lived by faith* in God.

Enoch (vv5-6): Enoch's faith is commended based on the fact **he pleased God**. This is why, according to the writer of Hebrews, God **translated** or took **him** to heaven. Enoch is only one of two people who ever lived that went to heaven without going through the doorway of death. Elijah is the other. It may be that God has some special purpose for them yet in the future (Revelation 11:4-14) or it may be simply that it was his will that they alone should not experience physical death. Either way, the writer of Hebrews takes the opportunity afforded by Enoch's example to explain that faith is absolutely necessary if we wish to please God. Enoch not only **believed that He is** (that he exists) but he also believed that God is **a rewarder of them that diligently seek Him**. The reward for Enoch was a ride to heaven that bypassed the doorway of death. God, the Rewarder, can offer a wide variety of rewards to the faithful and he does so according to his wisdom, but the final destination is the same as Enoch's—the presence of Christ in heaven.

Noah (v7): Noah's faith is commended because he **prepared an ark**. He did so, the text tells us, because he was moved with reverent **fear**. He probably had a healthy fear of the coming worldwide flood. He probably had an appropriate fear for the safety of his family. The fear in this verse, however, is directed toward God. He did what he did (built a massive boat) because he feared the Lord. His faith in God was exercised even though what was coming was **not seen as yet** nor ever had been seen. This is a recurring theme in Hebrews 11—obedience to God despite the lack of empirical evidence that offers *seeing is believing* proof-positive confirmation that what is promised is going to happen. This kind of obedience is called **faith** and it is pleasing to God. Verse 7 tells us that Noah's boat-building project **condemned the world** and at the same time made him an **heir of righteousness**. This is another example of the stark contrast between people who put their faith in God and those who do not. Noah and his family were saved from the flood waters. He was also granted a righteousness that came from outside of himself, much like an inheritance comes to someone from another. The rest of the inhabitants of the world, however, perished in the flood due to their lack of faith. They did not believe that a flood was coming, nor did they believe that the ark was their place of safety. This is all because they did not have faith in God.

> **This is a recurring theme in Hebrews 11— obedience to God despite the lack of empirical evidence that offers *seeing is believing* proof-positive confirmation that what is promised is going to happen.**

Patriarchal Faithfuls (vv5-22)

Abraham & Sarah (v8-19): Abraham's faith is commended as a result of his willingness to **go out** from his home and **sojourn** in a distant land. He is further commended for the faith he exercised when he **offered up Isaac** as a sacrifice. Likewise, Abraham's wife, Sarah, was commended for **judging** the Lord **faithful who had promised** her a son. Verse 8 refers to the command of God recorded in Genesis 12 to Abraham to leave his home and go to a place without knowing where he was actually going. We are told that Abraham **obeyed**. What the text does not include is that he was seventy-five years old and his wife was sixty-five years old at the time. We also are not told the home he is leaving is in Ur of the Chaldees, a settled, civilized area of the ancient world. We are not told any of this, only that he **obeyed**. That is what faith looks like whether you are young or old—obeying God no matter how strange or difficult his command may be. Verse 9 further tells us that he lived in this **land of promise as in a strange country, dwelling in tabernacles** (tents) **with Isaac and Jacob**. Abraham lived like a foreigner and a nomad in the land God had given him as an **inheritance** (v8). He was content to do this because he was looking past even the inheritance God was giving to him and his descendants and toward a city designed and built by God himself (v10). Two thousand years before Revelation 21 was written, Abraham had faith to believe a New Jerusalem was coming where he would live with the God who called him out of idolatry and into a special relationship. Sarah is the focus of verse 11. No mention is made of her initial unbelief when she first heard she would become a mother in her old age (Genesis 18) or the role she had in bringing about the birth of Ishmael through her handmaiden (Genesis 16). Rather, what is mentioned is her faith that God would cause her to **conceive** and her appraisal of God as **faithful** who had **promised** her that this very thing would come about. Verse 12 refocuses on Abraham. At age one hundred Abraham is referred to **as good as dead**. That is not meant to be an insult to his age but is merely a reference to his inability to father a child. The writer is saying as far as his ability to be a father is concerned, he might just as well be dead (Romans 4:19). Yet, Hebrews tells us that this one man, who was barely alive, was given descendants as numerous as **the stars of the sky and sand which is by the sea**. The recipients of these promises, however, did not live to see the multiplication of their descendants as they were promised—they died before the promises became a reality. Yet they saw them through eyes of faith as if from a great distance (**afar off**) and were **persuaded of them and embraced them**. Their faith was such that it was as though the promises were close enough to reach out and touch. This, all the while they admit to being **strangers** (foreigners) and **pilgrims** (exiles) **on the earth** (v13; 1 Peter 2:11). This, of course, is an apt description for all believers. This world is not our home, *our citizenship is in heaven* (Philippians 3:20). The writer of Hebrews goes on to say that people who openly acknowledge their status as strangers and pilgrims are indicating that they are looking for their homeland (v14). Additionally, if the homeland they were thinking of were the country they came from they would be able to return to it (v15). However, the writer concludes, that it is not the country they left behind they are thinking of but rather a **heavenly** one. The text seems to be saying because of this attitude of faith that longs for a heavenly home to be with God, he is not ashamed to be called their God—the God of Abraham, Isaac,

> Their faith was such that it was as though the promises were close enough to reach out and touch.

and Jacob (Exodus 3:6)—and that he has prepared a homeland for them in the form of a **city** (v16). Abraham is further commended for being willing to offer up his son Isaac as the Lord commanded him. Isaac is referred to as **his only begotten son** (v17) even though he had another son named Ishmael. This is not a factual error or an oversight by the writer of Hebrews. It is, in fact, very purposeful. It is the same language used by the Lord in Genesis 22:2 in giving the command to Abraham. Simply put, Isaac is the child of promise, the son of faith, the one born by the will of God instead of the will of man. As far as God was concerned, Isaac was the son through whom God's promises would be fulfilled. In that way, he was Abraham's only son. The text tells us that it was through **Isaac** that Abraham's **seed** would **be called** (v18). In other words, Abraham understood that the promise of God to him was to be fulfilled in Isaac and no one else. The way we say it is that all his eggs were in one basket. But Abraham showed that his hope was not fixed on the son God gave him but on God himself. That is why he was willing to obey the LORD and offer up Isaac as a sacrifice. He believed that God was able to raise Isaac from the dead, even if he were the victim of a burnt offering resulting in nothing of his body being left besides ashes (v19). That is what faith looks like—trusting God with your most valued possession, with the one on whom all your hopes and dreams rest. Abraham did that and was commended for it.

Isaac (v20): Isaac's faith is commended because **he blessed** his sons **Jacob and Esau**. Genesis 27 tells us of the deception Jacob, with the help of his mother, Rebekah, used to get his father, Isaac, to give him the greater blessing. The writer of Hebrews does not reference any of that dysfunctional family behavior in this verse. His purpose is to show that Isaac offered blessings on his sons because of the faith that he, Isaac, had in the promises of God given through his father, Abraham. Isaac believed that God was a promise-keeping God and the blessings he offered his sons, reflected that. As such, he is included as a man of faith who pleased God.

Jacob (v21): Jacob's faith is commended because he **blessed** the two **sons of Joseph**. Jacob, like his father, Isaac, believed that God's promises to Abraham would one day come to pass. As such, he offered blessings to Ephraim and Manasseh that he knew he personally would never see come upon them. Nevertheless, he had the faith to offer them even **when he was dying**. What a man shares when he knows he is dying is usually what is most important to him. Jacob's dying words indicate that what was most important to him was clinging to and expressing the promises of God in faith.

Joseph (v22): Joseph's faith is commended for giving **commandment concerning his bones**. We read in the closing lines of Genesis that Joseph said to his brothers near the time of his death, *God will surely visit you, and bring you out of this land unto the land which He swore to Abraham, to Isaac, and to Jacob. And Joseph took an oath of the children of Israel, saying, God will surely visit you, and you shall carry up my bones from hence* (Genesis 50:24-25). Joseph believed the promise God made to his great-grandfather, Abraham, to give his descendants the land of Canaan. Instead of being permanently entombed in a pyramid or among the great leaders of Egypt, he desired to be laid to rest in the land of promise. This was a statement of faith in God which the writer of Hebrews rightly recognized.

Promised Land Faithfuls (v23-31)

Amram & Jochebed (v23): The faith of Moses' parents is commended because they **hid** (him) **three months** directly after his birth. *They saw that the child was beautiful* (ESV) and **they were not afraid of the king's commandment**. One might conclude that the courage to defy the king came from the natural love and protective instincts of parents who want to do everything they can to keep their children safe. That may have played into the actions of Moses' parents, but the text tells us that their main motivation was faith in God. It is this faith that connected them and their actions to the many others in this chapter who lived long before them or long after them.

Moses (v24-28): Moses' faith was commended because **he refused to be called the son of Pharaoh's daughter**. In addition, he **kept the Passover** just as the Lord commanded. When Moses became an adult, he **refused** to be identified as an Egyptian any longer. More than that he **refused** to be called the adoptive son of Pharaoh's daughter any longer. He chose to **suffer affliction** over enjoying **pleasures** and receiving **reproach** over receiving **treasures**. Many a man throughout history have had to make the same choice. Jesus told of a rich man who made the wrong choice and has been paying for it ever since (Luke 16:19-31). Moses made the right choice and has been benefiting ever since. Bible scholars debate whether or not Moses was right to intervene in the violent struggle that ended in his killing of an Egyptian slave master. Among other things, it showed that he identified more with God's people than with the Egyptians. It was **through faith** that Moses **kept the Passover and the sprinkling of blood** (v.28). There is no logical connection between wiping the blood of a lamb on the doorposts of a house and the protection it will bring to those inside, particularly the first-born males. Yet that is what the Lord commanded of Moses and the Israelites—and that is what they did. Consequently, when the death angel came through the land, the Israelites were spared and the Egyptians were not. The difference was that one group operated in faith while the other did not.

> **He chose to suffer affliction over enjoying pleasures and receiving reproach over receiving treasures.**

Israelites (v29-30): The Israelites' faith is commended because **they passed through the Red Sea** when the Lord divided the waters for them. Forty years later **they compassed about** (marched around) **the walls of Jericho seven days** in obedience to the LORD. The account of the Israelites walking through the midst of the Red Sea in Exodus is rather dramatic, to say the least (Exodus 14). The scene describes a multitude of men, women, and children, plus countless livestock walking between a wall of water on their right and left. This was the same generation of Israelites who were forbidden from entering the promised land a short time later due to their disobedience. Yet, in this instance, they moved forward through a space that would be considered unsafe for humans to go by any sane person. They are commended for their obedience which was motivated by faith. The Egyptians attempted the same thing but were not commended for it as an act of faith. The difference between the two parties was direct disobedience to the Lord exhibited by the Egyptians as they pursued the Israelites to bring them back to Egypt to serve as slaves. They were not in the Red Sea as a result of faith in God but rather because of their rebellion against him. As a result, the Israelites escaped and the Egyptians perished. The next generation of Israelites were given the most unusual instructions by the Lord. They were to march around the city of Jericho once a day for six days and around it seven times on the seventh day. This was quite an unorthodox battle plan and one which required faith to obey. The Israelites obeyed and God gave them a great victory when he rewarded their faith in him by supernaturally causing the **walls of Jericho** to **fall down** (Joshua 6).

Rahab (v31): Rahab's faith is commended because **she received the spies with peace**. Rahab was a Canaanite woman, formerly a pagan idolater and a **harlot** on top of it all. Yet, she is included by name as one of only two women in Hebrews 11. The reason for this is that her actions bore witness to the fact she had become a woman of faith in God despite her lineage. When the spies came to her home, she hid them and helped them on their way, testifying that she believed the Lord had given the land of Canaan to his chosen people, the Israelites (Joshua 2).

Prevailing Faithfuls (v32-35a)

Gideon, Barak, Samson, Jephthah, David, Samuel, prophets: The faith of these servants of the Lord is commended for obeying the Lord in various conflicts and winning great victories as a result. The first listed are from the period of the judges before Israel's monarchy was established. They are not listed in chronological order but rather in order of significance. So too, with David and Samuel. David comes after Samuel in chronology, but he represents the good kings of Judah while Samuel represents the prophets who will come after him. The Lord asked them all to do challenging things and helped them accomplish victories that could not have been accomplished without him. David **subdued kingdoms** and he and some of his line, such as Hezekiah and Josiah, **wrought righteousness**. Daniel **stopped the mouths of lions** (Daniel 6), and his three friends, Shadrach, Meshach, and Abednego **quenched the violence of fire** when they were thrown into Nebuchadnezzar's fiery furnace (Daniel 3). David again **escaped the edge of the sword** on many occasions against both the Philistines and King Saul. **Women who received their dead raised to life again** included the widow of Zarephath (1 Kings 17) and the Shunamite woman (2 Kings 4). There is an old hymn entitled "Faith Is the Victory." In the case of these saints, faith brought victory.

Persecuted Faithfuls (v35b-40)

Unnamed Sufferers: The sufferers' faith is commended for **not accepting deliverance** when given the chance because it would mean turning their back on God. Many commentators ascribe much of these descriptions to the intertestamental period when Israel was under the reign of the Greeks including the wicked Antiochus Epiphanes. There are numerous accounts from the historian Josephus and the apocryphal books of terrible cruelties rendered on those Jews who refused to submit to Greek pagan practices. The point is that these dear saints who suffered so are in the same category as those mentioned earlier who won great victories. The common thread is remaining faithful to a faithful God. The world considered these people **unworthy** to receive mercy and unworthy to live. The writer of Hebrews says it is the world that is **unworthy** of them (v38). They, like so many men and women of faith before them, died before receiving **the promise** (of the Messiah, v39). The reason they are made to wait is due to the addition of the ranks of the faithful. **They without us should not be made perfect** (complete) (v40). The time is growing ever nearer when the total number of those who live by faith will be complete. Until then, let us remain faithful just as those who came before us.

Conclusion

An entire chapter in Hebrews is devoted to telling us what faith is and what it looks like in the life of the believer. For some it will result in tremendous blessings poured out from heaven. For others, it will mean tremendous suffering coming from the world. For all believers, it involves the opportunity to serve and worship the Lord in a way that is unique to life on this earth. When a believer arrives in heaven, his faith becomes sight (2 Cor. 5:7). Faith, as it is exercised in the here and now, will no longer be necessary. It will be similar to suffering for Christ in that way. These experiences are for a limited time only. As such, they will be considered precious, much like things in our world are considered valuable because "they just don't make those anymore." Now is the time to join the list of those who lived by faith, suffered in faith, and died in faith. In heaven, those things will be talked about in the past tense only.

My youngest son suffered a severe injury to his shoulder while playing high school football. Following surgery and a year of physical therapy, he opted to return to the gridiron. His mother and I tried to talk him into switching to another sport, one where there would be less chance of serious injury. Despite our best arguments, we could not change his mind. He explained to us that this was the only window of time he would have the opportunity to play a full-contact sport such as football. One day he would be too old and the opportunity would be gone forever. Serving Christ in this life is infinitely more important than playing a high school sport. It is a special privilege to be able to give glory to Christ by exercising faith in him right now, the only time throughout all eternity in which we can do that. May we take full advantage of the window of time the Lord has given us to live by faith.

ADDITIONAL COMMENTS

Hebrews 11:1-3
Faith:
  I. Is Future-Oriented – "things hoped for"
  II. Has Foresight – "things not seen"
  III. Is Factual – "substance" and "evidence"
  IV. Is Foundational (v2, 3)
(Spink)

Hebrews 11:13-16
God's Hall of Faith - Pilgrims
  I. The Assurance of Faith (v13)
    A. Its Object – "the promises"
    B. Its Focus – "having seen them afar off"
    C. Its Perseverance – "These all died in faith, not having received the promises"
  II. The Application of Faith (v13b)
    A. With the mind – "persuaded"
    B. With the heart – "embraced"
    C. With the Mouth – "confessed"
  III. The Attitude of Faith (v13-16)
    A. Foreign Friends (v13) – "strangers"
    B. Traveling Through (v13) "pilgrims"
    C. Heading Home – "This world is not my home…"

    D. Seeker Sensitive (v14) "they seek a country" (not Canaan but heaven)
    E. Forward Focus (v15) No turning back – "if they had been mindful ..."
    F. Delightful Desire (v16) "but now they desire a better country" – heaven!
IV. **The Advantage of Faith (v16)**
    A. A Permanent Relationship - "God is not ashamed to be called their God"
    B. A Precious Reward – "he hath prepared for them a city"
(Spink)

Hebrews 11:32-40
Triumphant Faith
 I. **The Many Examples Enumerated (v32)**
 II. **The Miraculous Exciting Events (v33-35)**
 III. **The Multiplied Evils Endured (v35b-38)**
 IV. **The Master's Evaluation Expressed (v39-40)**
(Spink)

STUDY GUIDE QUESTIONS

How is faith defined and what role did it play in the lives of Old Testament believers?

Choose one of the individuals emphasized in this chapter for their faithfulness and outline the fears they could have faced. Considering the individual you've selected, what is the suitable relationship between fear and faith?

A prevailing modern belief suggests that God protects people of faith from hardships and grants wealth and prosperity to the devout. How does this chapter challenge the notion that a life of comfort is assured for the faithful?

Can you identify someone from your personal life whom you would describe as faithful and deserving of a characterization like "of whom the world was not worthy"? What qualities led you to perceive them as faithful? Likewise, what characteristics might lead someone to perceive you in a similar light?

How does the faith demonstrated by figures such as Abraham and other saints from the Old Testament, who came before you, provide hope and inspiration as you face challenges in your current circumstances?

15

DISCIPLINED ENDURANCE

Hebrews 12:1-17

Patrick Odle

Introduction

When was the last time you were tempted to quit? You may be able to think of a specific event that led to that temptation. Or you may recall the cumulative weight of multiple trials in your life that brought you to the brink of giving up. Anyone who has ever been part of an athletic competition knows the feeling of wanting to quit. It is no wonder that in the Bible the Christian life is frequently referred to as a race. And it isn't just a sprint, it is an endurance race, perhaps a marathon.

Several years ago, I had the opportunity to watch one of my cousins participate in a race. At the time, Gregory was a semi-professional mountain biker. Specifically, he competed in cross-country mountain biking. Being somewhat ignorant of the sport, I didn't quite know what to expect on race day. I think I expected a cross-country mountain biking event to be the opposite of downhill mountain biking, an event on a fairly flat course. I guess I forgot that it is called mountain biking for a reason. The venue was a ski resort in the middle of the summer, and the course didn't just traverse the base of the mountain. It traversed the entire mountain, up and down and across the rugged terrain. After the pre-race formalities, we were excited to watch Greg race from a venue that allowed us to get good glimpses of him traversing the mountain. The race started with the usual fanfare for the first few minutes, and Greg found himself in the middle of the pack of racers. But then something extraordinary happened. A thunderstorm unleashed a deluge of water on the mountain, turning the course into a nasty mess of mud and water. You can imagine how this changed the race. Bikers who were unable to navigate corners careened off course and into the trees. Others struggled to stop and flew over their handlebars in a mess of both broken bones and bicycle parts. Many riders elected to quit the race rather than risk their health or their expensive bikes. Not Greg! He kept racing. As a matter of fact, as others were walking off the mountain, we watched Greg pick up his bike and put it over his shoulder while crossing the most treacherous parts of the course. Then he would get back on and ride only to dismount a few minutes later to carry his bike again. Employing this unique method of racing, Greg quickly pulled ahead of many other frustrated and forlorn bikers, finishing in third place at this national event. What did Greg do when a deluge of rain threatened to ruin his race? He just kept racing. He refused to quit. That is disciplined endurance. When it rains on your life, you keep racing!

One of the recurring themes of Hebrews is having an enduring faith in a superior Savior (2:1-3; 3:12-13; 6:11-12). The context of Hebrews 11 reminded the author's readers of amazing examples of enduring faith. Even before that, Hebrews 10:36-38 stated that we **have need of endurance.** In light of this recurring emphasis, the writer of Hebrews pivoted by beginning this portion of Scripture with **wherefore.** In light of all that had already been written about faith and endurance, we are told in 12:1 to **run with endurance.** The word for endurance employed here is *hupomone*, which literally means to remain under. A fitting description of the term is to wait patiently and hopefully. Another way to think of this disciplined endurance is the determination to keep going even when you desperately want to stop. It is the kind of endurance that remains faithful in the face of impossible obstacles and intimidating opposition, until reaching life's finish line. The marathon of the Christian life can be agonizing, yet faith energizes us to keep running. Faith is the catalyst for endurance. This passage clearly teaches us that God wants us to run the Christian race with faith-energized and hope-filled endurance. How can we run with that kind of disciplined endurance?

> **The marathon of the Christian life can be agonizing, yet faith energizes us to keep running. Faith is the catalyst for endurance.**

The writer of Hebrews provides us with four essentials that answer that question:

Lay Aside the Encumbrances (v1)

The first essential to running with endurance involves setting aside those things that would slow us in the Christian race. Three ideas are emphasized in these verses:

1) **The testimony of the encouragers (v1a)**

   Hebrews paints a word picture for us by describing believers as being **compassed about with so great a cloud of witnesses.** However, what many may picture is not exactly what the text is teaching. Many read this verse and envision a *Family Circus* cartoon image of angels or deceased grandparents peering down from heavenly clouds or through the portals of heaven like spectators to our Christian lives. That is not what this text is teaching. The word for **witnesses** here is *marturon*. It should be thought of like we would think of someone being a witness to others about what they have experienced. Hebrews is looking back to the previous chapter of witnesses who testify to us about a life of faith and faithfulness. They have faced great adversity and through faith and faithful obedience have been commended by the Lord. The idea that we are surrounded by such a great **cloud of** witnesses is designed to motivate us to trust God and be faithful to Him, no matter what we are facing.

2) **The weights that encumber (v1b)**

   In light of the witnesses, we are told to do two things. First, we are told to **lay aside every weight.** This refers to anything in the Christian life that slows you in running your race. In light of the next phrase in this verse, this is not referring to sinful things. Rather, these are matters that may slow your pace. One writer reflects, "Whatever... impairs the tenderness of your conscience, obscures your sense of God, or

   > "Anything that weighs you down, diverts your attention, saps your energy, or dampens your enthusiasm for the things of God needs to be removed!"

takes off your relish of spiritual things." Another comments, "Anything that weighs you down, diverts your attention, saps your energy, or dampens your enthusiasm for the things of God needs to be removed!" In our spiritual lives this may be a habit, a hobby, what we view or listen to, or even waste inordinate amounts of time doing. If it slows us down, we should get rid of it. The believer who wants to run well must live with the mindset that anything that slows him down in the race of the Christian life must be set aside.

3) **The sin that ensnares (v1c)**
We are also told to **lay aside... the sin which doth so easily beset us.** It is significant that the writer chose to include the definite article, **the.** He is not referring to sin in general. So, what is **the sin**? The context would point to the fact that the writer is emphasizing **the sin** of unbelief. One of the believer's greatest struggles is with unbelief. Disobedience is directly tied to disbelief. Every time we choose to sin, we are choosing to not believe God and his promises. When we choose our own way, we are choosing to not believe that God's way is best. Every act of disobedience is at its core a crisis of unbelief! It is no wonder that this sin is described as one that **besets** us. **Besets** is a word that could be translated *ensnares* or *entangles*. The original word paints a picture of being surrounded by something.

I can't help but think of a personal experience while deer hunting. I was hunting on a beautiful Iowa winter day with a fresh layer of snow covering the ground when I came across a massive set of deer tracks in the snow. Because of the size of the print, I was completely convinced that it had to have been made by a massive, trophy buck. But there was one problem—the track headed right into a small opening into a massive bramble of thorny vines. Struck by buck fever, I headed into the thicket opening with the hope of harvesting my trophy buck. Within a few steps, I quickly realized that the passageway into the bramble was growing narrower and shorter with every step. But I was determined! At first, I only had to bend over a little bit to pursue the track that kept leading me onward. Then I had to bend down. Then I had to walk on my knees. Then I had to crawl. And as I went farther and farther into the thicket, the thorns increasingly began to shred my hunting gear. Finally, I had endured enough and turned around without ever seeing the wily buck. That is exactly what sin does to us when we follow it, in hopes of some kind of pleasure or illicit satisfaction. The sin of unbelief tears us up. That is why we must **lay it aside.** Being mindful of our encouraging witnesses, setting aside slowing habits and getting rid of the entangling sin of unbelief are all vital to running this endurance race of the Christian life.

Look to the Example (v2-3)

The second essential to running with endurance is looking to Christ. Where one looks while racing is so important. The writer of Hebrews emphasizes four concepts.

1) **His person (v2a, 2c)**

We are challenged to be **looking unto Jesus the author and finisher of our faith.** The word **author** here refers to a person who blazes a trail. **Finisher** speaks of someone who has completed the course. Both of these terms continue to use the metaphor of a race. Jesus has blazed the trail and completed his race. He knows the pitfalls and even sympathizes with our struggles. There is no better person to look to or stay focused on than Jesus Christ. So, how does a believer keep their eyes on Jesus? We can certainly do that by regularly reading the Gospels while reflecting on the life of Christ. We should also be cautious not to become too focused on other people who will disappoint us and maybe even hurt us. Christ alone is worthy of unguarded allegiance and undying affection.

2) **His perspective (v2b)**

Part of the reason that we should keep looking to Jesus is because of his perspective while facing the cross. Christ faced the cross with **joy.** There was nothing joyful about the cross. It was what was on the other side of the cross that brought Jesus joy. That joy was rooted in what the cross would accomplish—our eternal salvation. Christ endured the agony of crucifixion and the misery of separation from the Father because it was the only way to pay the price for our sins and provide for our salvation. Jesus was so focused on this outcome that he is described as **despising the shame.**

Crucifixion was a horribly shameful means of execution. Victims were publicly humiliated by being marched through the streets while crowds mocked and jeered. Then they were made a public spectacle by being hung in view of passing spectators who ridiculed them even more over the hours they hung on crosses. Jesus despised **the shame**. The term despising is the Greek word *kataphroneo*, which is a compound word that literally means *to mind against*. It refers to thinking little of someone or something. Jesus despised the shame of crucifixion by refusing to be humiliated by the cross. As the humble and sinless Son of God, Jesus could not be shamed. While the words are similar, humiliation and humility are far different concepts. Only a proud person can be humiliated when they perceive themselves to be treated in a manner that is below or shames them. On the other hand, a truly humble person cannot be humiliated because (without self-will) they accept even injustice as a part of God's plan. Jesus humbly despised the shame of the cross and set a challenging example for each of us to follow.

3) **His pattern (v3a)**

Verse three provides additional insight into the suffering of Jesus. It states that he **endured such contradiction of sinners.** Other versions state that he "endured such hostility from sinners" (NKJV). The word **endured** is that familiar term that describes remaining under. Jesus did not escape the cross even though he possessed the ability to escape. Instead, *when he was reviled, reviled not again; when he suffered, he threatened not; but committed himself to him that judgeth righteously* (1 Peter 2:24). Christ did nothing to retaliate against those who tortured him! Is that how you respond when you are mistreated? Or do you retaliate or respond in kind? Christ's pattern is worthy of emulation.

4) **His plea (v3b)**

The fourth concept for consideration when looking to Jesus presents us with the very practical charge: **lest ye be wearied and faint in your minds.** Failing to focus on Christ will cause us to quit. Sadly, many professing Christians quit before the finish line because they focus on people or circumstances rather than the Lord. Focusing on Christ is essential to not quitting the race. Who or what is your life focused on? Who or what do you default to when you are alone with your thoughts? Keep looking to Jesus!

Learn from the Exhortation (v4-11)
The third essential to running with endurance is found in verse 5 where we are told: **My son, despise thou not the chastening of the Lord.** One of the great puzzles in many believers' minds is the question of why believers have so many struggles, problems, and trials. That was certainly the case for the Hebrews (cf. 10:32-36). Because of their mere affiliation with Christ and subsequent departure from Judaism's traditions, they were ridiculed, mistreated, and alienated by friends and family. That was also at least part of the reason the Hebrews were tempted to turn back to Judaism instead of being steadfast in their commitment to Christ. Amid their suffering, they struggled to see God's purposes for the trials. Our passage emphasizes five things related to the training ground of trials and **the chastening of the Lord.**

1) **A reminder (v4)**
To paraphrase verse 4, none of the readers had yet died for their faith. As a side note, this probably rules out Jerusalem as the home for the recipients of the book because by the time Hebrews was written at least Stephen (Acts 7:60) and James (Acts 12:2) had been martyred. While being told that none of them had been martyred may seem like little consolation, it still served as a good reminder that life is rarely as bad as it could be or maybe even isn't as bad as we think it is. Growing up I had the privilege of being very close to my maternal grandfather. An eternal optimist, one of his favorite and frequently repeated life mottos was, "It could always be worse!" That is certainly true of our lives, too. Maybe you need that reminder today like the Hebrews did.

2) **A reason (v5-6a)**
In the next several verses we are introduced to a crucial concept, **chastening.** Some form of this word is used eight times in our text. Unfortunately, the English word **chastening** fails to communicate the fullness of the meaning of the original. The Greek word *paideia* is employed here. *Paideia* is a term for child training that encompasses all that

parents do "to train, correct, cultivate, and educate children in order to help them develop and mature as they ought" (MacArthur, p. 385). The nature of such child training is <u>both</u> instructive and corrective but not always punitive! Our tendency is to think of **chastening** solely in terms of punishment. So why do we endure trials? To be trained by them! Believers may wonder, "What did I do to deserve this?" when going through a difficult time. The answer may be that you haven't done anything wrong. Or maybe we ponder, "Why am I going through this?" The answer in the passage is because your Father loves you (v6a). While child training can be the result of sin (rebuke—v5b, scourges—v6b), that is not always or exclusively the case. Why does God allow great difficulty in the lives of his children? Because our Father loves us.

3) **A relationship (v5b, 6b-8)**

His love makes even more sense when we ponder our amazing relationship with him. We are his children and his discipline actually proves that relationship. These verses teach that the absence of Fatherly discipline in the life of someone who professes to be a child of God is evidence of their illegitimacy! I can't help but read these verses and think of people I know who

> **We are his children and his discipline actually proves that relationship.**

profess Christ yet have been living for many years and in some cases decades, in a manner that is ungodly and contrary to the clear teaching of Scripture. Yet despite their persistent and unrepentant condition, these individuals claim to be believers. How does that align with these verses? If such professing believers are legitimately born again, the Father will not allow them to persist in unrepentant sin without corrective consequences. If they do not suffer corrective consequences, they have every reason to question the legitimacy of their salvation. To be as bold and blunt as the Bible, they aren't true believers! However, on the positive side, if we experience the corrective and instructive hand of God in our lives to train us to be godly and more mature, we can know that we are God's children and that he is demonstrating his love for us.

4) **A response (v9)**
The fourth important thing to consider is God's desired response from his children when he disciplines them. The two words that summarize that response in verse 9 are **reverence** and **subjection.** These attitudes are the result of being **corrected.** The Greek word for **corrected** is another form of the word **chastening.** A literal rendering of the Greek would read, "fathers as ones who discipline." Training is designed to change children (and us), especially our attitudes. Those attitudes should be **reverence** and **subjection. Reverence,** as it is used here, is not the more common Greek word *phobeo* from which we derive our word *phobia.* Instead, the word is *entrepo,* which means to hold in very high regard, esteem, or respect. Think about your relationship with your dad. My dad didn't become a believer until I was a teen, yet he was a consistent disciplinarian, and I respected him for it. Why? Because even as an unbeliever, my dad wasn't about to let his son become someone who lied, stole, swore, or was lazy or disrespectful. As a result, I respected him. Even as a child, I knew he wanted me to do what was right. Consequently, I submitted to him; I was in **subjection** to him. That must be our response when we are being trained by our Father's divine discipline. Are those your typical attitudes when God is training you through trials? With what attitudes are you more likely to respond when patiently enduring your Father's **chastening**?

5) **A result (v10-11)**
Fifthly, God's design for discipline is a life that is typified by **holiness** and **righteousness.** More precisely, the goal is that we would become **partakers of his holiness,** not a culturally conceived concept of our holiness. Verse 11 describes this in beautiful terms as **the peaceable fruit of righteousness.** However, enduring discipline does not automatically result in such traits in our lives. We must be **exercised thereby**. **Exercised** comes from the Greek word *gumnadzo,* a term that refers to athletic training through strict self-discipline. God's discipline will only train us if we let it change us. Sadly,

many believers refuse to allow God's discipline to have such an effect on them. In high school, I was an offensive left tackle who had the job of protecting the blind side of our right-handed quarterback. I remember well the constant drills and the accompanying yelling from my coach as I was being trained to improve my pass blocking techniques. I might have been tempted to think that the drills were monotonous or pointless or that my coach didn't like me because he was yelling at me and others while engraining the techniques in our brains. But rather than thinking that, I realized that the drills were designed to make me a better football player. I allowed the coach to train me. God's discipline is designed to train us. When we respond with reverence and submission and allow the discipline to change us, we become more like Christ – holy and righteous.

Look Out for Everyone (v12-17)

Finally, it is essential that we look out for the spiritual needs of others, if we are going to finish the race and help others to join us in crossing the finish line. The writer of Hebrews returns to his racing metaphor with three clear instructions.

1) Strengthen the weary (v12-13)

These verses portray a weary runner who is about to collapse from fatigue. His hands hang limply at his sides and his **knees** are **feeble.** He is about to quit the race. Trials have a way of exhausting even the strongest of believers. Who of us has not heard someone else say, "I just don't think I can take any more of this?" They might be facing cancer, a shattered family life or financial disaster and want to just throw in the towel. What is our responsibility to such fellow believers? We are called to do all that we can to point them down the right path (v 13). The term for **paths** that is used here probably refers to a running path or running lane. It reminds us of how Proverbs 3:5-6 is translated in some modern versions. We are challenged to trust the Lord, knowing that he will make our paths straight. He does that when we keep our eyes focused on him (12:2-3). Who is there in your circle of fellowship who is on the verge of quitting spiritually? Who cares for them on a heart level?

Perhaps God wants you to come alongside them to strengthen them and help them keep going.

2) **Seek peace and holiness (v14)**
Verse 14 almost seems out of place unless you understand its meaning in the context. What does following **peace with all men, and holiness** have to do with disciplined endurance in the race of the Christian life? Is this just a random instruction about positional peace and holiness, or is it tied to the idea of helping others finish the race? Scripture demands that we understand this verse in its context. The verse concludes with the key interpretive idea—without peace and holiness **no man shall see the Lord.** Because the context focuses on helping others finish well, this verse refers to relational peace with others and practical holiness that is evident to others. Relational peace and practical holiness are what every believer must pursue in order for others to see God in their lives. Why do so many professing believers quit the faith? Many people stop running because of the hypocrisy they see in the lives of believers. Believers who can't get along with each other, or whose lives are unholy, become stumbling blocks to the weary

> **Believers who can't get along with each other, or whose lives are unholy, become stumbling blocks to the weary person's faith.**

person's faith. This verse is teaching that our concern for relational peace and Christ-like holiness is also a concern for the souls of those who are watching our lives to see the presence of God in them. This fits perfectly with the next verse, where we are told to be **looking diligently lest any man fail.**

3) **Stay alert for unbelief (v15-17)**
The third instruction calls us to be alert for unbelief in our own lives and the lives of others. The concern is that nobody would **fail of the grace of God.** The Bible is not referring to someone "falling from grace," as some would put it. Rather, these verses describe someone who is closely affiliated with Christianity but is not yet converted to Christ. Such people,

because of their closeness to believers, have ample opportunities to observe the hypocritical lives of professing Christians (no relational peace or Biblical holiness), and become embittered by it and turn away from Christ. Their unbelief is nourished by the root of bitterness, caused by the hypocrisy of believers. Such unbelief is illustrated by the life and values of Esau. Esau was so close to salvation as Abraham's grandson and Isaac's son, yet he cared only for the immediate, **(profane)** sensual, and temporal rather than what mattered far more (Genesis 25:29-34). Being the firstborn, he was entitled to a double portion of the inheritance and would have served as the family priest. He gave up his birthright for a bowl of stew and was an example of Old Testament apostasy. John MacArthur appropriately comments that such unbelief "wants God's blessings without wanting God" (MacArthur, p. 408). Esau grieved over his foolish choice; **he sought it with tears.** Even though he regretted his decision greatly and even showed great remorse (v17), he was rejected (by Isaac) and found no place for a change of mind (**repentance**) from Isaac (Gen. 27:34-35). It wasn't that Esau didn't regret his choice. It was that Isaac couldn't change his mind (repent) after already blessing Jacob. These verses serve as a warning to us. Every one of us is capable of abandoning what we believe and teach. This is why we are commanded to look diligently, to watch out for bitterness and unbelief in our hearts and the hearts of others. May we heed this sober warning.

Concluding Thoughts

All of us want to finish strong! We want to run with endurance, leaning into the tape at the finish line of life! But are we going to finish the race by faith? Will we run with disciplined endurance? In order for us to finish well we must lay aside the encumbrances, look to the example, learn from the exhortation, and look out for everyone. What weights or sins do you need to lay aside in order to run well? Are you keeping your eyes on Jesus as you face trials? Are you remembering that trials are God's training tools for the children he loves? What are you doing to model peace and holiness to help strengthen those who are struggling? God wants us to run the Christian race with faith-energized and hope-filled endurance. Run well!

ADDITIONAL COMMENTS

Hebrews 12:5-11
God's Discipline
  I. **The Distinction** ("chastening" vs. judgment)
  II. **The Dangers (v5)**
      A. Carelessness- "ye have forgotten the exhortation"
      B. Confusion – "children, My son" – legitimate children
      C. Complaining – "despise not"
      D. Casualness – "despise" may mean to have little regard for; to regard too lightly
      E. Caving In – "nor faint"
  III. **The Details (v6-11)**
      A. It is Painful (v6, 11) "scourgeth" "grievous"
      B. It is Proof (v7, 8) of sonship
      C. It Has Purpose (v9, 10) Correction, Prevention, Education
      D. It Has Profit (v11)
(Spink)

STUDY GUIDE QUESTIONS

"Therefore" is used to highlight the need to act upon the truths already discussed. Why is it justified for Jesus to be the primary focus of our attention? What types of issues typically draw our focus?"

In what ways does the analogy of a runner in a race serve as a beneficial representation of the Christian journey?

How does discipline relate to the concept of endurance?

The lines referenced in verses 5-6 are taken from Prov. 3:11-12, conveyed from a father's perspective to his son. What motivates a father to discipline? And why does God discipline us?

Verse 16 mentions Esau, who hastily exchanged his inheritance for instant gratification. In what ways do you personally tend to trade eternal matters for temporary satisfaction?

In what ways have you experienced God's corrective guidance in your life? Did this encounter draw you nearer to him or create distance?

16

UNSHAKABLE KINGDOM

Hebrews 12:18-29

Bill Kopas

Introduction

Playing *Follow the Leader* on the playground is a fun game, so long as everyone gets an opportunity to be the leader. To perpetually be the follower is boring, tedious, and inevitably leads to some falling away, especially when there are so many other participation-oriented opportunities available. Jesus spoke plainly regarding what it meant to follow him in Luke 9:23: *If any man will come after me, let him deny himself, and take up his cross daily, and follow me.* The recipients of Hebrews have discovered that to *follow the leader*, Jesus, means perpetual following with no opportunities to lead. In addition, sometimes following Jesus means he leads into difficult places at incredible costs. The writer of Hebrews has been seeking to encourage his readers to not fall away, especially recognizing their temptation to be drawn back to the participation-oriented opportunities afforded under the Old Covenant.

When everything in your life has been turned upside down, and nothing seems to be marked by stability and security, to what or to whom do you turn? For those to whom Hebrews was written, that is the question they are facing. All people tend to return to where they last felt secure—a return to the place, to the people, or to the system that may not have been perfect but is preferable to the discomfort currently being experienced.

The Hebrews tended to return to the imperfect but preferred

system of the Old Covenant of the Law. After the Exodus, the people of Israel faced the unknown and difficult challenges of following the Lord to the Promised Land. They were inclined to return to Egypt. Forgetting the slavery and oppression from which they were freed, they only remembered the security and stability of water, food, and housing. Here, too, the readers of Hebrews are forgetting the slavery and oppression to sin and death from which they had been freed in Christ and were contemplating a return to the former, imperfect system.

In this passage, the writer takes them back to the very time and place that the Old Covenant was ratified under Moses' leadership at Mt. Sinai. He contrasts that historical event with their present reality under the New Covenant in Christ at Mt. Zion. He does so to demonstrate the superiority of what they now have in Christ. As with the rest of the book, this passage demonstrates that Christ is above all.

Considering a Return to the Law

According to Albert Mohler, "This passage is the climactic point the author has been building toward for the last eleven chapters" (p. 207). The introductory word **for** of verse 18 not only ties this passage to the immediate context but the greater context of the book as a whole. Here is provided the rationale behind the encouragement **to lift up the hands which hang down, and the feeble knees; And make straight paths for your feet** (v12-13) and the reason to do so. However, the great question of 2:3 is also in mind here: **How shall we escape, if we neglect so great salvation?** In this passage, the writer of Hebrews contrasts Mt. Sinai with Mt. Zion to remind the readers of what was encountered in both experiences with the intent of both encouraging and warning the readers.

Verse 18 begins by drawing the reader back to the base of Mt. Sinai. While the mount is never explicitly named, it is clear from the context that the writer has the events of Exodus 19-20 in mind. Those chapters coincide with the graphic description provided here of what was encountered by the people of Israel at the base of Mt. Sinai, **the mount that might be touched** (v18). Exodus 19 tells us that the people had spent three days preparing themselves for this event. Three days of consecration included washing their garments and abstaining from sexual relations. They were also commanded to set boundary limits around the mountain to prevent anyone or anything from drawing near. All of this was done in anticipation of

God coming down to meet with them. He did so in **fire** (v18). The pillar that had gone before them, providing light and direction was now settling on the mountain. The same God who had brought the ten plagues upon the Egyptians, who had passed over them on the fateful night before their deliverance, who had parted the Red Sea, was now coming down to meet with them. And as he does so, the experience is truly awful! A mountain **that burned with fire** (v18), yet described as manifesting **blackness, and darkness, and tempest** (v18). This was an event that was overwhelming in every way and shook all in attendance that day.

The Lord was not just coming down to meet with them. He had come to speak to them (Exodus 19:9). The Lord's voice was preceded by **the sound of a trumpet** (v19). Included in God's commands to Moses was the making of two silver trumpets. They were to be used in both calling assembly and in giving directions. Here a heavenly trumpet is calling a great assembly of both the host of Israel as well as the host of heaven. Moses remembers this day in Deuteronomy 33:2 saying,

> *The LORD came from Sinai,*
> *and rose up from Seir unto them;*
> *he shined forth from mount Paran,*
> *and he came with ten thousands of saints:*
> *from his right hand went a fiery law for them.*

They heard **the voice of words** as the Lord spoke the Ten Commandments in their hearing. This is an astonishing thing! Until this point, Moses and Aaron had served as the mouthpiece of God (Exodus 4:15-16). The announcement of each new plague, every promise of protection, and all the words of hope the people had ever heard from the Lord came through the lips of their leaders. But now the people were hearing from the Lord himself. What Moses had experienced at the burning bush was now being experienced by an entire nation—a fire that did not consume, a voice that shook to the core, and a holiness that defied approach. The immediate results of this experience are shared in verse 19, **They that heard entreated that the word should not be spoken to them any more**. Verse 21 even shares **so terrible was the sight, that Moses said, I exceedingly fear and quake.**

Here for the first time, the people of Israel were meeting and hearing the Lord directly without a mediator or a distractor. To this point, they have witnessed the Lord's mighty power at work on their behalf against the Egyptians who experienced the blackness, darkness, and tempest, but now it is they who must encounter the same God in those same elements. The same God who had worked so mightily on their behalf was the God with whom they now must reckon. Far removed from the *comforts* and distractions of Egypt, they now find themselves face to face with the Lord himself as he speaks to them. The people of Israel like the people of Egypt were experiencing the self-revelation of God making clear who he is.

> **Here for the first time, the people of Israel were meeting and hearing the Lord directly without a mediator or a distractor.**

This was a real experience. This was a tangible mountain with real darkness, real smoke, real rumbling, and the very real threat of death pungent in the air. The result was real fear. The people understood they were entering into covenant with a fearful God as he declared, *I am the LORD thy God, which have brought thee out of the land of Egypt, out of the house of bondage. Thou shalt have no other gods before me* (Exodus 20:2-3). The stone tablets were the official terms of the covenant with his people into which God entered. The events at Mt. Sinai were the official ratification of that covenant.

It's important to note here the purpose of the Old Covenant of the Law. Like all of Scripture, it is God's self-revelation to man. The Law was specifically intended to reveal and exalt God's righteousness. In doing so, the Law actively condemned man as it revealed man's unrighteousness. However, through the centuries the Israelites had turned that around. They began to view the Law as having less to do with God's righteousness and more as proof of their own. It is against this self-righteous pride that God sent the prophets again and again. Jesus Himself both identified and condemned this pride so often in his interactions with the religious leaders of his day (Matthew 23:13-33). It is this same spiritual pride that Paul bemoans of his fellow Jews in Romans 7:7-11 as he writes of the condemning effect of the Law.

> *What shall we say then? Is the law sin? God forbid. Nay, I had not known sin, but by the law: for I had not known lust, except the law had said, Thou shalt not covet. But sin, taking occasion by the commandment, wrought in me all manner of*

concupiscence. For without the law sin was dead. For I was alive without the law once: but when the commandment came, sin revived, and I died. And the commandment, which was ordained to life, I found to be unto death. For sin, taking occasion by the commandment, deceived me, and by it slew me.

The very law to which the reader is contemplating a return is the very means of condemnation—condemnation and death that was evident from the very beginning at Mt. Sinai. Everything about the Sinai experience was permeated by fear, trembling, distance, and death. Like the Israelites of the Exodus, the readers of Hebrews were forgetting the weight of slavery they had experienced under the Law, choosing only to remember the comforts of the familiar. To them, familiar slavery was more preferential than formidable salvation.

> To them, familiar slavery was more preferential than formidable salvation.

Reflection

Here we must pause to acknowledge our tendency to do the same. We too are prone to construct our own mini Mt. Sinai's. In an effort to manage our spiritual growth or measure it against others, we create our own list of rules and regulations. In doing so we take the immense and glorious relationship so deeply desired by God and reduce it to a formulaic set of rules with expectations of blessing. For the Hebrews, it was a temptation driven by a desire to escape the difficulties of oppression and persecution. For us, it is a temptation driven by the same self-righteous pride as that of the religious leaders of Jesus' day. Like the original recipients of Hebrews, we too *ought to give the more earnest heed to the things which we have heard, lest at any time we should let them slip* (2:1).

Old Experience to New Reality

In seeking to discourage his readers from returning to the Old Covenant, the writer of Hebrews turns his attention from what had been their experience, to what is now their present reality. He reminds them that they have come to **Mount Zion** (v22). Originally a stronghold of the Jebusite people, King David invaded, conquered, and took occupation. He renamed it *the city of David* (2 Samuel 5:6-9). It was most commonly known as Jerusalem and became the center of David's kingdom. Later as King Solomon both erected and dedicated the Temple, Jerusalem became the center of Israel's spiritual activity becoming synonymous with the dwelling place of God (2 Chronicles 6:2). However, the writer has something more in mind here than the tangible *city of David*. This mount to which we have come contrasts with **the mount that might be touched (v18)**.

In verses 18-19 the writer lists seven elements of the Mt. Sinai experience:

1) **might be touched**

2) **burned with fire**

3) **blackness**

4) **darkness**

5) **tempest**

6) **the sound of a trumpet**

7) **the voice of words**

Now in verses 22-24, he lists seven elements of the Mt. Zion experience to which **ye are come** (v22). Each of these elements builds in demonstrating the contrast and superiority of Christ above all.

1) First, the reader finds that they are coming to **the city of the living God, the heavenly Jerusalem** (v22). Solomon himself acknowledged in his prayer of dedication at the Temple in 1 Kings 8:27, *But will God indeed dwell on the earth? behold, the heaven and heaven of heavens cannot contain thee; how much less this house that I have builded?* Yet here the writer proposes the truth that for those in Christ under the New Covenant, they have come to the heavenly dwelling place of God. Paul emphasizes this truth in his letter to the Ephesians, *And (God) hath raised us up together, and made us sit together in heavenly places in Christ Jesus* (2:6). Further, he writes in Philippians 3:20, *For our conversation (citizenship) is in*

heaven; from whence also we look for the Saviour, the Lord Jesus Christ. The mount to which the Hebrews have come is not a physical mountain in the wilderness, but the heavenly dwelling place of God from which he reigns.

2) Second, the reader is told they have come **to an innumerable company of angels** (v22). Angels have already been discussed in the first chapter of Hebrews as the writer demonstrated the superiority of Jesus, but here the emphasis is contrasting a mount burning with fire to a vast number of God's angels described as *His ministers* (made) *a flame of fire* (1:7). Even the first mention of an angel in Genesis 3:24 demonstrates this truth: *at the east of the garden of Eden he placed the cherubim and a flaming sword that turned every way to guard the way to the tree of life.* The term **innumerable** is evidenced in previous Scripture:

- David writes in Psalm 68:17, *The chariots of God are twice ten thousand, thousands upon thousands.*

- Elisha's young assistant was given a glimpse of this in 2 Kings 6:17 where *the LORD opened the eyes of the young man, and he saw, and behold, the mountain was full of horses and chariots of fire all around Elisha.*

- In Daniel 7:10 a vision of the angelic company is described as *a thousand thousands served him, and ten thousand times ten thousand stood before him.*

3) Third, the reader discovers they have come **to the general assembly and church of the firstborn, which are written in heaven** (23a). The readers of Hebrews are no longer simply identified by their ethnicity, but rather by their salvation. Their connection is not just to a religious system or system of laws, but to Jesus himself identified by Paul as *the firstborn among many brethren* (Rom. 8:29). Paul continues this teaching in Colossians 1:15-18:

> *Who is the image of the invisible God, the firstborn of every creature: For by him were all things created, that*

> *are in heaven, and that are in earth, visible and invisible, whether they be thrones, or dominions, or principalities, or powers: all things were created by him, and for him: And he is before all things, and by him all things consist. And he is the head of the body, the church: who is the beginning, the firstborn from the dead; that in all things he might have the preeminence.*

The weary and worn readers of Hebrews who have been cut off from fellow countrymen and despised by the world are being reminded of their participation and unity with a vast network of brothers and sisters in Christ. No longer simply castaways of a local synagogue, they are members of the global family of the church. A church that Jesus himself had promised to build *and the gates of hell shall not prevail against it* (Mt. 16:18). Not only are the gates of hell powerless against it, but the library of heaven also records it. There is a book in which the name of each and every saint is recorded (Rev. 20:15) having been written *before the foundation of the world* (Eph. 1:4) from which no name can be erased (Jn. 10:28-29). Revelation 21:27 reveals this certainty as it speaks of the church as *they which are written in the Lamb's book of life.*

4) The fourth characteristic of Mt. Zion identified in verse 23 to whom the reader comes is **to God the Judge of all** (23b). The reader of Hebrews has not just come to **the city of the living God** (v22) but to God himself—the very one who called Abram to himself, the very one who commissioned Moses, and the very one who had descended on Mt. Sinai with boundary markers all around. It is to this very one to whom they have now come. The dread of Mt. Sinai was not just in response to the sights and sounds of God's descent upon the mount, but most directly to the presence and voice of God. Here the writer continues the theme of our ability to draw near or come to God because we have received *so great salvation* (2:3).

The Greek word *proserchomai* translated **ye are come unto** (22) is used by the writer of Hebrews to continually describe the relationship now enjoyed with God through Jesus as contrasted with that which was experienced under the Law. This is now the seventh time the writer has used it.

4:16: *Let us therefore <u>come</u> boldly <u>unto</u> the throne of grace, that we may obtain mercy, and find grace to help in time of need.*

7:25: *Wherefore he is able also to save them to the uttermost that <u>come unto</u> God by him, seeing he ever liveth to make intercession for them.*

10:1: *For the law having a shadow of good things to come, and not the very image of the things, can never with those sacrifices which they offered year by year continually make the <u>comers thereunto</u> perfect.*

10:22: *Let us <u>draw near</u> with a true heart in full assurance of faith, having our hearts sprinkled from an evil conscience, and our bodies washed with pure water.*

11:6: *But without faith it is impossible to please him: for he that <u>cometh to</u> God must believe that he is, and that he is a rewarder of them that diligently seek him.*

12:18: *For ye are not <u>come unto</u> the mount that might be touched*

12:22: *But ye are <u>come unto</u> mount Zion*

The use of the title connected to God as **the Judge of all** (v23) is significant here. It's both an encouragement to those feeling abused, oppressed, and awaiting justice, as well as a warning to those contemplating a rejection or abandonment of God's great salvation. Direct and immediate access to God is a cause of great rejoicing and sheer delight, but it is not to be taken casually, since he is **the Judge of all.**

5) Fifth, the reader is reminded they have come **to the spirits of just men made perfect** (23c). This language is meant to take us immediately back to those listed in Chapter Eleven who are summarily described as those who *having obtained a*

good report through faith, received not the promise: God having provided some better thing for us, that they without us should not be made perfect (11:39-40). They are declared just because of their faith as Paul explains of Abraham in Romans 4. But under the Old Covenant, based upon the Mt. Sinai experience, they were not made perfect. Their perfection only came as a result of Jesus' salvation work. He was *the promise* for which they looked and *the author and finisher of our faith* (12:2). The writer intends for the faithfulness of the Old Testament saints recorded in Chapter Eleven to serve as either an impetus to the reader's own faithfulness or as an indictment against the reader's unfaithfulness as he considers neglecting such a great salvation.

6) Sixth, the reader is pointed **to Jesus the mediator of the new covenant** (24a). The reader has come to Jesus because Jesus came to the reader. Jesus lived the righteous life the Law demanded, but no reader could fulfill it. Jesus died the sacrificial death the reader deserved. Jesus rose victorious over sin and death, freeing the reader from his bondage. Unlike the Mt. Sinai experience which could only produce fear, trembling, and a short-lived obedience, the Mt. Zion experience produces righteousness, hope, and endurance.

> **Unlike the Mt. Sinai experience which could only produce fear, trembling, and a short-lived obedience, the Mt. Zion experience produces righteousness, hope, and endurance.**

It is this very endurance the writer of Hebrews compels upon his readers that is both demonstrated and guaranteed by Jesus:

Looking unto Jesus the author and finisher of our faith; who for the joy that was set before him endured the cross, despising the shame, and is set down at the right hand of the throne of God. (12:2)

Wherefore he is able also to save them to the uttermost that come unto God by him, seeing he ever liveth to make intercession for them. (7:25)

7) Finally, the reader is reminded he has come **to the blood of sprinkling, that speaketh better things than that of Abel** (24b). The blood of sprinkling is the shed blood of Jesus that has already been explained in Chapters 9-10 as being the very cause for the reader's confidence in 10:19-22.

Having therefore, brethren, boldness to enter into the holiest by the blood of Jesus, By a new and living way, which he hath consecrated for us, through the veil, that is to say, his flesh; And having an high priest over the house of God; Let us draw near with a true heart in full assurance of faith, having our hearts sprinkled from an evil conscience, and our bodies washed with pure water.

Notice the phrase **speaketh better things** (v24). That phrase alone would be sufficient to draw the reader's mind to Genesis 4, but including Abel's name removes all doubt. After Adam and Eve had disobeyed God's clear command, plunging the world into sin and death, they were removed from the Garden of Eden and driven from the presence of the Lord. Over time, Eve bore two children: Cain and Abel. Cain was a farmer while Abel was a shepherd. Both had brought an offering to the Lord, but only Abel's was met with acceptance. Rather than respond to God's gracious rebuke and warning, Cain lured Abel into a field where he killed him.

And the LORD said unto Cain, Where is Abel thy brother? And he said, I know not: Am I my brother's keeper? And he said, What hast thou done? the voice of thy brother's blood crieth unto me from the ground. And now art thou cursed from the earth, which hath opened her mouth to receive thy brother's blood from thy hand; When thou tillest the ground, it shall not henceforth yield unto thee her strength; a fugitive and a vagabond shalt thou be in the earth (Genesis 4:9-12).

The cry of Abel's blood resulted in Cain's condemnation: a life marked by loneliness, wandering, and hardship. Contrasted with that is the salvation work of Jesus' blood: a life marked by companionship, assurance, and endurance. While the readers of Hebrews may have felt as though their current situation more closely resembled the life of Cain, the writer assures them of **better things** (v24). Their loneliness is only from the world, never from their Father, their Savior, and the Church. Their wandering is only in this world, where they are *strangers and pilgrims* (1 Peter 2:11). Their hardship is only in this world, so *lift up the hands which hang down, and the feeble knees; And make straight paths for your feet* (v12-13).

Responding to the Word of the Lord

It is for all these reasons the writer now makes his appeal in verse 25, **See that ye refuse not him that speaketh**. The writer is not putting himself in the position of being the speaker here but pointing the reader back to the Lord. The writer of Hebrews is aware of the reality that as he writes, these are not his words or his thoughts, but rather the word of God: *quick, and powerful, and sharper than any two-edged sword, piercing even to the dividing asunder of soul and spirit, and of the joints and marrow, and is a discerner of the thoughts and intents of the heart* (4:12).

Verse 25 is an example of what is called in logic and law an *a fortiori* argument, meaning a logical or legal argument stating what is true in a lesser case will be even more true in the greater. For those at Mt. Sinai, they learned that the Word of God is meant to be responded to in obedience and worship. The original response of the people was a favorable one as recorded in Exodus 24:7-8.

> *And he took the book of the covenant, and read in the audience of the people: and they said, All that the LORD hath said will we do, and be obedient. And Moses took the blood, and sprinkled it on the people, and said, Behold the blood of the covenant, which the LORD hath made with you concerning all these words.*

However, it wasn't too long afterward that the people disobeyed God's clear command and created a golden calf, proclaiming it to be their god, and worshiping before it (Exod. 32). The swift result of judgment came from the Lord resulting in the death of three thousand men falling by the sword, and countless others from a plague (32:28, 35). Based on that example, the writer of Hebrews observes **if they escaped not who refused him that spake on earth, much more shall not we escape, if we turn away from him that speaketh from heaven** (v25). This is not the first time the writer has spoken with such severity regarding the expectant response to God's Word of obedience and worship.

> *Therefore we ought to give the more earnest heed to the things which we have heard, lest at any time we should let them slip. For if the word spoken by angels was stedfast, and every transgression and disobedience received a just recompence of reward; How shall we escape, if we neglect so great salvation; which at the first began to be spoken by the Lord, and was confirmed unto us by them that heard him* (2:1-3).

> *He that despised Moses' law died without mercy under two or three witnesses: Of how much sorer punishment, suppose ye, shall he be thought worthy, who hath trodden under foot the Son of God, and hath counted the blood of the covenant, wherewith he was sanctified, an unholy thing, and hath done despite unto the Spirit of grace?* (10:28-29)

Unshakable Kingdom

The writer of Hebrews not only directs the readers' attention to the past as a warning to be heeded but also reminds them of the prophetic word yet to be fulfilled. Just as the voice of God shook the earth at Mt. Sinai, God has promised he will do so **yet once more** (v26). In quoting Haggai 2:6, the writer practices some expositional preaching in verse 27 explaining the meaning of the text. Unlike the shaking of Mt. Sinai, this shaking will result in **the removing of those things that are shaken** (v27). Mt. Sinai was shaken, yet it remained. The people of Israel were shaken, yet they remained. The shaking that is to occur **yet once more** will mean the removal of all that can be shaken **that those things which cannot be shaken may remain**. The things that cannot be shaken are the very things the writer highlighted as those to which they have come in verses 22-24. Implicit then is the promise that for those who have come to these things, they too cannot be shaken. Those who have come to Mt. Zion can echo the words of Paul from 2 Corinthians 4:8-9, *We are troubled on every side, yet not distressed; we are perplexed, but not in despair; Persecuted, but not forsaken; cast down, but not destroyed*. The writer of Hebrews encourages his readers to turn to their Hebrew Psalms and sing together Psalm 42.

The writer practically shouts in praise the fact that we have received **a kingdom which cannot be moved** (v28)! It is not a kingdom that has been earned or captured by any of its readers. It is a kingdom received. It has been granted to us only by the Father's gracious promise, the Son's gracious purchase, and the Spirit's gracious provision.

> It has been granted to us only by the Father's gracious promise, the Son's gracious purchase, and the Spirit's gracious provision.

For those who have come to Mt. Zion, which cannot be touched or shaken, what is the expected response? Verse 28 reads, **let us have grace whereby we may serve God acceptably.** The literal Greek rendering is *let us continually have grace*, meaning this is to be a constant state of dependence upon and rejoicing in our great salvation in Christ. The grace that we have received is the same grace that holds us fast, therefore let us hold fast to grace. This is in contradiction to the musings of the reader to *neglect so great salvation* (2:3). Thus, the need for endurance and the reason for the admonitions throughout the book to not give up, but to persevere.

- *Hold fast the confidence and the rejoicing of the hope firm unto the end* (3:6b)

- *Hold the beginning of our confidence stedfast unto the end* (3:14)

- *Let us therefore fear, lest... any of you should seem to come short of it* (4:1)

- *Let us labour therefore to enter into that rest* (4:11)

- *Lay hold upon the hope set before us* (6:18)

- *Hold fast the profession of our faith without wavering* (10:23)

- *Cast not away therefore your confidence* (10:35)

- *Run with patience the race that is set before us* (12:1b)

Final Thoughts
There is a bit of mystery here as we consider both truths of God's sovereign grace to draw and to keep as well as man's responsibility to endure. Both are clearly taught in Scripture and while difficult to reconcile in our mind, it is not too difficult for God to manage and reveal in his Word. Knowing that there is security in Christ coupled with admonitions to work, labor, and hold fast should create within the follower an attitude of **reverence** and **godly** fear. Those attitudes are exactly what the writer says is the manner of acceptable service. Those attitudes are not only appropriate given our position in Christ but also in light of how the writer concludes this section in verse 29, **For our God is a consuming fire.** The writer now brings us full circle back to **the mount that might be touched** (v18). While the covenant has changed, God has not. The same God who descended in majesty and holiness upon the top of Mt. Sinai calling the ancient Hebrews to worship and obey is now issuing the same call to the Hebrews of the New Testament. Our only hope is found in the grace available to all those who trust in Christ above all.

ADDITIONAL COMMENTS

Hebrews 12:18-29
When God Speaks
  I. **PAST (v18-21)** – Justice Warning
  II. **PRESENT (v22-24)** – Justification Welcoming
  III. **FUTURE (v25-27)** – Judgment Waiting
(Spink)

STUDY GUIDE QUESTIONS

The previous covenant required the people to maintain a separation from a holy God, while the subsequent covenant removed that barrier. Consequently, modern believers may occasionally lack a reverence for God and unintentionally adopt a too casual approach. What kind of relationship should be formed between the Old Testament concept of fearing a holy and unapproachable God and the New Testament concept of unrestricted access (particularly in light of verses 28-29)?

The author of Hebrews often alternates between encouraging perseverance and warning against the consequences of not enduring. What does he urge his readers to remember in verses 25-26?

According to verses 26-27, what can be shaken? What cannot be shaken?

According to verse 28, what is the proper response to understanding that God will one day judge heaven and earth?

How closely do our modern ideas of worship match the depiction presented in verses 28-29? How might our worship take on a unique quality if we viewed God as a consuming fire?

17

LIFE IN CHRIST

Hebrews 13:1-25

Robb Fowler

Introduction

As the writer comes to a conclusion, keep in mind the overall focus of the letter: **Christ Above All**. But, if Christ is above all, what difference does that make in the here and now? Having demonstrated at every turn that Christ is above all others, this final instruction challenges the follower of Christ to live with Christ above all in his or her life. Chapter Twelve concluded with a vivid description of the sheer magnitude of the holiness and supremacy of God, and an accompanying call to serve/worship God in response to his greatness and grace toward us.

In light of this, how does the reverent believer live with godly fear? The writer challenges us in a variety of areas: our personal lives, our conduct in the Body of Christ, our relationship with spiritual leadership, and our testimony in the community where God has placed us.

Christ Above All in Personal Life (v1-6)

Verse 1

We may recall, from **6:9-10**, that the readers were known for their demonstration of love for one another. Although the writer was dismayed over their lack of spiritual knowledge and ability to understand truth beyond the basics, their authentic love for each other was unmistakable evidence of genuine faith. There is a danger, sometimes, that as a believer pursues a greater understanding of truth, that passion for truth may displace compassion for others. We must allow our growing understanding of the person, nature, and heart of God to fuel compassion and love toward others, rather than reducing theology to cold academia. Indeed, Paul hails love as the greatest of virtues (1 Cor. 13:13) because it is what must govern our thoughts and actions toward each other. So, our worship response to the greatness of God is not merely another song or another prayer or another testimony. We must include actions of love toward our brothers and sisters in Christ.

> **There is a danger, sometimes, that as a believer pursues a greater understanding of truth, that passion for truth may displace compassion for others.**

But, this expression of love is not to be exclusive toward believers. Indeed, there is no such modifier here. While elsewhere in Scripture there is express command to actively love fellow believers, the worshiper of Christ is to *do good to everyone, and especially to those who are of the household of faith* (Gal. 6:10). Let love begin in the household of faith, but let it overflow to the world outside, that they may see the beauty of Christ in his people.

Verse 2

The idea of **be not forgetful** is not to neglect or overlook. Rather than thinking of it as the result of a poor memory, we should see it as taking responsibility. **Entertain** is the word *philoxenia* (consider that "brotherly love" in verse 1 is *philadelphia*), literally meaning "love of strangers." This extends beyond our modern, Western concept of trying to efficiently move people along. As Guthrie notes, "Another practical matter of considerable importance for Christians is hospitality. In the environment of the early church, it was essential, since alternative facilities for travelers were such that Christians would not choose to make use of them. Wayfarer's hostels, where they existed, were notorious for immorality. But the New Testament concept of hospitality has a much wider application than this. In the Middle East, hospitality is a means of friendship. To invite a person to a meal is to extend fellowship to him" (Guthrie, p. 269). The writer observes **for thereby some have entertained angels unawares.** This is not suggesting we seek to determine if the stranger we just met is an angel. Rather, we simply practice hospitality. Show them love that meets their needs, whether it is a safe place to sleep, a meal, a listening ear, or some other help. Since we don't live for this world, and our inheritance in heaven is both infinite and guaranteed, we must not live with the fear that they will take advantage of us. Rather, love generously, entrusting the investment to the God who sees and provides.

Verse 3

Remember is to bring to mind. As the persecution persisted against the early believers, they were frequently incarcerated for their faith. Thus, it is essential to 'remember' them; however, the writer admonishes that they be remembered as if we were **bound with them**. This introduces a deeper level of compassion for and identification with those who are imprisoned. And this compassion is also for **them which suffer adversity**, for there were also many who were not imprisoned but endured ostracization, financial difficulty, verbal and physical abuse, displacement, and threats. The compassion is felt **as being yourselves also in the body**, in that believers are all one Body in Christ, and therefore when one suffers, all share in that suffering. It is "to act as though they themselves were in the bodies of those undergoing such hardship" (Johnson, p. 341).

Verse 4

Marriage is a God-ordained covenant and is to be held in respect and honor. **Honorable** is something precious or valued, and so the covenant of marriage is to be considered such. The believer should champion the marriage relationship not only of his or her own spouse, but among all others as well. Within the greater understanding of Scripture, it is clear that God intended marriage to be only between a male and female, and that covenant is intended to endure until broken by death. So, the body of believers must support marriage, encouraging each other in our marriages while fortifying our own covenant relationship with our spouse. The Body of Christ should be a community that nurtures, strengthens, restores, and celebrates marriage. And, **the bed undefiled** indicates the exclusive nature of the sexual relationship in marriage. Simply put, within the marriage relationship, sex is a beautiful part of God's gift to a married couple, and they are free to enjoy it in devotion, service, and intimacy with each other; but, there is to be no sexual activity or relationship outside of a marriage partner. The world has often sought unfettered sex by encouraging it at any time in any way with any other person as the individual feels in the moment. This is error. But, in the Christian community, sex has often been so stigmatized that a married couple may still see it as shameful, selfish, or even sinful. This is also error. While it is best considered private, remember that private does not indicate shame. Rather, the intimate nature of sex indicates it is to be held sacred between the husband and wife, enjoyed without shame, yet only between them.

Whoremongers (unmarried sexual activity) and **adulterers** (sexual activity by a married person outside of the marriage) will face God's judgment. This demonstrates how seriously God takes this command about human sexuality, and therefore how seriously humanity, and specifically the believer, should take it as well. For the believer, knowing this is behavior that brings God's judgment, it must be avoided if we are to live a life of authentic worship service to God.

Verses 5-6

There is also the matter of money—and our desire for it. The believer must avoid **covetousness**, that is, the love of money, and rather pursue contentment, or simply to be satisfied with what God provides. Money must never be the central pursuit of our lives. But this command comes with a sense of action—the believer must choose and practice contentment with what has been provided. Here the believer is reminded of the transience of this world and all that belongs to it because the basis of true satisfaction is the presence and faithfulness of Jesus Christ. The reader is emboldened by Jesus' promise: *I am with you alway, even unto the end of the world* (Matt 28:20). Indeed, such boldness is a thread woven through this letter (4:6; 10:19) and demonstrates confidence in the promise and power of God, not in any sense of self-sufficiency in man. Thus, contentment is rooted in resting in the faithful and loyal presence of our Savior, as in such we find there is no need to fear what any person could do to us, as the Psalmist wrote: *I will not fear. What can man do to me? The Lord is on my side as my helper* (Ps. 118:6-7).

So, this first section could be summarized as this: Love for our fellow believers. Love for strangers that meets their needs. Compassion for and identification with those facing hardship for their faith. Faithfulness in our marriages and supporting faithfulness in other marriages. And not allowing money to take priority in our lives, but rather trusting in the faithful presence and loyalty of our Savior.

Reflection

- Have you allowed your pursuit of greater knowledge of Christ to diminish your love for others?

- In what ways are you actively loving others around you?

- What about people you don't know? How are you demonstrating Gospel hospitality toward strangers?

- What are some practical ways we could demonstrate Gospel hospitality in your current cultural setting?

- Are you aware of others who are suffering for the Gospel? How do you identify with them? How could you encourage them as they endure?

- If you are married, how is your marriage going? Are you invested, or have you checked out?

- What are some practical ways you encourage others in their marriage?

- Are you actively protecting the sexual aspect of your marriage? How about the marriage of others?

- What is your attitude toward money? Do you manage it, or does it manage you?

- How do we navigate the responsibility of earning money to meet our obligations (providing for our family, access to necessities, etc.) without giving money too prominent a position in our priorities?

- Are you content with what God has provided, or do you find yourself pursuing more money and sacrificing satisfaction in Christ?

Christ Above All in Church Life

Verse 7

Church leadership bears a significant level of responsibility and accountability before God. Indeed, the writer continues applying the practice of worship from Chapter Twelve to the relationship of the believer with spiritual leaders. This is not to say such leaders are to be worshiped; indeed, such would be blasphemy. Rather, the response of a church member to a church leader is a reflection of that believer's worship of God. But, how so?

First, the believer is to **remember**, to "recall information from memory, but without necessarily the implication that persons have actually forgotten" certain individuals (Louw and Nida, p. 346). Such individuals **have the rule over**; (*hegoumenon*—regard, consider, lead) that is, they are identified as the leaders within the Body, and they are the ones that teach God's Word. The word **rule** here is the idea of leading, directing, or influencing. This imperative indicates the believer is to be intentional in thinking about their spiritual leaders. What to think of them? That is indicated with the command **whose faith follow.** The leaders are to be recognized as being ordained by God and provided to the church by his grace to accomplish his purposes, thus the mandate to remember them - call to mind their role and activity in your life, specifically that they have taught **the Word of God** to you. This is followed with the charge to follow their faith—let their life be an example and model for yours, as you reflect on the results of their lifestyle (**the end of their conversation**). While every believer stands personally before God through Jesus Christ alone, it is God's plan and provision that Godly leaders will teach and model Godly living for his people. As we connect in the body of Christ, it is appropriate to pattern our lives after those who demonstrate spiritual wisdom and maturity, particularly those whom God has placed in positions of spiritual leadership in our lives. Consider Paul's words: *Be ye followers of me, even as I also am of Christ* (1 Cor. 11:1).

Verse 8

The doctrine of the immutability of Jesus Christ seems a silent undercurrent throughout Hebrews. While more often the writer has spoken of events that led to the "perfecting" or completing the necessary qualifications to be the better High Priest, it must be noted that he remains the same in nature, character, and indeed his very deity—**yesterday, today, and forever**. The unchanging nature of Christ should be reflected in the "conversation" or life of the spiritual leaders of the Body. And, because he remains the same, the truth about him remains the same.

Verse 9

Therefore, don't be led astray, or **carried about** (remember, the believer is anchored in Christ), **with diverse and strange doctrines**. When new ideas come along, be on guard. Don't be enamored by every new thing that comes along. Bring it back under the scrutiny of the Doctrine of Christ. This does not mean the Body must stick to tradition—just that it must stick to the truth. Mere decades after Christ's ascension, there were already multiple false teachers and their written twisted heresies circulating among the churches. Fast forward almost 2,000 years and those heresies and proponents have multiplied. Don't be enamored with *new* theories and doctrines.

> **Don't be enamored by every new thing that comes along. Bring it back under the scrutiny of the Doctrine of Christ.**

It would seem that false teachers were trying to draw the readers back into the restrictions of the Law, which the doctrine of the letter has demonstrated was set aside with the New Covenant and the Great High Priest, Jesus. Some of those restrictions include dietary—hence the reference to **meats**, or foods. The Law's ineffectiveness in producing forgiveness and cleansed consciences has been repeatedly demonstrated, and thus further adherence to such restrictions and practices can bring no benefit. Any attempt to bring those restrictions into the New Covenant provided no benefit to those who practiced them. Rather, our hearts are to be established in grace. That **grace** is rooted in the unchanging Christ, who by his sacrifice secured grace for all believers of all ages. What a blessing that now the believers can live solely by the grace of Christ, rather than still seeking God through the mandates of the Law!

Reflection

- With the abundance and ease of access to so many religious teachers today, what are you doing to ensure you remain committed to the unchanging truth of Jesus Christ?

- Who are your spiritual influencers? How do you evaluate their faithfulness to sound doctrine?

- Do you have spiritual influencers who actually know you? Are you connected in a local church that recognizes you as part of their spiritual oversight?

- How do we differentiate between tradition and truth? Is tradition always good or bad? How do we determine the value of tradition?

- Have you allowed anyone or anything to pollute your understanding of the grace of Christ?

Christ Above All in Our Priorities

Verses 10-11
Verses 10-14 provide a parenthetical thought that further argues against the inclusion of the Law in the redemption of Grace provided by Christ.

In worship, **an altar** serves as a powerful symbol. It is the place where a sacrifice is offered, and through that sacrifice, the worshiper seeks favor with the deity being worshiped. Under the Old Covenant, the altar was the place of such sacrifice, and by those sacrifices, the worshipers received God's mercy. Ordinarily, the priests were permitted to eat the meat sacrificed. In fact, it was one of the chief ways God provided for the needs of the priests. But, on the Day of Atonement, the offered animals were not to be eaten, but rather taken **outside the camp** and **burned**. This demonstrated that the priests would not identify with the sins of the people, which were associated with the sacrifices.

The **we**, then, is a reference to the fellow Jews to whom Hebrews was written. **They... which serve the tabernacle**, would be identified as the priests, who offered the sacrifice on the Day of Atonement but did not eat it as they would the other sacrifices throughout the year. The sin associated with those offerings must be removed from the camp.

Verses 12-13
To carry the analogy to the readers, the writer now observes that Jesus was offered **outside** the camp. Thus, the sin divinely attributed

to him, and the atonement he accomplished, is outside the system of the Law and outside the city as prescribed. To be put outside the city was considered shameful to the Jews, as if the individual were unclean, or had violated the community expectations to such a degree the individual would no longer be permitted to participate in community life. For the one who would then believe in Christ, he or she must be willing to go outside the Old Covenant (with its emphasis on the impenetrable barrier of sin and the constant reminder of that barrier through the sacrificial system) and outside the community of the Jews who were identified as a people in that Covenant. Once outside, there the believer would find Christ, with all the **reproach** and rejection of the Jewish community that still held to the Old Covenant. By extension, the Gentile who would come to Christ must also go outside any other system of works and self-achievement and identify with the weakness and scandal of a crucified Savior.

In the end, the point must be observed: Redemption is only available through Jesus Christ. This requires separation from any other belief or system, and through him the believer is sanctified and set apart from the world to live in worship of the God who has saved us.

> **Redemption is only available through Jesus Christ. This requires separation from any other belief or system.**

Verse 14

For the one who still longs for the systems and practices and familiarity of this world, note this: The believer is looking for a different **city**. This was repeatedly emphasized in Chapter Eleven, where those men and women of faith chose to pursue something different. Abraham *looked for a city which hath foundations, whose builder and maker is God* (Hebrews 11:10). Abraham and Sarah *confessed that they were strangers and pilgrims on the earth. ¹⁴ For they that say such things declare plainly that they seek a country. ¹⁵ And truly, if they had been mindful of that country from whence they came out, they might have had opportunity to have returned. ¹⁶ But now they desire a better country, that is, an heavenly: wherefore God is not ashamed to be called their God: for he hath prepared for them a city* (Hebrews 11:13-16). And Moses chose *rather to suffer affliction with the people of God, than to enjoy the pleasures of sin for a season;*

Esteeming the reproach of Christ greater riches than the treasures in Egypt (11:25-26). The Law and sacrifices pertain to earthly Jerusalem, which would soon be destroyed. Here we have **no continuing city**. It has an end, and so do all the treasures and pleasures that it offers. But **we seek** a city that is not yet available, but which will be our home for eternity.

Reflection

- Are you still holding on to something of this world?

- Do people ever criticize your stand for Christ? What does it look like?

- How do you handle when people criticize your stand for Jesus Christ?

- How do you set your mind on things above (Col. 3:2)?

Christ Above All in Christian Community

Verse 15

The writer now returns to the statement of Christ's unchanging nature, with this response: **By him therefore let us offer the sacrifice of praise to God continually**. It is by Christ himself that believers are able to now worship God. It is only through the grace that he has provided that there is access to the New City and the hope of eternity as the people of God. In addition to the activities of love, devotion, and obedience, believers must voice their praise to God for his grace and greatness. **Praise** is to speak of the excellence of a person, and this must be the subject of the believer's speech - the excellence of God. This is the sacrifice of the believer; not the blood of an animal, but the **fruit of our lips;** speech that flows from hearts and lives of gratitude. The authentic worshiper continually praises God through hearts, lives, and words of gratitude to him. Disobedience is a failure to show gratitude. Complaining is a failure to show gratitude. Lack of contentment, returning to sin, and attempting to include the dead works of the law in our salvation; all indicate failure to show gratitude.

Verse 16

After this section of reflection on the nature of Christ, with the resulting command to offer praise and gratitude, the writer returns now to corporate life. As the worshiper celebrates the grace of God through praise to him, he must keep in mind **(forget not)** two important behaviors in the Body. First, to **do good**, or good deeds. The book of Acts is replete with accounts of practical deeds done in love toward others. Where modern Western culture is more inclined to place the responsibility on individuals to purchase goods and services to meet their needs, the community of Christ has the opportunity to give to and serve others in tangible, practical ways to help meet needs.

A second behavior is **to communicate**. This is translated from the familiar word *koinonia*, and in several other translations is rendered "to share" (e.g. ESV, NASB, NKJV, NIV). Thus, while doing good may focus more on acts of service toward others, sharing emphasizes the giving of tangible goods to help meet needs.

Along with the sacrifice of praise, these two are also associated with **sacrifices** that please God. What is it that God desires from us? Not the blood of animals, or any other offering brought to the priest, for the offering presented by the great High Priest Jesus Christ is sufficient. Instead, perhaps the words of the prophet echo here: *He has told you, O man, what is good; and what does the Lord require of you but to do justice, and to love kindness, and to walk humbly with your God?* (Mic. 6:8, ESV).

Reflection

- What are you doing to cultivate gratitude toward God?

- What is the connection between gratitude and doing what is good? How might our gratitude to God fuel our response toward others?

- If the idea of sharing is an expression of our gratitude to God, how will that shape our perspective on our personal resources?

Christ Above All in Leadership

Verse 17

Peitho means to trust or to be persuaded by someone or something. The translation to **obey** implies confidence in someone which results in following someone. **Them that have the rule** (see v7) does not necessarily imply absolute authority as in a dictatorship, but it elicits a strong sense of authority granted to those charged with responsibility for us. This is further strengthened by the imperative to **submit yourselves.** A Biblical understanding of submission is that one chooses to place oneself under the leadership or authority of another. It is modeled in the perfect submission of Jesus to the Father (Philippians 2), and to be repeated in the life of every believer in a variety of relationships (e.g. Ephesians 5:21, 22; Philippians 2:3-4).

As noted in the discussion of 13:7, these leaders are God's ordained provision to his church, and as such are charged with responsibility and accountability for those in their assigned sphere. It should be noted that each of these is still human, and therefore no leader will be without fault. But in this the sovereignty of God still holds. Even in human failure, God provides what is good to accomplish his divine purpose in each life.

In that confidence, submit. This is not a charge to blind obedience without boundary or restriction. This is about God-appointed leaders who are charged with shepherding the souls God has entrusted to them. The responsibility of the leader is present here—spiritual leaders will account for those under them. The responsibility of the reader then is to have confidence in God's ordained structure and servants of leadership, and then submit to those leaders.

Also, note these leaders must account for their shepherding of the **souls** under their care. So, submit in such a way that when they **give an account, they may do so with joy and not grief**. The picture of grief (*stenazontes*) is groaning or sighing. Imagine, in the accounting, the next name is announced, and the leader responds with a sigh or groan over the choices of that believer. The result of that account will be **unprofitable**, or to no advantage, for that believer.

Verse 18-19

The writer now begins the closing of the letter, but there seems to be a strong tie to verse 17. This is a request/command for the readers to **pray for** the writer and companions. As those who have been spiritual leaders for the readers, this connection to verse 17 demonstrates one way a believer might honor the leader God has provided—through faithful prayer on that leader's behalf.

The writer strengthens the request for prayer through the evidence of lifestyle. A **good conscience** flows from honest living. As was discussed throughout the letter, redemption provides for the believer a cleansed conscience, the effect of the New Covenant that writes the law of God on the heart of the believer. With humility, the writer acknowledges a need for prayer that his commitment to and practice of integrity would continue.

There is additional motivation for this prayer, and that is the hopeful soon reunion of the writer with the readers. This suggests the writer may still have been incarcerated (10:34 indicates the writer had been imprisoned at some point) although that is not certain. Thus, prayer for this spiritual leader included elements of prayer for character and spiritual power, as well as prayer for immediate physical concerns.

Reflection

- Who watches for your soul? Do you perceive them to be God's provision for you?

- How do you demonstrate submission to those spiritual overseers?

- What happens in a church when the spiritual overseers don't demonstrate integrity in life?

- How can you be supportive of those who have spiritual oversight for you?

Christ Above All in Us

Verse 20

In this formal benediction, the writer invokes God as **the God of peace**. In the tumultuous times that serve as the background for this letter, peace may often have seemed elusive. And certainly, while the imminent destruction of the Temple was unknown to the writer and readers, the events of the ensuing years would have felt very disruptive to any peace they may have known. But this God of peace is not merely a God who loves peace, but the God who can create peace. God is further identified as the one who resurrected **our Lord Jesus**, reminding them they serve a master who had died and now lives. And this Jesus is the **great shepherd of the sheep**. He is the ultimate overseer of the souls of all believers, a role he has earned **through** his **blood** that secured the **covenant** which has been a primary subject throughout the letter.

Verse 21

This benediction helps shape an understanding of the purpose of the letter. There are three sections to the writer's prayer for them. First is the <u>expectation</u> of what will happen. The prayer is that God would **make you perfect**, that is, complete you **in every good work to do His will.** The idea of perfect here is not blameless, but rather, a finished product. Paul noted: *For we are his workmanship, created in Christ Jesus for good works, which God prepared beforehand, that we should walk in them* (Eph. 2:10 ESV). The result of salvation is the believer is now equipped to do good works, and it is only by the power of God that such good works can be done. There is such assurance here. God will finish in the believer what he begins. This transformation is to work, or make, in the believer that which is **wellpleasing** in the **sight** of God.

The second section is the <u>means</u> by which this will happen. Shortly put, it is **through Jesus Christ.** The entire letter has demonstrated how Christ is the means for God to accomplish the work of the New Covenant in the believer, and here in the final prayer, this is once again brought before the reader. God is in the process of transforming the believer to do the good works for which God created him, and this happens only through Jesus Christ.

The third section is the <u>purpose</u> for this transformation. It is for the **glory** of Jesus Christ. While the benefits of redemption are infinitely immeasurable for the believer, it should always be known that the glory of God is the primary purpose for man's existence, and for his redemption.

Verse 22

The writer now has a request for the readers—essentially, that they would **suffer**, or endure, this **word of exhortation**. While it may seem to have some length, the writer apparently kept it shorter than it could have been. It would seem he desires that the readers would do more than simply sit through a reading of it but rather that they would embrace it for the doctrine, reproof, correction, and instruction it is intended to be. For any reader or hearer of biblical teaching, there is a responsibility to actively engage with the material. This is clearly what the writer has in mind. It must be more than passively experiencing the delivery, whether by written or spoken word; instead, the listener must choose to mentally interact, and allow God's message to accomplish his transforming work.

Verse 23

Timothy is well known from Paul's writings, and while his relationship with the readers is not described, he is well known to them as well. Timothy, it would appear, had been incarcerated as well, though seemingly not with the writer of this letter. The writer is not clear on Timothy's plans and movements, however, as **if he come shortly** indicates. While the writer desires to travel and visit the recipients with Timothy, clear plans had not yet been made, and such plans await Timothy's possible reunion with the writer. Nevertheless, we see the writer desires to visit the readers, reminding us of the affection that existed in the early church, which hopefully characterizes churches today.

Verse 24

A common formal farewell is given here. **Salute** literally means 'to be happy about' and was used as a form of greeting. This greeting is directed both to the spiritual leaders, mentioned earlier in this chapter, as well as to **all the saints**. And the salutation is conveyed from those who appeared to be companions of the writer - Italian believers. Whether this is referring to specific Italians (perhaps Aquila and Priscilla, cf. Acts 18:2), or indicating the writer was currently in **Italy** and thus surrounded by Italian believers, is unclear, but not crucial to the understanding of the letter.

Verse 25

This final statement repeats with a prayer for **grace** for the recipients, common among the New Testament epistles. And the final **Amen** is a fitting conclusion. Let the words be so.

The AV text includes the statement **Written to the Hebrews from Italy by Timothy**. It should be noted this has come under some speculation as to whether this is in the original letter, or added later, as earlier manuscripts do not include it. The inclusion also raises some potential conflict with the discussion on Timothy in verse 23—if Timothy were not with the writer at the time of the writing, then how could he be either the author or an amanuensis? But again, this presents no theological addition or perspective on the letter as a whole.

Reflection
The final greetings and benediction of a letter have meaning for us. First, the blessing conveyed in the benediction reflect the blessings God desires to pour out on us, as well as model for us how we ought to pray for and bless others. Second, the greetings reflect the love that existed between the writers and readers, which ought to instruct and motivate us to pursue similar love for our fellow believers. Third, it demonstrates the connection that existed among the Christian community, even when it was spread out across different regions.

- Do you love other believers around you?

- Do you express that love through words AND actions?

- Are you aware of the followers of Christ in different places?

- How can you build meaningful connections with believers in other places?

ADDITIONAL COMMENTS

It should be noted that I am indebted to John MacArthur's explanation of verses 10-14. There were several other possible explanations, but this seemed to me to best explain the passage in light of the overall argument and flow of the letter. While I did not directly quote him, his observations served as a guide for my writing, and thus credit should be given to him. (Fowler)

Hebrews 13:1-3
I. **Love For Saints (v1)**
   A. Commanded
   B. Common – "brotherly"
   C. "Continue"
II. **Love For Strangers (v2)**
   A. Must Be Remembered – "Be not forgetful"
   B. May Be Rewarded
III. **Love For Sufferers (v3)**
   A. Embrace the Command
   B. Express Compassion   (Spink)

Hebrews 13:4
I. **The Marriage Bond is Honorable**
II. **The Marriage Bed is Holy**
III. **The Moral Breaches are Harmful** (Spink)

Hebrews 13:5, 6
I. **The Curse of Covetousness (v5)**
II. **The Cure of Contentment (5)**
III. **The Confidence in Christ (v6)**
   Greed is a weed that grows inside
   It's a hideous monster we try to hide;
   It pokes and prods, contorts the soul
   It sucks you into a deep dark hole

The 10th commandment states very clearly: "Thou shalt not covet." Yet, the apostle Paul warned that the last days would be marked by covetousness. This 10th commandment is the only one which addresses an attitude rather than a deed. Thus, it shows that mere rules, regulations, and laws could never suffice to police the human race! This law is designed for the heart rather than the visible, external acts of a person. How can such a command be enforced? Who can accurately assess one's level of coveting?

The American system has refined the art of coveting and capitalized on it big time! TV commercials are aimed especially at children to nurture that natural lust for things. Every child grows up in a culture which has become intoxicated with materialism. The more our culture provides, the more we tend to lust. The more we lust, the more we grasp. The more we get, the more we want. It is a vicious cycle which sedates and empties the soul! (Spink)

Hebrews 13:7-9
Following the Right Faith
  I. **The Faith of Our Fathers (v7)**
  II. **The Faith Founded Upon Christ (v8)**
  III. **The Faith Fastened Firmly to the Foundation (v9)** (Spink)

Hebrews 13:10-16
What Pleases God?
  I. **Our Will (v10-14) – Surrender**
  II. **Our Words (v15) – Sing**
  III. **Our Works (v16) – Serve** (Spink)

Hebrews 13:22
... bear with the word of exhortation; for I have written a letter unto you in a few words

The "word of exhortation" is the usual expression for a sermon. Some sermons are long and hard to "bear with" or suffer. This phrase usually applied to the exposition and application of the Scripture which had been read aloud to the assembled congregation. Do not get weary of Bible exposition—entertainment is more fun. Drama is more exciting. Topical sermons and stories are easier to listen to. Upbeat music pumps you up more. Visuals keep your attention better. But do not get weary of Bible exposition.

One man was talking about a particular preacher—"he puts the goodies down on the lower shelf where they are easy to reach." Everybody wants the goodies to be easy to reach, so you don't have to work too hard!

This epistle (the word of exhortation) is not on the lower shelf! You've got to do some hard work to find the goodies here! Mature believers must endure such words of exhortation and faithful pastors must deliver sound doctrine and biblical exposition. 2 Tim. 4:2—*Preach the Word* (not your opinions, experiences, anecdotes, stories, nice comforting religious topics…). (Spink)

STUDY GUIDE QUESTIONS

While much of the guidance in Hebrews has been aimed at individuals, Chapter Thirteen shifts its focus to our responsibilities toward others. What specific activities are mentioned in this list, and what are the reasons for their inclusion?

What is the rationale behind the caution against being attached to wealth in verses 5-6, which is subsequently reinforced by references to Deuteronomy 31:6 and Psalm 118:6? How does this concept tie into the overarching theme of the book of Hebrews?

In verses 13, 15, and 16, the writer highlights three types of offerings that are pleasing to God. What are these offerings, and which one do you believe demands the most attention in your current phase of life?

In the text, the writer personally urges believers to show respect to those in positions of authority within the church. What is his explicit request? Moreover, what benefits arise from demonstrating such respect? Additionally, what are some typical ways in which we unintentionally pose challenges for church leaders in their leadership roles?

BIBLIOGRAPHY of Works on HEBREWS

A Select Library of Nicene and Post-Nicene Fathers of the Christian Church. Edited by Philip Schaff and Henry Wace. 28 vols. in 2 series. 1886–1889. Repr., Buffalo, NY: The Christian Literature Company, 1892.

Allen, David L. *Hebrews*, The New American Commentary. Nashville, TN: B & H, 2010.

BBC Monitoring. *Ukrainian Man Survives Three Days at Sea on Inflatable*, 2017, https://www.bbc.com/news/blogs-news-from-elsewhere-40874668

Bellini, Jarrett. *Apparently This Matters: A Ghost Ship with Cannibal Rats*, CNN, 2014, www.cnn.com/2014/01/24/tech/web/apparently-this-matters-lyubov-orlova-ghost-ship/index.html

Berryman, Eric J. *Strange Things Happen at Sea*, Proceedings, U.S. Naval Institute, 1989.

Bruce, F.F. *The Epistle to the Hebrews*. Grand Rapids, MI: Eerdmans, 1964.

Catholic Church. *Catechism of the Catholic Church*, 2nd Ed. Washington, DC: United States Catholic Conference, 2000.

Chafer, Lewis Sperry. *Grace*. Philadelphia, PA: The Sunday School Times Company, 1922.

Cole, Steven J. Bible.org, 2004, https://bible.org/seriespage/lesson-28-total-forgiveness-hebrews-101-18

Constable, Thomas. *Thomas Constable's Notes on the Bible*, 2017.

Dods, Marcus. *The Book of Genesis*. The Expositor's Bible. Hartford, CT: S.S. Scranton Co., 1903.

Ellingsworth, P. *The Epistle to the Hebrews: A Commentary on the Greek Text.* Grand Rapids, MI: Eerdmans, 1993.

Gaebelein, Frank E., Leon Morris in *The Expositor's Bible Commentary: Hebrews Through Revelation*. Grand Rapids, MI:

Zondervan, 1981.

Ger, Steven. *Hebrews: Christ is Greater.* Twenty-First Century Biblical Commentary Series. Chattanooga, TN: AMG, 2009.

GotQuestions. www.gotquestions.org/eternal-security.html

Guthrie, Donald. *Hebrews: An Introduction and Commentary.* Tyndale New Testament Commentary. Westmont, IL: InterVarsity Press, 1983.

Hughes, R. Kent. *Hebrews: An Anchor for the Soul.* Preaching the Word. Wheaton, IL: Crossway Books, 2015.

Hughes, R. Kent. *The Perils of Apostasy.* The Gospel Coalition. 1992, www.thegospelcoalition.org/sermon/the-perils-of-apostasy/

Jeremiah, David. *What the Bible Says About Angels.* Sisters, OR: Multnomah, 1996.

Johnson, Luke Timothy. *Hebrews: A Commentary.* Louisville, KY: Westminster John Knox Press, 2012.

Kent, Homer. *The Epistle to the Hebrews.* Winona Lake, IN: BMH Books, 1972.

Krejcir, R.J. Into Thy Word Ministries, 2008.

Lane, William L. *Hebrews.* Vol. 47, Word Biblical Commentary. Grand Rapids, MI: Zondervan, 2015.

Lawson, Steven J. *Famine in the Land: A Passionate Call for Expository Preaching.* Chicago, IL: Moody Publishers, 2003.

Lewis, C.S. *Mere Christianity.* San Francisco, CA: Harper Collins, 1952.

Louw, Johannes P., Eugene Nida. *Greek-English Lexicon of the New Testament Based on Semantic Domains.* United Bible Societies, 1996.

MacArthur, John. *Hebrews.* The MacArthur New Testament Commentary Series. Chicago, IL: Moody Publishers, 2016.

MacArthur, John. *The MacArthur Study Bible.* Nashville, TN: Thomas Nelson, 2019.

MacDonald, William. *Believer's Bible Commentary.* Nashville, TN: Thomas Nelson, 2016.

Mohler, Albert R. *Exalting Jesus in Hebrew.* Christ-Centered Exposition. Nashville, TN: Holman Reference, 2017.

O'Brien, Peter T. *The Letter to the Hebrews.* The Pillar New Testament Commentary. Grand Rapids, MI: Eerdmans, 2010.

Owen, John. *Hebrews.* Vol. 4, East Peoria, IL: Versa Press, 2010.

Pentecost, Dwight D. *Faith that Endures: A Practical Commentary on the Book of Hebrews.* Grand Rapids, MI: Kregal Publishers, 2022.

Pfeiffer, Charles, Everett Harrison. Robert W. Ross in the *Wycliffe Bible Commentary.* Chicago, IL: Moody Publishers, 1990.

Piper, John. Desiring God. 1997, https://www.desiringgod.org/messages/perfected-for-all-time-by-a-single-offering

Poole, Matthew. *Matthew Poole's Commentary.* BibleHub, https://biblehub.com/commentaries/hebrews/4-9.htm

Reinecker, Fritz, Cleon Rogers. *Linguistic Keys to the Greek New Testament.* Grand Rapids, MI: Zondervan, 1980.

Roberts, Alexander, James Donaldson, A. Cleveland Coxe, Allan Menzies, Ernest Cushing Richardson, and Bernhard Pick. *The Ante-Nicene Fathers. Translations of the Writings of the Fathers Down to A.D. 325.* Buffalo, NY: The Christian Literature Publishing Company, 1885.

Smith, Joseph. *The Doctrine and Covenants: Of the Church of Jesus Christ of Latter-Day Saints, Containing the Revelations.* Salt Lake City, UT: Desert News, 1876.

Swindoll, Charles R. *Moses: A Man of Selfless Dedication.* Nashville, TN: Thomas Nelson, 1999.

Utley, R.J. *The Superiority of the New Covenant: Hebrews.* Bible Lessons International, 1999.

Waalvoord, J.F., R.B. Zuck. Z.C. Hodges in *Hebrews.* Vol. 2, The Bible

Knowledge Commentary. Victor Books, 1983.

Westcott, B.F. *The Epistle to the Hebrews.* Grand Rapids, MI: Eerdmans, 1980.

Wiersbe, W.W. *Hebrews.* Vol. 2, The Bible Exposition Commentary. Victor Books, 1996.

Wikipedia. https://en.wikipedia.org/wiki/Apostasy_in_Christianity

Wuest, Kenneth S. *Hebrews in the Greek New Testament for the English Reader.* Grand Rapids, MI: Eerdmans, 1947.

MEET THE EDITORS

SERIES EDITOR

KENNETH J. SPINK is the senior pastor of Berea Baptist Church in Berea, Ohio. He came to Berea in 1982 serving as youth pastor for 1-½ years before being called as senior pastor in 1984. He has served in leadership roles with the Hebron Association of Regular Baptist Churches, the OARBC, the GARBC and Baptist Mid Missions. He is the author of three books, *Prayer Force, A Love Story,* and *A Very Rich Man.*

GENERAL EDITOR

DARYL A. NEIPP is the associate pastor at New Community Baptist Church in Avon, Ohio. He came to New Community in 2001 and has served in a variety of roles including teaching, leading worship, small group leadership, and the organization of ministries and events. He also teaches for Liberty University where he helps professors develop course curriculum. Publications include articles such as, *Lost or Found: The Impact of Sin Upon the Death of a Child*, *The Problem of Genocide in the Old Testament*, and *Introverts in Ministry.*

COPY EDITOR

TIMOTHY McDIVITT is a deacon and Sunday School Superintendent at Berea Baptist Church in Berea, Ohio. He is a retired mechanical engineer who has been a faithful member of Berea Baptist Church since 1994, serving in multiple leadership roles. He is a regular adult Sunday School teacher and has also served on the board of the Berea Baptist Bible School. He is married and has three grown children.

Made in the USA
Columbia, SC
13 November 2024

daa67e40-5aa4-4992-9da4-3553bbd09a45R02